The Sanitary Arts

The Sanitary Arts

Aesthetic Culture and the
Victorian Cleanliness Campaigns

Eileen Cleere

THE OHIO STATE UNIVERSITY PRESS
COLUMBUS

Library of Congress Cataloging-in-Publication Data
Cleere, Eileen.
   The sanitary arts : aesthetic culture and the Victorian cleanliness campaigns / Eileen Cleere.
— First edition.
      pages cm.
   Includes bibliographical references and index.
   ISBN 978-0-8142-1258-5 (cloth) — ISBN 0-8142-1258-1 (cloth) — ISBN 978-0-8142-9362-1 (cd-
rom) — ISBN 0-8142-9362-X (cd-rom)
1. English literature—19th century—History and criticism. 2. Aestheticism (Literature) 3. Art and
literature—Great Britain—History—19th century. 4. Social values—Great Britain—History—
19th century. 5. Sanitation in literature. 6. Sanitation in art. 7. Sanitation—Social aspects—Great
Britain—History—19th century. 8. Hygiene—Social aspects—Great Britain—History—19th
century. I. Title. II. Title: Aesthetic culture and the Victorian cleanliness campaigns.
   PR468.A33C54 2014
   820.9'008—dc23

                              2013046161

Cover design by AuthorSupport.com
Text desgin by Juliet Williams
Type set in Adobe Minion
Printed by Thomson-Shore, Inc.

9 8 7 6 5 4 3 2 1

For John and for Max

CONTENTS

ACKNOWLEDGMENTS

This project began accidentally. A copy of Samuel Smiles's *Character* appeared in the hefty pile of Interlibrary Loan books I received one morning while working on my first book, *Avuncularism*, at my first job at Simmons College in Boston. I returned it after a quick read when I found it had nothing to do with uncles, but I was so haunted by Smiles's mysterious meanderings about Edwin Chadwick, John Ruskin and the filthiness of Venice that I kept a copy of *Character* on my desk for most of my time at Simmons and later at Southwestern University. For this reason, I first want to thank all of the fabulous librarians I have worked with over the years who sometimes know better than I do what book or which essay I should read, and who labor with limited resources to make sure I can have those materials in my possession for possibly unreasonable stretches of time. Some of these wonderful professionals are Lisa Anderson, Dana Hendrix, Carol Fonken, Lisa Hopkins and Laura Forbes Glass.

At both Simmons and at Southwestern I have had supportive colleagues who, in various ways, encouraged this project, and I would like to thank in particular Pamela Bromberg, Renee Bergland, Helene Meyers, Elisabeth Piedmont Marton, David Gaines, James Kilfoyle, Carina Evans, Walt Herbert, Thom McClendon, Laura Hobgood-Oster, Elaine Craddock, Alisa Gaunder, Dirk Early, Maria Lowe, Romi Burks, and Eric Selbin. Several research fellowships and sabbaticals from Southwestern enabled me to travel to archives and libraries in England to conduct crucial research, and I credit Dean James

Hunt and the Southwestern University Awards Committee for continuing to prioritize Humanities scholarship, and for making sure I had necessary resources for those trips to the British Library and the Bodleian Library in Oxford. President Edward Burger's commitment to faculty scholarship at Southwestern has been especially encouraging during the final phases of this book, and I look forward to enjoying that commitment in future endeavors.

Over the years, I also benefitted significantly from generous fellowships and travel grants from the Whiting Foundation, the Sam Taylor Foundation, Yale Center for British Art, the British Academy, and the Harry Ransom Humanities Research Center at University of Texas at Austin. Invitations to deliver early versions of these chapters from Roger Louis at UT, from Helena Michie at Rice, and from Claudia Nelson at Texas A&M, helped enormously as I imagined, extended and revised this book. Letters of support from these scholars as well as Teresa Mangum, Joseph Childers, and Robyn Warhol helped me as I moved from one archive and one chapter to the next. The British Studies community at University of Texas provided a convivial intellectual home for me as I was mapping out *The Sanitary Arts*, and I'm especially appreciative of Sam Baker for his enthusiasm and encouragement. I must thank the editors and readers at *Representations* for publishing the earliest version of my first chapter, and William A. Cohen and Ryan Johnson for finding the perfect home for my third chapter "Victorian Dust Traps" in their collection of essays, *Filth: Dirt Disgust and Modern Life*. To my readers for Ohio State University Press, Linda Shires and Barbara Leckie, I owe an enormous intellectual debt. Their careful, close readings of my manuscript allowed that final set of revisions to be both joyful and exciting. My editors at The Ohio State University Press, Sandy Crooms, Malcolm Litchfield, and most recently Lindsay Martin, have made the publication process as easy as possible, and I would like to thank them as well as all of my contacts at the press who helped to compile and print this project. More thanks goes to Natalie Zelt at the Harry Ransom Humanities Research Center for helping me obtain the cover image. My dear friends Kim Smith, Elizabeth Green Musselman, and Lisa Moses Leff have made the special challenges of the "second book" seem less impossible, less onerous, and certainly much more fun. Rebecca Stern's ongoing perspective and humor about all things professional were also much valued. As always, Caroline Levander provided the best advice, support, and friendship at the most crucial moments of the project's evolution. Members of my family have been uniquely supportive of my project too: my father sent me every clipping from *The Wall Street Journal* over the last decade that even remotely pertained to sewers or British museum culture, and my mother taught me everything I know about filth and cleanliness.

Finally, I thank my husband, John Pipkin, who vitally connects me with a robust contemporary literary culture and also makes me laugh, and my son Max, who is simply the best kid in the world.

Foul Matter

Edwin Chadwick, John Ruskin, and
Mid-Victorian *Aesthesis*

In addressing you on the subject of the Fine Arts in relation to Sanitary Reform, I am met by two difficulties, a Scylla and Charybdis that might well appall one who had not set out with a determined purpose, or was not sure of his way. The first difficulty is that the work of the artist and of the sanitary engineer seem to stand so very far apart in our minds, that I may be challenged with the question, "What have they to do with each other? Speak about either of the two things, and we will listen. But let us have one thing at a time." The second difficulty is that the two—Art and Sanitation—are so nearly identical, are so interwoven in their action and re-action, that it may be too hastily assumed that anything I may have to say regarding their relation to each other must necessarily be obvious and trite.

—Wyke Bayliss, "Sanitary Reform in Relation to the Fine Arts" (1889)

*I*t should already be apparent that Victorian ecclesiastical painter Wyke Bayliss and I have a few things in common. When I began my research for this project on the nineteenth-century sanitation reform movement and its connections with Victorian aesthetic philosophy, my hybridized topic seemed explicitly contradictory. While I have always intended to argue that Sanitation and Art were thrown into philosophical opposition, controversy, and resolution in a wide variety of Victorian texts and settings, the two things, as Bayliss observes, share no semantic domain, no commonplace history of mutual development, no obvious field of discursive reciprocity and collusion. On the other hand, as I quickly realized, in the wake of Foucault the singular topic of sanitation reform had been so thoroughly mapped upon Victorian culture that potentially nothing seemed beyond the reach of Edwin

Chadwick's invidious sanitary apparatus. In fact, to argue that Victorian aesthetic culture had shifted to accommodate the values and discourse of sanitation reform might very well seem "obvious and trite" under the methodological inevitability of Foucauldian New Historicism, where Chadwick's infamous "Sanitary Idea" had already been discovered to have widespread economic, political, social and sexual effects. Mary Poovey's groundbreaking work on British cultural formation, for example, contested standard Whig histories of Victorian reform by recasting Chadwick as a malevolent bureaucrat who "helped normalize what Michel Foucault has called disciplinary individualism, that paradoxical configuration of agency whereby freedom is constituted as "voluntary" compliance with a rationalized order, which is (not incidentally) as capable of producing irrationality as embodying rationality."[1] Following Poovey, scholars of Victorian culture came to recognize sanitation reform as encompassing a broad range of personal rituals and procedural regulations that allowed the modern state to gain control of both individual bodies and social bodies, disciplining through the dissemination of public health laws that discriminated, disproportionately, against the poor and against women.

Indeed, since the 1975 publication of Foucault's *Discipline and Punish*, the rise of governmental agencies, the proliferation of bureaucratic spaces, and the viral spread of state "carceral archipelagos" have become familiar features of mid-Victorian cultural studies.[2] Underwritten, most commonly, by Foucault's concept of "panopticism," much New Historical work on British reform movements has been methodologically dependent on a concept of vision and visibility that sometimes harnesses interest in Victorian cultural formation to the modes and metaphors provided by optical surveillance and the disciplinary gaze. In the case of Victorian sanitation reform, much has been made of Chadwick's investment in discursively revealing the poor to his middle-class readers, exposing their filth and fragility to the view of a sympathetic and eagerly interventionist public who would enforce codes of morality, civility, and cleanliness through charity work and philanthropy, to be sure, but also by embodying and performing morality, civility and cleanliness themselves. Joseph Childers has argued that Foucault's concept of panopticism was particularly instructive for understanding the observational techniques and habits that Chadwick's sanitary inspections introduced to middle-class readers of his 1842 *Report on the Sanitary Condition of the Labouring Population*: panopticism, Childers writes, "may indeed have been the means by which middle-class values such as 'respectability' or 'duty' became the disciplinary mechanism that helped to maintain dominant middle-class representations of its particular interests as those of the whole and that established to norms against which all society could be evaluated."[3]

It seems plausible that the observational habits of looking that Childers describes would have aesthetic implications, especially given the specific training in visual appreciation and responsiveness Chadwick required of his readers, and the taste for realist detail over generalization he hoped to foster for the purposes of social discipline in middle-class spectators. Childers explains that Chadwick insisted "observers must not avert their eyes, nor be satisfied with generalizations that dilute the specifics of the problem at hand, for the effects of their observations will go on making the world of the lower classes knowable to readers . . . their observations will help to police that world."[4] But one limitation of Foucauldian methodology is its tendency to repress aesthetic development under the hegemony of scientific revolution: the realist vision so associated with Victorian aesthetic concepts and practices is primarily, under New Historicism, a sensory apparatus without sensibility, harnessed to clinical observation, classification, and ameliorist narratives of social perfectibility.

I am certainly not the first to observe this, nor any other limitation of Foucauldian methodology. The New Historicist elision of a whole set of critical conversations about Victorian aesthetic forms has been of great concern to Caroline Levine, for example, just as the dominance of scientific over aesthetic models of cultural interpretation has been recently criticized by Rachel Teukolsky.[5] Furthermore, any assumption that optical surveillance in mid-Victorian Britain became a uniformly established and stable method of social control and identity formation has been variously thrown into doubt by art historians and literary critics like Jonathon Crary, Linda M. Shires, Janice Carlisle, Kate Flint and Meegan Kennedy, while the totalizing narrative of Victorian government centralization and Chadwickian bureaucratic discipline has been thoroughly challenged by Lauren Goodlad.[6] All of these critics and many others I discuss below and throughout have helped me to shape my argument in *The Sanitary Arts* around the unevenness rather than the hegemony of sanitary discipline, and the places of philosophical overlap and ideological collision that are the most interesting sites of cultural study. They have enabled me to argue here for a more volatile vision of the Sanitary Idea than is usually circulated in Victorian histories or genealogies, one that allows us to see not just an invidious narrative of disciplinary bureaucratic reform unleashed in the 1840s by a charismatic and megalomaniacal Chadwick, but a longer and more dilatory, more contradictory, more contested story of sanitation reform that inevitably confronted, at its inception, not just scientific technologies of vision but, as Wyke Bayliss implies, philosophical questions of taste.

Visual preferences, I will argue, were certainly sanitized by Chadwick's style of observation, but I am also suggesting that the ongoing work of sanitation reform in the nineteenth century was less concerned with mobilizing sophisticated technologies of vision than with galvanizing the baser senses of the British public to be more "instinctively" repulsed by dirt. The nineteenth-century cleanliness campaigns, as I have termed the wider variety of movements and controversies arising from Chadwick's mid-Victorian reforms, represent a crucial passage in the cultural history of taste that propelled a seemingly natural, seemingly instinctive sensitivity to filth into ideological and aesthetic coherence. Dominant models of sense perception and, indeed, dominant models of visual interpretation inherited from the eighteenth century, were actively displaced in order to make way for what I call the sanitary aesthetic: a more holistic understanding of beauty that submitted visual values to the smell test. Edwin Chadwick clearly understood and explained the more exalted stakes of sewerage and drainage, slum clearances and washhouses, in his writings and lectures, and represented the battle for cleanliness in Victorian London as a philosophical and intellectual choice between darkness and light, disease and health, and, perhaps surprisingly, dirt and art. In the middle of an 1862 address to the British Association for the Promotion of Science called "The Manual Labourer as an Investment of Capital," Chadwick asserts,

> We may, indeed, claim from professors of high art like Mr. Ruskin, that they have yet to take into account more of the economical being immersed in the physical and material in connection with the beautiful. I remember talking with him once on his search for works of art in Venice, on which he discourses so eloquently, and, describing to him my own feelings at the filth and squalor of the population, as suppressing any admiration for art amidst the foul and pestilential. I remember his admission that in that city the seats of ancient art were commonly centers of filth, so much so that his attendant in his explorations would sniff an ill odour, and when it was strong would say, 'now we are coming to something old and fine,' meaning in art. I would submit that the nose of the attendant gave a truer indication than the eye of the painter, for the right direction of labour, which must be for works of purification to produce the truly beautiful, which is always connected with the economical.[7]

This passage may certainly serve as further evidence of Chadwick's megalomania and apparently boundless self-regard, even twenty years after the

publication of the *Sanitary Report,* but it also succinctly isolates an important aspect of my argument: the Victorian sanitation reform movement was
a direct challenge to an established hierarchy of the senses, and a referendum
on traditional philosophies of *aesthesis* that favored "the eye of the painter"
over the more prosaic and more commonplace human sensitivities. "Abhor-
rence of smell produces its own kind of social power," Alain Corbin has
influentially observed, and in Chadwick's case, that social power was oppor-
tunistically (and I may add, retrospectively) recast as a natural human desire
for beauty over ugliness.[8]

Along with Corbin, Peter Stallybrass and Allon White have been central to my thinking about sanitation and *aesthesis,* not because they specifically focus upon art objects or write about art history, but because they insist
that the "discipline of policing and sanitation depended . . . upon a transformation of the senses" not limited to the "permanent visibility" embodied
by the Panopticon.[9] Visibility implies some distance, but the real source of
pollution anxiety for the Victorian middle class was physical intimacy, and
more anxiously focused upon the threat of both touch and smell. Smell was
particularly worrisome for Chadwick and fellow sanitarians, Stallybrass and
White explain, because it was transient but deadly, and could invade the middle-class body and the bourgeois home without warning: "It was, primarily,
the sense of smell which engaged social reformers, since smell, whilst, like
touch, encoding revulsion, had a pervasive and invisible presence difficult
to regulate" (139). Corbin has likewise pointed out the centrality of smell
over all other sensory experiences in eighteenth- and nineteenth-century
French sanitary reportage, and I would add that Chadwick's original *Sanitary
Report* is similarly occupied with the olfactory threat (Corbin 2). Featuring
long, repetitive quotations from well-known physicians like Thomas Southwood Smith and Lyon Playfair that testify to people being killed instantly by
unspecified putrid smells, the *Sanitary Report* crackles with anxiety about the
foul vapors and noxious miasmata emanating from organic decay.[10] Crucially,
Chadwick even warns that foul odors are so ubiquitous in urban slums and
working-class neighborhoods that "the sense of smell in the majority of the
inhabitants seems to be destroyed, and having no perception even of stenches
which are insupportable to strangers, they must be unable to note the excessive escapes of miasma as antecedents to disease" (Chadwick 23). The olfactory quality of the original *Sanitary Report* has been noted in passing by
many readers including Childers, and a variety of cultural critics have noted
that "olfactory reform of the poor was . . . intimately linked with their moral
reform."[11] But smell is as difficult to theorize as it is to regulate, and remains
an understandably neglected feature of sanitary history and experience. As

David Trotter explains, smell functions "consistently as a disintegrative and agonistic principle in the literature of sanitary reform" that works against narrative and against social meaning: "To understand the meanings and values attributed to it," he writes, "one must be able to think the pure negativity of the nausea it provokes."[12]

Smell also works against the panoptical model of social development, and, according to Trotter, requires a more phenomenological approach than can be provided by New Historicism: "The New Historicism's preoccupation with modernity's dominant visual regimes have produced some brilliant analyses of the moment at which these regimes falter," but they cannot adequately account for alternative models of sense perception so rooted in physiological disgust and cultural anxiety. While *The Sanitary Arts,* is not, in any way, a history of smell or even an alternative genealogy of sense perception, it recognizes smell as an oppositional aesthetic value that points to the more expansive capacities of sanitation as an imagined mechanism of social perfectibility in the long nineteenth century. As noted above, bad smells became a particularly disturbing category of social and bodily experience because sanitarians privileged smell as the most prophylactic and hygienic of the senses. Not only were the poor suffering under increasing pressures of abjection and dehumanization because they were losing the capacity to smell properly, even a highly trained art critic like John Ruskin, a master technician of vision and interpreter of visual codes, could be endangered, Chadwick warns, by a fundamental failure of *aesthesis,* a disregard of the lower senses in favor of dangerous visual pleasure. Predicated on a reverse hierarchy of sensitivities and underwritten by a fundamental distrust of outdated and "dirty" visual values, Victorian sanitation reform thus became part of an aesthetic conversation about beauty, culture, and shared social experience that predated the 1842 *Sanitary Report* and outlasted the 1870 discovery of the germ.

Interestingly, by ignoring baser forms of sense perception, panopticism extends the repressive work of a traditional strand of eighteenth-century aesthetic philosophy founded upon the devaluation of physical experience. Disinterest, that central tenet of what Linda Dowling and others have termed "Whig aesthetics," presumes that taste is a universal category of experience that can be reasonably expected to govern men's moral and social behavior.[13] Beginning with Lord Shaftesbury's 1711 *Characteristics of Men, Manners, Opinions, Times* and continuing through Edmund Burke, and, crucially, Immanuel Kant, beauty is a social instinct that represses individual, baser sensitivities in favor of civic harmony and communal pleasure. The significance of aesthetic disinterest to Western philosophy in general and to Victorian culture in particular has been emphasized by many contemporary critics like Dowling and Allison Pease, who notes that Kant's detached, intellectualized aesthetic of "pure pleasure" protected art from the sciences, from commercial need, and even from the subjective bias of individual sense perception.[14] For Terry Eagleton, moreover, the emergence of this particular strand of traditional eighteenth-century aesthetic philosophy is repressive not just because it represses the body and the body's instincts in favor of "a community of sensibility with others," but because it mobilizes *aesthesis* in the service of political hierarchy and aristocratic power. "If the aesthetic comes in the eighteenth century to assume the significance it does," he reasons, "it is because the word is shorthand for a whole project of hegemony, the massive introjection of abstract reason by the life of the senses."[15] He continues,

> What matters is not in the first place art, but this process of refashioning the human subject from the inside, informing its subtle affections and bodily responses with this law that is not law. It would thus ideally be as inconceivable for the subject to violate the injunctions of power as it would be to find a putrid odor enchanting. (Eagleton 43)

Eagleton's argument here highlights a Kantian conundrum about the basest of human senses that the philosopher explored in his 1798 *Anthropology from a Pragmatic Point of View*. Kant explains that smell is not an aesthetic sense because it is "contrary to freedom and less sociable than taste, where among many dishes and bottles a guest can choose according to his liking, without others being forced to share the pleasure in it."[16] Smells, bad or good, are socially coercive, and at odds with the seemingly instinctive and natural pleasure generated by more detached forms of sense perception. Because it is socially disruptive rather than formative and a reminder of repressed animal instinct, smell is the most "ungrateful" and "dispensable" sense for Kant. Yet there might be, he admits grudgingly, necessary physiological reasons for the nausea and disgust caused by foul odors:

> It does not pay to cultivate it or refine it at all in order to enjoy it; for there are more disgusting objects than pleasant ones (especially in crowded places) and even when we come across something fragrant, the pleasure coming from the senses is always fleeting and transient. But, as a negative condition of wellbeing, the sense is not unimportant, in order not to breathe in bad air (oven fumes, the stench of swamps and animal carcasses), or also not to need rotten things for nourishment. (Kant 60)

For Kant, bad smells register a radically individual regard for self-preserva-
tion and highlight the precarious quality of aesthetic disinterest; as Eagleton
interprets, bad smells are a violation of the regular and harmonious motions
and movements that produce social life as an aesthetic experience. "The maladroit or aesthetically disproportioned," Eagleton elaborates, always "signals
in its modest way a certain crisis in political power" (Eagleton 42). Revisiting
Chadwick's anecdote through Kant and through Eagleton, it becomes apparent that when Chadwick accuses John Ruskin of a penchant for putrescence
he is reframing the insanitary hazards of urban filth as an ongoing aesthetic
crisis, one that was enabled and institutionalized by the disinterested "eye of
the painter" in eighteenth-century Whig philosophy, at the expense of the
more common and self-preserving senses. Instead of ignoring bad smells,
avoiding them, teaching the body to repress the baser instincts that actually
protect individual health and the human species, Chadwick relocates smell to
the very center of aesthetic activity and demands that the higher senses follow the nose.

It may seem that this line of argument threatens to replicate and even
enhance the stories of sanitation reform that feature Chadwick as an malevolent disciplinarian who managed to dominate and restructure a variety of
cultural discourses with his Sanitary Idea; as Goodlad has pointed out, Chadwick's "success in portraying himself as the master agent of an all-embracing
sanitary idea was one of the most remarkable feats of self-promotion in the
nineteenth century" (Goodlad 92). However, Chadwick's self-aggrandizement
cannot be interpreted as complete bureaucratic authority or saturating ideological control. Chadwick eventually became "the most hated man in England" and lost his own position on the Board of Health in 1855; moreover, as
Goodlad reminds us, the *Sanitary Report* merely consolidated (albeit thoroughly and well) ideas already in wide circulation in the Victorian period,
thanks to the investigations of medical professionals like James Phillips Kay,
Neil Arnott and Southwood Smith (Goodlad 94, 101, 93). Goodlad, along with
critics like William A. Cohen and Michelle Allen, warns that the Foucauldian
impulse to rewrite positivist histories of sanitation reform as a repressive and
mechanistic genealogy of discipline too easily elides the real improvements
wrought by the cleanliness campaigns, as well as the specific injustices and
deprivations imposed by local sanitary "improvements."[17] Sanitation reform
was slow, moreover, and not triumphantly imposed upon willing Victorians
by the olfactory perspicacity of Chadwick's 1842 *Report*. As Carlisle cogently
explains in *Common Scents: Comparative Encounters in High-Victorian Fiction,* a central board of health was established in 1848, but "it was not until
1866 that local authorities were required to hire sanitary inspectors, and

not until 1871 that a new central department was created to oversee public health."[18]

Given the sluggish pace and uncertain effects of sanitation reform in Victorian England, I am cautious of suggesting an alternative genealogy for the Sanitary Idea that would imply either a strong theory of cultural development or a rupture narrative of aesthetic change. While I am arguing that sanitation reform enters British intellectual life as a challenge to traditional models of *aesthesis,* Chadwick is not the sole instigator of sanitary philosophy in Victorian England, nor is he the solitary advocate of the sanitary aesthetic as it travels through nineteenth-century public discourse and cultural controversy. In fact, I argue in *The Sanitary Arts* that the aesthetic dimensions of the cleanliness campaigns over the long nineteenth century were often and ably managed by artists like Wyke Bayliss, by novelists like George Eliot, and by architects like Robert Edis, seemingly unconnected Victorian figures who nevertheless collaborated on the cultural project of redefining taste as a mechanism of public health and social justice. Such collaboration was enabled but not authorized by Chadwick, who may have been a strong and avidly opportunistic producer of sanitary discourse in the 1840s, but was in no sense an orchestrator of the spontaneous, decentralized, and adaptive alliance between sanitary protocols and aesthetic reforms that engendered a series of complex cultural developments by the end of the nineteenth century. The inadequacy of direct intention or causation as a model of cultural change is nowhere more apparent than in the spontaneous development of the sanitary aesthetic across discourses and disciplines in the mid-Victorian period, and is especially vivid in the work of Chadwick's self-appointed nemesis, John Ruskin. Although Chadwick, in the above passage from 1862, positions Ruskin as someone who finds foul odors enchanting and thus represents all that is most threatening and antisocial about traditional aesthetics, Ruskin's enthusiasm for moral cleanliness and purity are self-evident throughout his writings. Moreover, the art critic's frank admiration for the less metaphoric, less spiritual aspects of hygiene have become infamous footnotes in the annals of sanitary history: "A good sewer is a far nobler and a far holier thing," Ruskin once declared, "than the most admired Madonna ever painted."[19]

Ruskin, in fact, began to sanitize Victorian aesthetic preferences as early as his first volume of *Modern Painters* where he privileged the bright colors and cleanly details of J. M. W. Turner and the Pre-Raphaelite painters over the picturesque browns and pestilential yellows of the Renaissance Old Masters. While every chapter in *The Sanitary Arts* reflects upon this distinctly Ruskinian contribution to the cleanliness campaigns, my first chapter is specifically concerned with a watershed moment in the production of what I'm calling the sanitary aesthetic, a confluence of events in the 1840s that first subjected fine art to hygienic scrutiny. In 1842, Edwin Chadwick published his *Sanitary Report;* the following year, John Ruskin published his first volume of *Modern Painters.* Seemingly oppositional, seeming incomparable, these texts nevertheless collaborated in challenging traditional models of *aesthesis* and imposing new standards of aesthetic sensitivity upon Victorian thought and experience. Under the bright clarity of sanitary science, an eighteenth-century artistic philosophy based on obscurity, darkness, and the metaphysical experience of sublimity came to be understood as a degraded obsession with filth. By the mid-forties, moreover, these philosophical ideas yielded material effects when a public controversy erupted over the cleaning and restoration of dirty paintings in the National Gallery in Trafalgar Square. Members of the public who were initially outraged by the cleansing process were eventually converted to the more sanitary perspective that the embrowned tones and shadowy backgrounds of many famous, highly valued art treasures were actually caused by a range of filthy and offensive organic substances. The high aesthetic preferences of Shaftesbury, Burke, Hazlitt, and other famed collectors, connoisseurs, and philosophers were suddenly contaminated, diseased, and offensive to the commoner senses, and Ruskin's more intellectual and abstract revulsion for the Old Masters was popularly and publicly affirmed. The sanitary aesthetic did, indeed, emerge as its own semantic field in the mid-Victorian period, challenging Whig darkness and disinterestedness as a dangerous threat to public health and individual wellbeing.

To reiterate, however, when I describe the connection between Edwin Chadwick and John Ruskin as collaborative, I am not implying that the sanitarian and the art critic together hatched a deliberate, intentional program for reinventing aesthetic culture as a mechanism of social perfectibility in the middle of the nineteenth century. Nor do I mean to suggest that the discourse of sanitation was so powerful and so totalizing that it redirected Ruskin's foundational aesthetic interests into Chadwick's grandiose pursuits. The limitation of a Foucauldian model of cultural change is more than apparent in the unstudied association between two domineering Victorian personalities who spoke to each other far less than they participated in a broad, spontaneous and adaptive conversation at the increasingly robust, increasingly porous interface between public health and aesthetics. Instead, my understanding of an interface rather than a border between sanitation and art has realized some help from Caroline Levine's notion of "strategic formalism," which challenges the structuralist idea of oppositional terms that "contaminate and destabilize each other," and also the and/or discovery that irreconcilable concepts actually mean something so nearly identical (and identically repressive) that they are not worth discussing separately. According to Levine, strategic formalism

> considers the ways that social, cultural, political, and literary ordering principles rub up against one another, operating simultaneously but not in concert. This method shows that it is in the strange encounters among forms—even those forms that are deliberate outcomes of dominant ide-ologies—that unexpected, politically significant possibilities emerge. Thus social change comes not so much from active and intentional agency as from the openings that materialize in the collisions among social and cul-tural forms." (Levine 633)

Similarly, I am arguing that Chadwick's *Sanitary Report* and Ruskin's *Modern Painters* were not intentionally, mutually coercive, but were simultaneously generative of significant cultural debate and aesthetic remapping at a crucial historical moment that produced new conventions and new preferences in not just visual art, but in architecture, interior decoration, and even literature.

On the other hand, I do not think it's entirely productive to relinquish intention as a functional category for understanding the process of cultural change; intentionality, I would argue, is a much more complex and adaptive system than either Foucault or Levine allow. In fact, the model of causality I am describing in *The Sanitary Arts* more closely resembles what biologists and economists would refer to as "self-organization," a term popularized by Paul Krugman, but best adapted for interdisciplinary use by bioethicist and philosopher Henri Atlan. In Atlan's assessment, self-organization offers a model of intention "in which intentionality is not assumed from the begin-ning, but is an emerging property of local causal constraints."[20] For scientists, self-organization explains the apparent coordination and complex develop-ment that arises spontaneously from local, unrelated biological systems. Self-organization is the methodology economist Krugman adopts to compare economic slumps to hurricanes; in doing so, Krugman is looking for par-allels between "seemingly disparate phenomena" to explain how it is that some systems that "start from an almost homogenous or even almost random state, spontaneously form large-scale patterns."[21] While Atlan and Krugman represent disciplines at some remove from both each other and the intellec-tual traditions of the Humanities, self-organization as they explain it relies on a notion of spontaneous but opportunistic collaboration that has signifi-cantly helped me understand both the features of multiple causality that are endemic to my interdisciplinary project, and the possibility that discourse is another system that functions adaptively, at times joining forces with diverse and seemingly oppositional semantic fields. While one of the most important critiques of self-organization targets the assumption that altruism and progress must necessarily accompany any example of spontaneous emergence (the best example here may be Adam Smith's infamous "invisible hand" of the free market), my own view is that the cultural collaborations I describe in this book are often robust and complex, but are fundamentally unpredictable and idiosyncratic over the long term.[22] Unexpected consequences of intentional actions are not necessarily better or more inherently progressive than predicted or desired short-term outcomes, but they are inevitable and potentially widespread.

Most appealingly, self-organization offers a model of causality that deemphasizes the rupture narratives of cultural change that dominate our stories about both Victorian sanitation reform and aesthetic development; after all, the suddenness of Chadwick's Sanitary Idea, the discovery of the germ, the rise of the Pre-Raphaelites, and the invention of Modernism have been long and well-known data points in the causal narrative of nineteenth-century cultural history. But when sanitation reform and aesthetic change are viewed as deeply collaborative, mutually constitutive discourses, each subject seems less revolutionary but more complex, and implicated in a far richer story of cultural development. In this way, the collisions among forms that Levine describes might be more robustly understood as productive and enabling collusions among *functions* that, in turn, make complex cultural developments possible. Cultural change emanates from the strength of certain discourses and eminent, charismatic producers of discourse like Chadwick and Ruskin, but also from dynamic, and unpredictable collaborations among discourses. Such collaborations are indirect and evolving, and need to be mapped over a much longer period of cultural history than singular stories of intellectual or aesthetic development are usually allotted. Thus, in the longer, slower view, Victorian sanitation reform can be seen as both a recognizable, coercive discourse and an open, idiosyncratic, mobile set of events that I reframe here as the cleanliness campaigns.

While my understanding of cultural development as collaboration is opposed to a structuralist understanding of collaboration as contamination or collapse, it still borrows usefully from structuralist methodology for an explanation of how contamination mythologies remain relevant, especially for anyone trying to tell a story about sanitation. For example, Mary Douglas's groundbreaking interpretation of the anthropological meaning of dirt has explained that "pollution dangers strike when form has been attacked," or when culturally dangerous ambiguities threaten pattern.[23] This is, in itself, a powerful metatextual inscription of the effect of stucturalist critique, but it is also, for my purposes, a fascinatingly antagonistic interpretation of the sanitary/aesthetic encounter at a particularly transformative moment in the nineteenth century. The formal conventions of painting and the metaphysical states associated with those conventions were challenged by the Sanitary Idea in the 1840s, and I argue in my first chapter that this cross-disciplinary collusion produced a set of pollution anxieties about old aesthetic forms, and replaced those forms with new, "healthful" aesthetic patterns and new experiences of *aesthesis*. The first three chapters of this volume, in fact, are specifically invested in the convergence of sanitary ideas with traditional aesthetic values in the mid-Victorian period, and the peculiar, even contradictory negotiations that developed a coterminous cultural discourse for artistic hygiene and sanitary beauty at the porous interface of two disciplines.

My second chapter identifies a specific subset of the nineteenth-century novel as "sanitary narratives": novels that articulate the social drama of sanitary reform as an aesthetic transformation of Victorian culture.[24] In the mid- to late-Victorian novel, moreover, this ideological transformation of dirt into art is often inscribed upon more dominant narratives of character growth and transformation, and the pollution anxiety Douglas theorizes becomes a driving mechanism of the plot. The sanitary narrative is, on the one hand, a formal commitment to social reconciliation and harmony as an aesthetic condition; thus I argue that canonical mid-Victorian reform novels like George Eliot's *Middlemarch* (1870–71) and Elizabeth Gaskell's *North and South* (1855) stage the ideological defeat of dirty, aristocratic visual preferences for picturesque landscapes and quaint people and put forward baser, sanitary sensitivities as realist vehicles for social reform and narrative closure. The marriage of art and sanitation in such fiction is often coterminous with the inexorable teleology of the Victorian marriage plot, and is even more visible in popular novels that explicitly assign ideological positions to their romantic leads. For example, George Halse's 1889 *Graham Aspen, Painter* and George Gissing's 1890 *The Emancipated* both conclude with a union between a formerly "dirty" artist to a woman who enforces hygiene and health through scientific knowledge or ethical principles. Moreover, in a variety of these lesser-known novels like Averil Beaumont's *Magdalen Wynard, or The Provocations of a Pre-Raphaelite* (1872) and Charlotte Mary Yonge's *The Pillars of the House* (1873), the revival of "true" art is imagined to be a process of purification that privileges the "healthy" gloss and bright "clean" colors of the Pre-Raphaelite painters over the degenerate tones and shadowy images of the Old Masters.

As we have seen, for Edwin Chadwick the connection between art and dirt was topographically obvious: art was dirty because its cherished environments were dirty. Venice, that revered paradise of aesthetic culture, was "pestilential and foul" in Chadwick's assessment, and the art it contained and inspired must necessarily be degraded and potentially contagious. But mapping the unsanitary status of distant European capitals was not the primary geographical effect of the Sanitary Idea; as Stallybrass and White have influentially argued, Victorian reformers like Chadwick and Henry Mayhew were central in the ideological mapping of London "fever nests" for the Victorian middle class. My third chapter argues that the slow development and uneven circulation of germ theories in the 1870s gradually forced sanitary geographies of the city inward, eventually producing analogous geographies of the over-decorated, architecturally busy Victorian interior. In these domestic geographies, the decorative "dust trap" supplemented the fever nest as an internal locus of pollution anxiety. Advocates of domestic health not only eschewed the nooks, crannies, tunnels, dark rooms, narrow hallways, and turrets cherished by Gothic revivalists, they also dismissed the favored features of Aesthetic decoration—dados, decorative carving, shelving, cornices, tapestries, curtains and carpets as "dust traps" or, in other words, "the forcing beds for disease germs." By century's end, the banishment of the dust trap from the Victorian home and the transition to a sleek, seamless Modernism in British art and architecture looks less like a rupture narrative of aesthetic revolution than the slow, collaborative work of the Victorian cleanliness campaigns.

While there is some temporal and ideological overlap between the first and second halves of this book, the last three chapters are more specifically focused on the impact of germ theory, laboratory science, and microbiology on the experience and understanding of *aesthesis*. Most studies of sanitation reform suggest a rather abrupt ending to the positivist, ameliorist notion that social perfectibility could be ensured for England through a serious, state-enforced commitment to environmental cleanliness and individual hygiene.[25] But in spite of various "germ theories of disease" that circulated fitfully and incompletely in the 1870s and 1880s, the familiar features and ideological meaning of the sanitary narrative lingered through the beginning of the twentieth century: still reliant on the pollution anxiety inspired by the reeking village and the picturesque landscape, sanitary fiction continued to promote the aesthetic promise of perfectibility, even when challenged by new and potentially contradictory information about microorganisms, bacteria, and genetics. The work of historians of science like Alison Bashford, Nancy Tomes, and David Wootton helps to make sense of these apparently anachronistic novels and narratives. Insisting that rupture narratives of scientific change and revolution radically misrepresent the sluggish pace of scientific discovery and adaptation, as well as the protracted resistance to germ theory that

lingered until well into the twentieth century, these historians make a case
for a longer, slower, more vacillating story of medical reform than positivist
histories of science admit. In turn, this allow me to argue in the second half
of *The Sanitary Arts* for the continued and continuing importance of Victorian sanitary philosophy to cultural forms and ideologies far beyond their
conventional domain. For example, germ theory is often acknowledged in
the design guides and domestic health manuals I discuss in Chapter Three,
represented by the invocation of both germs and microscopic "seeds" of disease. But pollution anxiety in these texts still pivots upon smells and vapors,
effluvia and miasma, spontaneous generation of illness, and a Gothic fear of
organic decay. Germ theory doesn't replace sanitary discourse simply and
efficiently in the 1870s; germ theory supplements (and at times contradicts)
the Victorian environmental hygiene program with a newly biological component, promising to deliver bodily health and social harmony one germ and
gene at a time.

My fourth chapter thus explores the so-called revolution in medicine that
occurred in the last decades of the nineteenth century as a protracted cultural
dispute about the human body that pitted the proponents of sanitary science,
or prevention, against the rising forces of laboratory and surgical science, or
cure. Here, I discuss medical fictions as a generic offshoot of what I've already
identified as the sanitary narrative; while, as I argue in my second chapter, the
late-Victorian sanitary narrative privileges clean art over dirty art and thus
forges a new social order based on aesthetic harmony, the medical narrative
fundamentally challenges that social order by contesting the faith in mutual
pleasures and collective pains that stabilized and sustained the sanitary aesthetic. In the medical narrative, Ruskin's sanitary philosophy is thrown into
opposition with Walter Pater's more physiological, more impressionistic, and
considerably less social theory of aesthetics: "A counted number of pulses
only is given to us of a variegated, dramatic life," Pater famously mused in
his 1873 *The Renaissance*. "How may we see in them all that is to be seen in
them by the finest senses?"[26] This decadent description of an aesthetic experience found in the local shifts and individual "pulses" of an atomized body,
develops contiguously with the anatomical sciences in the 1870s and 1880s,
when a new understanding of the human body as a potential site of surgical
penetration and dissection threatened to overthrow a vitalist concept of the
perfectible body defined by unity, beauty, and physical cleanliness. But medical fictions and surgical stories enter aesthetic controversy not through their
mobilization of "decadence" as a coherent philosophical category, I argue, but
through their perpetual inscription of "anesthesia" as the physiological and
philosophical opposite of aesthesia.

Anesthesia, first discovered and utilized in the 1840s, was coined linguistically by Oliver Wendell Holmes to underscore the deliberate repression of the very senses awakened and enjoyed through aesthetic experience. Late-nineteenth-century medical fictions like Edward Berdoe's *St. Bernard's: The Romance of a Medical Student* (1887), Roy Tellet's *A Draught of Lethe: The Romance of an Artist* (1891), and Grant Allen's *Hilda Wade* (1900), collectively indulge a cultural fantasy about medical perversion as a threat to sanitary philosophy by inscribing the numb, insensate, surgically prepared body as the ultimate corruption of traditional models of *aesthesis*. Anesthesia, it was widely believed, destroyed the need for empathy on the part of surgeons and doctors, numbing the social dimension of traditional aesthetic experience while expanding the uncivilized taste for asocial and even sadistic pleasures. Pitting surgeons against sanitarians, vivisectionists against holistic healers, mad scientists against valiant artists, Ruskinian philosophers against Paterian aesthetes, medical fictions expose and exploit moral confusion about the rise of pathology, revealing the shared territory of aesthetics and human health to be not the utopian, evolutionary platform of sanitary perfectibility, but the dystopian, degenerate nightmare of surgical interventions.

In my fifth and sixth chapters, I continue to explore the development of sanitation reform as it shifted from an environmental to a biological phase in cultural history, and examine that shift through the persistence of the sanitary plot in British "New Woman" fiction written well-after the discovery and general acceptance of microorganisms. "New Woman" fiction reinvented sanitation as a specifically female responsibility, not just through the rituals of domestic cleanliness and hygienic design I discuss in my third chapter, but through a new commitment to reproductive control and sexual selection found to be necessary in a post-germ theory England. In the late nineteenth-century novels of Grant Allen and Charles Reade, for example, the task of the female sanitarian retains its mid-Victorian ideological meaning and urgency: sanitary knowledge must purify the community by remaking the aesthetic, teaching the perverse landowning class, in particular, to recognize and appreciate a form of beauty found in healthy environments and beautiful people rather than in the picturesque poison of the decayed village and the degenerated human body. But the sanitary narrative in the late nineteenth century demands biological as well as affective reconciliation, teaching heroines to choose husbands based on virility, heredity, and cleanliness, and transforming the Victorian marriage plot into a more prescriptive, more contentious, and, in some ways, more feminist social arrangement.

"New Woman" novels that emphasize eugenic mating have been notoriously difficult for feminist critics to address as a crucial component of both women's history and socialist history, but the feminist, socialist program of "judicious breeding" is a distinct outgrowth of the sanitary aesthetic. "New Woman" fiction, I argue in my fifth chapter, articulates the troubling statistical and genetic program of social hygiene as an aesthetic appeal to the conscience, to the senses, to the virtuous necessity for beauty in all aspects of human existence. Mrs. Humphry (Mary) Ward's *The Mating of Lydia* is the text I discuss most thoroughly here as a very late sanitary fiction: published in 1913, Ward's novel absorbs many of the most notable features of those mid-Victorian sanitary narratives I discussed in the second chapter, and it eventually uses the marriage plot as a vehicle to banish environmental degradation, and to inspire a philosophical conversion to a sanitized, socialized aesthetic. But inscribed within the very title of Ward's novel is an acknowledgment of the somewhat refined responsibility carried by that closing tableau of affective reconciliation; if mid-century sanitary fictions cleanse and renew the social order through a harmonious reconciliation of opposites in marriage, late-Victorian and early-twentieth-century novels often emphasize not only marriage, but the biological and reproductive ritual of "mating" as a fundamental component of the new sanitary philosophy. The repudiation of the picturesque is a crucial ideological linchpin between sanitary and protoeugenic thinking, I argue, a trope that captures clearly an abiding effort to naturalize a set of specific social, political and economic problems as an aesthetic controversy.

The work of Pierre Bourdieu informs my thinking about aesthetic "naturalization," and the way taste functions politically in the construction of a cultural aristocracy. While my fifth chapter investigates the beginnings of a distinctly genetic phase in sanitary thinking that circulated as advocacy for aesthetic culture, my sixth and final chapter more fully explores the fin de siècle use of aesthetic philosophy as a mechanism for naturalizing the most distasteful and antisocial aspects of genetic engineering. In a variety of eugenic writings published at the end of the nineteenth and the beginning of the twentieth century I have discovered a common and artfully constructed genealogy of "race culture" in England, one that identifies the father and founder of British eugenic thinking to be not Francis Galton nor Herbert Spencer, nor even Edwin Chadwick, but, interestingly enough, John Ruskin. Ruskin's ongoing advocacy of what I've been calling the sanitary aesthetic in the Victorian period, his abiding investment in "clean" environments and strong, healthy bodies, is imported by racialists at the turn of the century, in an effort, I argue, to make the ugliness and unpleasantness of statistical thinking seem like an instinctive and even moral preference for beauty.

Opposed to what eugenicists like Caleb Saleeby would identify as the harsher, "Nietzschean" trend in social engineering, the Ruskinian eugenic program was "positive," emphasizing the preventive goals of hygienic breeding practices like healthy, state–approved "mating" rather than the more draconian methods of forced sterilization and infanticide. Of course, this insertion of Ruskin into eugenic philosophy is highly selective, and disregards, blatantly, Ruskin's social advocacy for the working classes, his investment in realist detail, his distaste for the "low" picturesque, and, most importantly here, his original intentions when he articulated social reform as an aesthetic philosophy. But a wide variety of these materials by both British and American eugenicists like Saleeby, Robert Reid Rentoul, Anna Mary Galbraith, and Scott Nearing, are organized, even self-organized around a set of protocols that invoke Ruskin as a powerful touchstone of aesthetic socialism, where the communal aspects of graceful, harmonious, and essentially Shaftesburian civil life seem to necessitate the sacrifice of dysgenic individuals and unhealthy types. What Saleeby calls "eugenic reconciliation" becomes a familiar feature of New Woman novels that explicitly advocate hygienic breeding as the ideological force of the marriage plot, and I argue in Chapter Six that Sarah Grand's two-part, post-Victorian trilogy *Adnam's Orchard* (1912) and *Winged Victory* (1916), advances eugenic reconciliation as a highly civilized, yet mysteriously natural aesthetic goal. Still channeling Ruskinian aesthetic revulsion through the stinking village and the picturesque landscape, Grand's novels nevertheless recuperate and revitalize that aristocratic strand of aesthetic philosophy that represses bad smells and ugly bodies through a process of prevention that begins at birth, and most resembles genetic elimination. Direct causality can be a misleading indicator in strong theories of cultural change, and the inherent long-term unpredictability of the initial collaboration between sanitary and aesthetic philosophies I foreground in *The Sanitary Arts* is especially visible in this disturbing late-century resuscitation of Ruskin for the purpose of eugenic advocacy. Under a longer, slower, more complex understanding of cultural change, even the best intentions are necessarily severed from unpredictable and morally ambivalent effects.

CHAPTER 1

Dirty Pictures

John Ruskin, *Modern Painters,* and the Victorian Sanitation of Fine Art

It must be remembered, also, how difficult it has become to define the term "filthy" with precision, in the present state, moral and physical, of the English atmosphere.

—John Ruskin, "On Usury" (1872)

When Edwin Chadwick denounced John Ruskin's insensitivity to filth in his 1862 address "The Manual Labourer as an Investment of Capital," he called attention to his own peculiar place in the history of Victorian aesthetics, a place unintentionally established twenty years earlier with his 1842 publication of the *Report on the Sanitary Condition of the Labouring Population of Great Britain* and the powerful ideologies of dirt and cleanliness that it shaped. Given that the *Sanitary Report* had forcefully argued that foul odors and miasmatic vapors were indicative of disease, poverty, and even crime, bad smells could only be the antithesis of beauty for the social scientist who admired robust health as a benchmark of individual and national prosperity.[1] For Chadwick, aesthetic reform must have seemed the natural byproduct of his cleanliness campaign: by producing a hygienic version of the truly beautiful, social science could eventually transform a reverence for Venetian darkness and decay into a celebration of English health, strength, and vigor, transforming at the same time Victorian aesthetic philosophy into a sanitized science of art. Moreover, it is evident that Chadwick, in 1862, believed such transformation was already in progress. Later in this same speech, he proudly takes credit for turning Ruskin away from his formerly foul aesthetic pursuits: "To do him justice, however, I might claim the honour

of having him as a disciple, even as an economist in this—that he now rec-
ognises the laws of health and the exercises of enjoined by them (which are
the true foundations of the beautiful), as sources of the national economy."[2]
While there is certainly a complex causal narrative at work in this story I am
trying to tell about sanitation and aesthetics, Chadwick is here opportunisti-
cally overstating his messianic influence on John Ruskin, identifying himself
as the originator of a complex discourse he would have needed to be a god to
design and to forward.

   Many scholars have influentially written about Chadwick's impact on mid-
Victorian social philosophy, contending that his "sanitary idea" helped to consolidate a variety of disciplinary mechanisms foundational in the formation
of the modern state. According to critics such as Mary Poovey and Joseph
Childers, for example, Chadwick's *Sanitary Report* not only inaugurated a
reform movement, it placed into circulation an entire discourse of public
health that would crucially inform nineteenth-century ideologies of domes-
ticity, morality, and subjectivity.[3] Yet while the social, political, and economic
effects of the sanitary idea have been well, even excessively, documented, the
sanitary reform movement of the 1840s also animated and reframed a series
of aesthetic transformations that have remained largely unexamined under
new historicist interrogation. The twinning of art and sanitation reform, the
pairing of Chadwick and John Ruskin, seems counterintuitive to a model of
history that has been so disciplined by discursive fields of meaning; indeed
the whole argument I am trying to advance in *The Sanitary Arts* points to a
series of aberrations in the smooth functioning of a discursive power that
can by definition move in only one direction and follow a (by now) static and
predictable genealogy. As I discussed in my Introduction, post-Foucauldian
critics have long been questioning the willingness of Victorian studies, in particular, to ignore events that contradict, or narratives that elide, Foucauldian
methodology. In this chapter I will specifically argue that when Chadwick's
original *Sanitary Report* inadvertently, even accidentally revealed that some
of the most idealized aspects of aesthetic decay were actually the commonest
forms of dirt, sanitation became a robustly invasive and self-organizing aesthetic apparatus, advancing a series of artistic changes under the banner of
public health.

   While my project is broadly interested in the interdisciplinary work of
what I will call sanitary art in nineteenth-century Britain, the chapter that
follows is primarily concerned with a watershed moment in the production
of that interdisciplinarity, a moment that subjected fine art to hygienic scrutiny. In 1842, Edwin Chadwick published his *Report on the Sanitary Condition
of the Labouring Population;* the following year, John Ruskin published the
first volume of *Modern Painters*. Incomparable in subject, genre, and style,

these texts would nonetheless participate in the same cultural project, producing between them a discourse of "dirty" art that challenged and eventually redefined nineteenth-century aesthetic standards. As we will see, Chadwick was partly correct when he counted Ruskin as a fellow sanitarian: indeed, the art critic employed the discourse and ideological necessity of sanitary reform from his earliest work, enforcing through his celebration of modern painters an aesthetic preference for the bright, clean colors of J. M. W. Turner and the Pre-Raphaelites over the pestilential tones and dark obscurity of the Renaissance Old Masters. Moreover, Ruskin's sophisticated preferences were circulated and popularized by a cultural event more generally accessible than *Modern Painters*. Isolating a mid-Victorian moment when the agitation for urban cleanliness began to interact with a variety of social discourses, this essay will also argue that Chadwick's powerful sanitary idea was channeled through a public controversy in the mid-forties about the aesthetic status of "picture cleaning" in the National Gallery at Trafalgar Square. When the dust from this debate finally settled, it had significantly destabilized a set of "dirty" aesthetic theories that had accumulated over previous centuries. What emerged was a more complex model of *aesthesis* driven by the pollution discourse of *Modern Painters,* and a shifting, at times contradictory, standard of aesthetic hygiene for Victorian art.

I. Filth, Formlessness, and Modern Painters

Ruskin's officiation at the marriage of art and sanitary reform becomes more imaginable if we reassess the aesthetic implications of Mary Douglas's groundbreaking description of the anthropological meaning of dirt. For Douglas, the pollution behavior and discourse of a given culture "is the reaction which condemns any object or idea likely to confuse or contradict cherished classifications."[4] Describing dirt in the now famous phrase as "matter out of place" (Douglas 35), Douglas explains that cleaning is a process of selecting and ordering the world in order to reduce ambiguities that arise in various cultural contexts. She writes that "Uncleanness or dirt is that which must not be included if pattern is to be maintained" (Douglas 40), later adding that "ritual pollution also arises from the interplay of form and surrounding formlessness. Pollution dangers strike when form has been attacked" (Douglas 104). Of course, Douglas's observations are particularly germane to the Victorian period, when ordering, selecting, and categorizing was a fundamental cross-disciplinary occupation. But her equation of formlessness and ambiguity with cultural uncleanliness also illuminates the pollution discourse endemic to the work of Ruskin, the eminent classifier of ancient and modern art. As David

Carroll has noted with reference to Douglas, *Modern Painters* "was Ruskin's most systematic attempt to present, codify, and justify his own 'science of aspects' to a world colonized by a host of other sciences. The subdivisions into volumes, parts, sections, chapters and sub-sections is evidence enough of this extraordinary attempt to categorize the visible world."[5]

In Carroll's assessment, the vocabulary of dirt and decay that proliferates in *Modern Painters* would arise from the art critic's need to defend the unity of God's creation from the divisive and calculating spirit of modern progress, and especially the industrial tendency to defile the earth's surface with railroads and narrow England's ancient legacies into a dirty path of factory production and commerce (Carroll 63). While it is certainly true that Ruskin's religious beliefs inform his association of dirt with contemporary religious decay, I am more interested in Douglas's assessment of dirt as a threat to pattern and a signifier of culturally dangerous ambiguities of form. If the pollution discourse of *Modern Painters* attacks the increasing spiritual impoverishment of England, it also attacks aesthetic formlessness in order to distinguish between the foul and the fair in art, and to dismiss the landscapes of the Old Masters in favor of those of contemporary artist J. M. W. Turner.[6] The first volume of *Modern Painters* divides artists into two main classes: "one aiming at the development of the exquisite truths of specific form, refined colour, and ethereal space, and content with the clear and impressive suggestion of any of these, by whatsoever means obtained; and the other casting all these aside, to attain those particular truths of tone and chiaroscuro, which may trick the spectator into a belief of reality" (*Modern Painters* I, 79). In paintings of the first class (primarily by Turner), form is preserved in everything from the specificity of the vegetation in the foreground to the precise time of day evoked by light and shadow; conversely, in the second class all effects are ignored except the one conferred by a brown or "green stain on their surfaces" (*Modern Painters* I, 164). Ruskin writes: "The old masters, content with one simple tone, sacrificed to its unity all the exquisite gradations and varied touches of relief and change by which nature unites her hours with each other" (*Modern Painters* I, 107).

Understanding how Ruskin manages to classify Turner in the first camp thus requires some special attention to the connections made in *Modern Painters* between color, form, and filth. While the brown and green stain variously imposed on paintings was dubbed "the veil of perversion" by Ruskin, he considered one of Turner's greatest triumphs to be the artist's discovery that "there is no *brown* in Nature . . . what we call brown is always a variety either of orange or purple."[7] On the contrary, Turner's landscapes were true to nature's use of a pigment despised by eighteenth-century connoisseurs, white. Jack Lindsay writes that by 1813 Turner was experimenting with white "to drive his tonality up and bring it finally to the brilliance of daylight itself," despite the ridicule he endured from Sir George Beaumont and the other disciples of the murky picturesque.[8] As the first volume of *Modern Painters* indicates, Ruskin considered pure white light essential for classifying and even quantifying nature's minute gradations of color, tone, and perspective.

> Turner starts from the beginning with a totally different principle. He boldly takes pure white (and justly, for it is the sign of the most intense sunbeams) for his highest light, and lampblack for his deepest shade; and between these he makes every degree of shade indicative of a separate degree of distance, giving each step of approach, not the exact difference in pitch which it would have in nature, but a difference bearing the same proportion to that which his sum of possible shade bears to the sum of nature's shade; so that an object half-way between his horizon and his foreground, will be exactly in half tint of force, and every minute division of intermediate space will have just its proportionate share of the lesser sum, and no more. . . . Hence, where the old masters expressed one distance, he expresses a hundred, and where they said furlongs, he said leagues. (*Modern Painters* I, 102–3)

For Ruskin, white light allows the potential ambiguity and obscurity of a Turner painting to be mathematically proportioned, regulated, measured: even the most ephemeral subjects like shadows and clouds are shown to be circumscribed by mathematical and scientific certainties, or the "hard edges" of truth. On a bright, sunny day in winter, Ruskin argues, there are no objects outlined so sharply as shadows, and Turner's shadows reflect this:

> Whatever is obscure, misty or undefined, in his objects or his atmosphere, he takes care that the shadows be sharp and clear; and then he knows that the light will take care of itself, and he makes them clear not by blackness, but by excessive evenness, unity and sharpness of edge. (*Modern Painters* I, 118)

This celebrated "sharpness of edge" provides one of the most obvious justifications for Ruskin's preference for both Turner and the later Pre-Raphaelite painters, a preference, which Ruskin was often called upon to explain and defend.[9] Conversely, the Renaissance old masters perpetually violate this natural truth, eliding the reassuring boundary of obscurity and fact: "they blacken their shadows till the picture becomes quite appalling, and everything in it invisible; but they make a point of losing their edges, and carrying them off by gradation, in consequence utterly destroying every appearance of sunlight" (*Modern Painters* I, 118). Ruskin admitted the "metaphysical" dimension of these aesthetic principles in an 1870 lecture delivered at Oxford on "Light" when he argued that the perception of light and darkness was connected to human character and to morality. But he also made clear the extent to which an imposition of form upon ambiguity was a necessary step in the production of knowledge, and that formlessness itself was symptomatic of not only ignorance but also death.

> The way of light and shade is . . . taken by men of the highest powers of thought, and most earnest desire for truth; they long for light, and for knowledge of all that light can show. But seeking for light, they perceive also darkness; seeking for truth and substance, they find vanity. They look for form in the earth,—for dawn in the sky; and seeking these, they find formlessness in the earth and night in the sky. . . . And, as I said, the school of knowledge, seeking light, perceives, and has to accept and deal with obscurity: and seeking form, it has to accept and deal with formlessness, or death.[10]

Reading the first volume of *Modern Painters* through Ruskin's more self-conscious later work, is easy to understand why the venerable Old Masters are so willfully discredited as ignoramuses, deceivers and, above all, inferior artists. In *The Literate Eye*, Rachel Teukolsky brilliantly argues that the formalism lurking in Ruskin's earliest work is a sign of the continuity between Victorian and Modern aesthetic sensibilities and evidence of the influence of scientific observation; here, it helps explain the way that Ruskin's subsequent attacks on brown formlessness and dark ambiguity soon yield the ideological associations with filth and decay theorized by Douglas.[11] In 1844, when Ruskin penned the Preface to the second edition of *Modern Painters,* Chadwick's sanitary idea had already provided ample aesthetic and even ethical justification for preferring Turner's bright sun and white lights to the Old Masters' murky darkness and vague shadows. The Old Masters were not only false and inferior to Ruskin, they were also debased and diseased. Instead of effective gradation of color, the Old Masters were guilty of de-gradation; where Turner displayed unity of composition, the Old Masters depicted only de-composition. This intensified pollution discourse is perhaps most vivid in the second edition Preface to *Modern Painters* when Ruskin explains the real problem with Salvator Rosa's ambiguously painted foregrounds:

There is no grandeur, no beauty, no beauty of any sort or kind; nothing but destruction, disorganization and ruin, to be obtained by the violation of natural distinctions. The elements of brutes can mix only in corruption, the elements of inorganic nature only in annihilation. . . . [I]t is the generalization of a defeated army into indistinguishable impotence—the generalization of the elements of a dead carcass into dust.[12]

Just as Ruskin's distaste for the Old Master's habit of formlessness or generalization is likened to death and "decomposition," his scorn for the habitual use of dark backgrounds in landscape painting is often attributed to "degradation" in all three of its definitions. In Victorian art dictionaries, "degradation" signifies the opposite of "gradation," a term that describes the judicious separation of parts from the whole in a painting; to "degrade," therefore, is to lower or "enfeeble" the tone in a painting until the parts are indistinguishable from the whole.[13] Within a variety of Ruskin's writings, this definition also resonates with its two non-aesthetic meanings available in the *OED*, the lowering in character or quality, or the wearing down of any surface, allowing the art critic to conclude with impunity that erosion of truthful distinctions among objects in a painting is indicative of the impure feelings and low intellectual capacities of the artist (*Modern Painters* II, 40). "The enormous majority of all good and true men will be *clear* men, he explains, "and the drunkards, sophists, and sensualists will, for the most part, sink back into the fog bank and remain wrapt in darkness, unintelligibility, and futility" (*Modern Painters* IV, 75). In his 1860 *Elements of Drawing*, moreover, Ruskin even links the degradation of dark colors with bad bodily and mental health when he advises potential artists that their "power of colouring will depend much on your state of health and balance of mind; when you are fatigued or ill, you will not see colours well."[14]

However, it is probably the third definition of "degradation" as the wearing away of surfaces that resonates most pointedly with the kinds of dusty pestilence denounced by sanitary reformers. Florence Nightingale warns in her 1860 *Notes on Nursing*, that "there is a constant *degradation*, as it is called, taking place from everything except polished or glazed articles," recommending sunny, airy rooms and smooth, polished wall-coverings that wouldn't absorb the effluvia normally saturating the atmosphere in a house.[15] This model of degradation is Ruskin's chosen metaphor for describing the pressure put on young artists like John Constable to reproduce the venerated darkness of the Old Masters: the young artist may paint, explains Ruskin in 1865, but he "is not even sure if the thoughts are his own; for the whole atmosphere round him is full of floating suggestion; those which are his own he cannot keep pure, for he breathes a dust of decayed ideas, wreck of souls of dead nations, driven by contrary winds."[16] If Ruskin here compares learning to paint by studying the Old Masters to breathing the unhealthy effluvia of decomposition, he will eventually suggest in the same essay that merely looking at a Rembrandt painting produces the kind of unsanitary experience so abhorred by writers like Nightingale. Assessed by Romantic art critic William Hazlitt, the effect of absorbing Rembrandt's sublime colour is intensely pleasurable, even though he describes it as staggering "from one abyss of obscurity to another."[17] Under Ruskin's scrutiny, however, Rembrandt's style of illuminating his paintings with a small circular patch of yellow light is both unromantic and unhygienic:

> The sky, with the sun in it, does not usually give the impression of being dimly lighted through a circular hole; but you may observe a very similar effect any day in your coal cellar. The light is not Rembrandtesque, usually, in a clean house; but it is presently obtainable of that quality in a dirty one . . . it is the aim of the best painters to paint the noblest things they can see by sunlight. It was the aim of Rembrandt to paint the foulest things he could see—by rushlight." ("The Cestus of Aglaia" 499)

Throughout his long, prolific career, Ruskin would continue to use the tropes of degradation, decomposition and decay to argue that noble art could only be produced in clean houses and countries, and that the revival of true art in England would require its own version of sanitation reform. In fact, by 1871, Ruskin was voicing the environmental perspective that would eventually associated with William Morris, writing that "the beginning of true art was to get your country clean and your people lovely."[18] Reshaped by Ruskin's evocative language of degradation and decomposition, Victorian fine art eventually found a way to accommodate the cleanliness campaigns, and with the banishment of dirt, disorder and decay came the reshuffling of fundamental aesthetic theories of previous centuries.

II. Sanitizing Sublimity: Romantic Art/Victorian Dirt

Ruskin's desire to establish a contemporary school of aesthetic cleanliness had been directly stimulated by what he interpreted as an eighteenth-century reverence for "foulness," otherwise, a delight in ambiguity and dark, shadowy tones in painting. Such preferences had philosophical roots in what was perhaps the most influential aesthetic treatise of the period, Edmund Burke's 1756 *Essay on the Sublime and the Beautiful*. Here, Burke identified "sublimity" as the fundamental characteristic of all forms of high art, celebrating a style of visual representation that best approximated poetry's ability to conjure up feelings of terror and awe: "It is our ignorance of things that causes all our admiration, and chiefly excites our passions," Burke explains, and while poetry always raises obscure images that spark the imagination,

> Painting, when we have allowed for the pleasure of imitation, can only affect simply by the images it presents, and even in painting, a judicious obscurity in some things contributes to the effect of a picture; because the images in a painting are exactly similar to those in nature; and in nature, dark, confused, uncertain images have a greater power on the fancy to form the grander passions, than those have which are more clear and determinate.[19]

Burke's preference for dark, mysterious images that stimulate the viewer to respond with narratives of imagined meaning ensured a privileging of the Old Masters, otherwise the "brown" or even "black masters," in a majority of pre- and early Victorian art criticism. Mellowed by a patina of age, warmed by a fine golden tone, works by Rembrandt, Claude, and Rubens were admired by critics through the early nineteenth century for their ability to trick the spectator with an apparent darkness and vacancy that gradually yielded shape, color, and even movement. Describing a Rembrandt painting as late in the century as 1842, art historian Anna Jameson declared that its shadowy background is "positively peopled with life . . . figure after figure emerges, and another and another; they glide into view . . . as if they grew out of the canvas; even while we gaze, we rub our eyes, and wonder whether it be the painter's work or our own fancy."[20]

The experience of sublimity Jameson describes is thus provided by the dissolution of specific form and the proliferation of shifting, subjective images: as Douglas explains, the power and danger of disorder is that it "by implication is unlimited, no pattern has been realized in it, but its potential for patterning is indefinite" (Douglas 94). Indeed, Ruskin especially disliked this "imaginative" school of landscape painting because it suggested that the experience of sublimity could be released in the beholder by not only grand or noble scenes of nature, but by "works that have in them no imagination at all. A few shapeless scratches or accidental stains on a wall, or the forms of clouds, or any other complicated accidents, will set the imagination to work to coin something out of them" (*Modern Painters* II, 166). Ruskin's suspicion

that dirt and stains had been the foul occasion for fine art is hardly an exag-
geration; in fact, the method had been codified by Alexander Cozens in his
1785 treatise "A New Method of Assisting the Invention in drawing Original
Compositions of Landscape." In search of an expeditious system for teaching
his most promising students to draw from the imagination, Cozens, a drawing master at Eton, had a fortuitous "accident" that produced what he aptly
dubs his "blot theory":

> At this instant happening to have a piece of soiled paper under my hand,
> and casting my eyes on it slightly, I sketched something like a landscape
> on it with a pencil, in order to catch some hint which might be improved
> into a rule. The stains, though extremely faint, appeared upon revisal to
> have influenced me, insensibly in expressing the general appearance of a
> landscape. This circumstance was sufficiently striking: I mixed a tint with
> ink and water, just strong enough to mark the paper; and having hastily
> made some rude forms with it, (which, when dry, seemed as if they would
> answer the same purpose to which I had applied the accidental stains of
> the aforementioned piece of paper) I laid it, together with a few short hints
> of my intention, before the pupil, who instantly improved the blot, as it
> may be called, into an intelligible sketch, and from that time made such
> progress in composition as fully answered my sanguine expectations from
> the experiment.[21]

The creation of potentially unlimited pattern was certainly the aesthetic objective behind Cozens's blot theory. To better unleash the creative potential of the
artist, moreover, Cozens recommends stains and blots that are more deliberately created, citing as support Leonardo da Vinci's description of a similar, if
"inferior," process in his *Treatise on Painting*:

> If you look upon an old wall covered with dirt, or the odd appearance
> of some streaked stones, you may discover several things like landscape,
> battles, clouds, uncommon attitudes, humorous faces, draperies, &c. Out
> of this confused mass of objects, the mind will be furnished with an abun-
> dance of designs and subjects perfectly new.[22]

Cozens's treatise suggests that fine art did, indeed, have a close connection
with dirt in the minds of Renaissance artists as well as eighteenth-century
academicians, and that painters and connoisseurs alike found the connection far from repulsive. Cozens was the protégé of Sir George Beaumont,
a wealthy connoisseur and art patron whose 1823 promise of his collection

of Old Masters paintings to the nation essentially inaugurated what would become the National Gallery. Beaumont's strong preference for "an old Cremona fiddle for the prevailing tone of everything" often enforced the use of brown tones and colors even in the work of contemporary artists ("Preface" lxi). Ruskin records John Constable's anecdote of Beaumont looking over his shoulder while he painted, and finally asking the painter, 'Where do you put your brown tree?' as a "melancholy instance of the degradation into which the human mind may fall when it suffers human works to interfere between it and its Master" ("Preface" lxi). Yet such degrading study was common in eighteenth-century studios. Theorist of the picturesque William Gilpin records his struggle to achieve the old master brown in his first attempts at drawing: "I well remember . . . when a boy I used to make little drawings, I was never pleased with them till I had given them a brownish tint: And, as I knew no other method, I used to hold them over smoke till they had assumed such a tint as satisfied my eye."[23] Even tourists and travelers could embrown nature's tones with the help of a portable convex mirror known as the "Claude Glass": as Malcolm Andrews explains, the mirror captured Romantic landscape in the proportion and feeling of an Old Master painting, temporarily blending particularities and details within the circumference of a smoky, golden lens (Andrews 28–29). Some of Ruskin's most vituperative language is reserved for this "balc [sic] convex mirror, one of the most pestilent inventions for falsifying nature and degrading art which was ever put into an artist's hand" (Elements of Drawing 297).

If aesthetic formlessness is dirt, the "sharp edges" and bright lights of a Turner painting must somehow be its opposite. Inevitably, the era that revered dirt and stains as the vehicles of sublimity, reviled the so-called "White Painter" for his apparent promise of cleanliness: "The sea looks like soap and chalk," scorned a critic for The Sun in 1803 in reference to Turner's painting of Calais Pier, and in 1842, The Snow Storm was likewise reckoned "a mass of soapsuds and whitewash."[24] "Soapsuds and Whitewash!" Turner is reported to have exclaimed, "What would they have? I wonder what they think the sea's like? I wish they'd been in it."[25] Aesthetic impressions of cleanliness were a negative virtue in the pre-Chadwickian period, just as artistic depictions of healthy bodies were a rude violation of the laws of subtle color and harmony. Describing an exhibition of modern paintings at Somerset House in 1814, Romantic critic William Hazlitt writes that

the eye in vain seeks relief from the glitter of the frames in the glare of the pictures; where vermilion cheeks make vermilion lips look pale; Indeed, the great error of British Art has hitherto been a desire to produce popular effect by the cheapest and most obvious means and at the expense of everything else;—to lose all the delicacy and variety of nature in one indistinguishable bloom of florid health, and all precision, truth and refinement of character in the same harmless mould of smiling, self-complacent insipidity.[26]

For Hazlitt and other champions of the Old Masters, the form, clarity, and brightness of modern imitative art was a commercial corruption of true aesthetic philosophy. Depictions of "insipid" bodily health excluded feeling and imagination, reducing, in Hazlitt's words, "all nature and art, as far as possible to the texture and level of a china dish—smooth, glittering, cold, and unfeeling!"[27] In Hazlitt's assessment, the finest art captured and evoked in the mind of the viewer not smiling health and cleanliness, but the terrifying and euphoric moment of bodily putrefaction, when the spirit is released from its material prison. "The sense of final, inevitable decay humanises," he famously declares in his *Essays on Art,*

> all the petty, meretricious part of the art is dead in them; the carnal is made spiritual, the corruptible has put on incorruption, and amidst the wreck of colour and the mouldering of material beauty, nothing is left but a universe of thought, or the broad, immanent shadows of calm contemplation and majestic pains.[28]

But when an "indistinguishable bloom of florid health" became not an artistic crime but a social imperative under sanitary philosophy, the sublimity of decay and shadow so revered by Hazlitt and his contemporaries began to lose its privileged status in nineteenth-century art appreciation.

Ruskin's own cleansing of sublimity began, of course, with reclassification. Sublimity has both a high and a low manifestation in *Modern Painters:* firstly, a pure feeling inspired by an artist's empathy with the suffering and misery engendered by picturesque decay, and secondly, an emotion that arises merely from artistic contemplation of the decay itself. "Outward sublimity" was low because it was "heartless":

> The lover of it seems to go forth into the world in a temper as merciless as its rocks. All other men feel some regret at the sight of disorder and ruin. He alone delights in both; it matter not of what. Fallen cottage— desolate village—deserted village—blasted heath—mouldering castle—to him . . . all sights are equally joyful. Poverty, and darkness, and guilt . . . the shattered window, opening into black and ghastly rents of wall, the foul

rag or straw wisp stopping them, the dangerous roof, decrepit floor and stair, ragged misery, or wasting age of the inhabitants,—all these conduce, each in due measure, to the fullness of his satisfaction . . . he yields to his destiny, enjoys his dark canal without scruple, and mourns over every improvement in our town, and every movement made by its sanitary commissioners, as a miser would over the planned robbery of his chest.[29]

Ruskin's critique of such degraded aesthetic pleasure positions him firmly on the side of those sanitary commissioners, who identified and vilified the low picturesque with every exposure of urban decay, dirt and disease. Moreover, as early as the 1840s, the improvements wrought by engineers and scientists ensured that the sanitation of sublimity had a more material and public locus than Ruskin's erudite volumes of art criticism: the walls of the National Gallery in Trafalgar Square.

III. Dirty Pictures in the National Gallery

By 1844, just as Ruskin's distaste for the Old Masters' habit of generalization was engaging sanitary discourse, the reverenced "patina of age" warming the surfaces of the ancient paintings was discovered to be common dirt, and public concern began to be expressed about the health of England's national art collection. In the pages of *The Times,* for example, Punch rechristened the National Gallery the "Hospital for Decayed Pictures," lampooning the "melancholy interest" inspired by so much impending decrepitude:

Here is provided an asylum for the Old Masters during their progress to decay, which its arrangements are in every way calculated to expedite. They may be seen, in their respective wards, resting against the wall; an incrustation of dust, dirt and mildew quietly forming over them, and no attempt at disturbing their latter days being made by interfering with it. . . . Age is daily creeping upon Vandyke and Rembrandt; Rubens is fast breaking up, and poor Sir Joshua looks very ill. . . . Might we venture to suggest a little soap and water occasionally, a gentle dusting now and then, would really do the patients no harm, and improve their looks considerably![30]

Whether to answer Punch's petition, or in response to changing cultural views about cleanliness, that same year a series of paintings in the National Gallery were indeed subjected to soap and water during the long vacation under the direction of the current keeper, Sir Charles Eastlake. The public took little notice of Eastlake's sanitary project until 1846 when four important paintings (among others) were cleaned during the summer months: Titian's *Bacchus and Ariadne,* Rubens's *Peace and War,* Cuyp's *Evening Landscape,* and Velasquez's *Boar Hunt.*[31] Punch may have been quietly satisfied with the results, but many other gallery patrons loudly objected. Still attached to the eighteenth-century aesthetic preference for brown tones and hazy images, Victorian art critics like Morris Moore and William Coningham launched a series of public vituperations in the pages of *The Times* that would eventually bring Eastlake and his picture cleaners under parliamentary investigation.

Both Moore and Coningham accused members of the Royal Academy of attempting to deform (rather than discipline) the artistic tastes of the British people by suggesting that the revered qualities of tone, shadow, and aerial perspective were actually conferred by age and applications of varnish. Under the pseudonym of Verax, Moore denounced "The mutilation of the national pictures in the ignorant and impudent attempt to improve them by a process vulgarly called 'cleaning' and 'restoration.'"[32] In the very language of Hazlitt, Moore insisted that the "vigour and vivacity" of Rubens's *Judgment of Paris* in particular had been "reduced to smooth and monotonous insipidity by the scouring, which has had the effect of enervating those last masterly finishing touches which gave point and variety to the whole" (Moore 16). The brighter colors revealed in Rubens's painting suggested a form of medieval torture to Coningham, who dubbed National Gallery custodians "The Skinners Company," and insisted the forms of women "no longer resembled human flesh, but more nearly that of a freshly skinned calf; the warrior now has the jaundice; the children are covered with yellow and reddish streaks."[33]

In 1847, a Select Committee on the Fine Arts was formed to investigate the charges that the custodians of the National Gallery were wantonly flaying valuable old pictures in the name of art restoration; by that time, Sir Charles Eastlake had resigned his post as Keeper of the National Gallery and had been replaced by Thomas Unwins. Eastlake, Unwins, and a legion of experts were called upon over the next few years to testify about the process and effects of picture cleaning, and one after the other they responded, like their denouncers, with narratives of bodily health and disease. Yet rather than bestowing a fanciful corporeality upon the oil paintings in order to argue for picture cleaning as productive of aesthetic "health," Eastlake and his supporters defended the process of art restoration with the scientific findings of the sanitation engineers. Citing not only the polluted atmosphere of Trafalgar Square, but also the constantly circulating human effluvia of gallery patrons, the National Gallery custodians transformed an aesthetic debate about tone, color, and perspective into a battle over ventilation, contamination, and the healthfulness of public spaces. Almost immediately, the sublime brown tones, rich textures, and hazy images so celebrated by Burke, Beaumont, and Cozens became little more than dirt, and the main anxiety of Commissioners and parliamentarians became not the "flaying" of the national pictures, but the possibility of building a new National Gallery on a healthier spot in Kensington-gore and limiting the access of the dirtiest visitors.

As Unwins testified on 17 June 1850, the National Gallery was normally visited by over three thousand people per day, and many of them did not come to look at the pictures: "Mondays, for instance, are days when a large number of the lower class of people assemble there, and men and women bring their families of children, children in arms, and a little train of children around them and following them, and they are subject to all the little accidents that happen with children, and which are constantly visible on the floors of the place."[34] In addition to the unclean deposits left by working-class children, crowds of adults seeking shelter from bad weather, a pleasant place to picnic, or simply a convenient gathering spot also purportedly contaminated the National Gallery. These unruly crowds of working-class families became sites of real anxiety for Commissioners when scientist Michael Faraday, a respected authority on electricity and magnetism, testified that the darkening of oil paintings could certainly be the result of the "sulfurous vapours" so abundant in London; moreover, that "miasmata" from human perspiration, saliva, and "ammoniacal exhalations" was absolutely capable of producing the greasy substance adhering to the surface of the Old Masters (*Reports from the Select Committees and Commissioners on Fine Arts and on the National Gallery* 74).

This phobia about the unhealthy and contaminatory viscosity of so many working-class bodies was not confined to government Blue Books. "The National Collection will remain exposed as long as the indiscriminate admission of the public is continued," declares C. R. Leslie's 1855 *Handbook for Young Painters*: "Why might not an office, not far from the Gallery, be established, at which tickets should only be given to those who can write their names? It may be safely affirmed that fine pictures can afford no instruction to those who cannot."[35] In an article that appeared in *The Art-Journal,* German art authority Dr. Gustave Frederick Waagen agreed that the freedom of admission to London galleries was indeed too permissive. In Berlin, Waagen explained, children under ten were not admitted to the national galleries, and museum officials had the right to refuse entry to anyone whose dress or body was dirty enough to "create a smell obnoxious to the other visitors."[36] One of the most offensive practices in England, according to Waagen, was the transformation of the National Gallery into a large nursery, with "wet-nurses having regularly encamped with their babies for hours altogether," suckling their charges in uncomfortable proximity to the pictures (Waagen "Thoughts on the New Building to be Erected for the National Gallery in England" 123). "Falling like vapour upon the pictures," Waagen writes, the multiple exhalations of this class of people poses a serious impediment to art preservation" (Waagen "Thoughts" 123).

While the scapegoating of the working classes is the most obvious by-product of sanitary reform in the National Gallery, the anathemization of non-white races is a subtler, but nonetheless significant, effect. The vocabulary in the Select Committee Report casually invokes the specter of race when it repeatedly dubs the atmospheric incursion of soot within the National Gallery "the admission of blacks from the smoke" (*Reports from the Select Committees and Commissioners on Fine Arts and on the National Gallery* iv). But outside government blue books, this metaphor explodes into more pointed racial anxiety. In 1857 an unsigned article appeared in *The Art-Journal* that consulted one Mr. S. P. Denning, the long-standing curator of the art collection at Dulwich College, about the current crisis in art preservation. The article concluded that atmospheric pollution was indeed a problem for urban galleries, glibly noting that "Mr. Denning hates and despises 'the blacks,' as if he were a man from Missouri." [37] Punch described the "medieval" tortures of picture cleaning from the perspective of the victimized paintings in a similar manner:

> We've read a great deal of late in the Blue Books, and read in the papers,
> How much you fear for us from the fogs and the blacks and the vapours;
> But we'd rather endure all the blacks that e'er came out of Uncle Tom's
>   Cabin,
> Then stand your sand-papering and scraping and scouring and scrubbing
>   and swabbin'. [38]

Although it is hardly unusual to find racial anxiety embedded within a variety of writing about cleanliness and health, [39] the impetus behind picture cleaning at mid-century may have been particularly charged by general alarm over the fact that dirty pictures necessarily meant darkened human figures within pictures: white European subjects transformed by "decomposition" and "degradation" into brown-skinned entities. For Ruskin, such degradation even threatened to corrupt contemporary artists who tried to reproduce the foul browns of Titian, Caravaggio, and Spangnoletto, and he dubbed such artists "the black slaves of painting" (*Elements of Drawing* 297). Paradoxically, cleaning the working-class dirt from the national pictures implied the restoration of racial integrity to the visual history of European culture, as well as "white emancipation" [40] for the artists who traditionally learned their sense of color from dirty canvases. Curators like Denning and Eastlake were thus charged with protecting the national pictures from a virtual miscegenation of pigment. At the root of much picture-cleaning advocacy was an ardent belief like the one Henry Mogford expressed in 1851 that the Old Masters had not actually meant to paint brown or black people: "In the historical pictures of the ancient Italian school; it would be a gross absurdity to imagine that these great artists ever painted the shades of flesh of the intense brown and black in which we now find them." [41]

These various threats to the purity of European art made the dirtiness of working-class visitors to the Gallery a profound source of concern for the Fine Arts Commissioners; ironically, however, the potential cleanliness of these same gallery patrons was also deeply troubling. According to the testimony of Unwins, the deposit of soot, matter, and dust upon the paintings had been exacerbated by the relatively recent construction of a set of tall chimneys located at the rear of the National Gallery: these chimneys were connected with the water-works that not only powered the fountain in Trafalgar Square, but also the public baths and wash-houses that working-class families were encouraged to utilize (*Reports from the Select Committees and Commissioners on Fine Arts and on the National Gallery* 9). The act of cleansing one source of contamination seemed only to create a more pernicious site of pollution, as working-class filth reentered the atmosphere in the guise of steam-engine waste. One member of the Commission who resided in the neighborhood of Trafalgar Square contributed his own testimony that the new steam-engines made "everything in his possession more blackened and more soiled in every way than it was previously" (*Reports from the Select Committees and Commissioners on Fine Arts and on the National Gallery* 19). After the Great Exhibition of 1851, moreover, the danger of working-class effluvia and industrial exhaust was virtually lost in the greater threat of unclean foreign respiration: "We had the combined ammoniacal exhalations of Russia, Austria, France, Italy, Belgium, and America condensed upon the pictures, supervening upon our own National Exhalations," trustee William Russell dramatically reported, "and I think at the close of that year, the pictures became in as bad a state as it was possible for pictures to be in." [42]

In the context of such comprehensive xenophobia, most of the trustees concluded that the obvious solution was to move the National Gallery away from the especially polluted Trafalgar Square to a less industrialized area of London, and by implication, an area less frequented by the dirtiest classes of visitors. In his own testimony to the Select Committee in 1857, Ruskin described the destructive effects of dirt, and suggested that two galleries be established: an easily accessible gallery for second-rate art, and a gallery off the beaten path for fine art, making it more difficult for crowds to descend upon the pictures by accident. [43] Yet Commissioners were ultimately unwilling to abandon the goal of social perfectibility through art education that had been articulated by reformers from Prince Albert to Henry Cole, and decided to retain the Trafalgar Square location for its accessibility to the "fullest tide of human existence" (*Reports from the Select Committees and Commissioners on Fine Arts and on the National Gallery* ii). Better ventilation for the National Gallery was instead recommended by the Commissioners, as well as the use of glass for covering as many pictures as possible.

Moreover, for the first time in the history of the Gallery, Commissioners stipulated that the cleaners hired to care for the national pictures possessed knowledge of not only art history, but also chemistry. This decision largely resulted from the apparently startling discovery that the mysterious brown varnish used by Sir George Beaumont and past Gallery custodians to keep the Old Masters "well-toned" was a mixture of licorice water and brown glaze that actually hastened rather than halted the process of degradation and decay. When chemical knowledge was perceived as central to the preservation of paintings, categorization and classification again functioned as a ritual of cleansing. Artists themselves began to be held responsible for the chemical compounds they employed in their work; in fact, the long-deceased Sir Joshua Reynolds was fulsomely repudiated during the Victorian period for using colors, vehicles, and varnishes likely to decay because "sitters paid for their portraits prices calculated on the theory of their infinite duration, not of their evanescence in the course of a few years." [44] The aesthetic "health" of the Old Masters was to be judged by a more scientific standard, and picture-restorers were noted to be "as important a class in Art as physicians and surgeons in Life" (Leslie 216). Consequently, as scientific knowledge became a prerequisite for artistic production, renovation, and appreciation, the aesthetic issues that had originally so troubled opponents of picture cleaning were largely elided. Thoroughly interpolated by sanitary philosophy, the Select Committee dismissed the aesthetic concerns of so-called "Brownmaniacs" as a remnant of the dark ages, a holdover from a pre-reform era of bad health and indifferent hygiene.

If aesthetic standards dramatically shifted under the sanitary idea, transformed too was the commercial principle behind aesthetic evaluation. While Hazlitt had argued that the clearness and discernible imagery of contemporary art was a sign of its commercial corruption, sanitary standards revealed that the true commercial villain was the brown stain of past connoisseurs.

Before sanitary reform, dirt under a different name added considerable pecu-
niary value to pictures, encouraging repairers, restorers, and especially picture
dealers to enhance the market value of imported Old Masters through an
accelerated aging process. Eighteenth-century connoisseurs of fine art, Richard Redgrave explained in 1865,

> believed that pictures, like coins, obtained a patina from age, which mel-
> lowed their tone, and made them more valuable than in the state they left
> the painter's easel. . . . If a picture came from abroad in a fine fresh state of
> preservation, the dealers were too wise to let it be seen until its pure tints
> were subdued to the established hue.[45]

Although Anne McClintock has suggested that dirt was the imagined antithesis of commercial value in the Victorian period, "what is left over after
exchange value has been extracted" (McClintock 153), dirt euphemized as
"tone" or "chiaroscuro" was the very substance of marketability for early-
nineteenth-century art dealers. In his testimony to the Select Committee,
Mr. Unwins admitted that the preference for dirty pictures originated with
National Gallery founder Sir George Beaumont, and recollected a dealer
named De la Hante who unwillingly catered to his and other connoisseurs'
desire for brown hues.

> De la Hante . . . had his pictures in a room in Pall Mall, and when certain
> persons, who he knew were tinctured with this Cremona fiddle mania,
> were coming to see his pictures, he used to take a quantity of ox-gall in a
> cup, and mix it with Spanish liquorice which he passed over the surface of
> his pictures to present them in a proper state to the amateurs of that partic-
> ular tone of colour; and I must say to the credit of De la Hante, the moment
> those persons were gone, he washed it off again, with as much earnestness
> as he had employed putting it on; to him it was the greatest horror, but
> he did it from the necessity of selling his pictures. (*Reports from the Select
> Committees and Commissioners on Fine Arts and on the National Gallery* 8)

Ironically, it was not De la Hante, but John Seguier, Eastlake's chief cleaner,
who became the whipping boy for these dirty past practices when he revealed
that he was also guilty of "toning" some of the very paintings he was later
employed to restore. A noted expert on varnish, Seguier admitted in his 1853
testimony to the Select Committee that since 1843, when he was first hired
by Eastlake, he was in the habit of contributing to the aesthetic preference
for brown tones by coating the Gallery pictures with his own special glaze: a

mixture of boiled oil and varnish that was especially dark and absorbent. "It is my opinion," Seguier confessed, "that this oil varnish has a great tendency to attract dirt, and that, if it continue any length of time on a picture, it will get yellower and blacker from day to day" (*Reports from the Select Committees and Commissioners on Fine Arts and on the National Gallery* 41–42). While this glaze was primarily applied as a protective coating over cracked and eroding old paint, Seguier admitted he had sometimes used the varnish after the pictures had been too enthusiastically cleaned in an attempt to restore "tone" to newly brightened Old Masters. The critics quickly demonized Seguier, and in the process came to devalue the aesthetic standards that the restorer had been laboring to preserve: "Toned, indeed!" scoffed one critic for *The Art-Journal* in 1853, "Which implies either the scumbling of dirt, or adding foul, hard glazings over the colour, which was as clean as when the painters considered their works completed."[46] Marveled Waagen:

> Glazing, scumbling, and toning have been held to constitute painting; while real painting has been discountenanced as if it were a foundation for the after impure practices. . . . If they are not to be cleaned because the market value, given by the veil of impurity, is diminished, and pictures are only to be valued for so many pounds sterling, it were better to turn their faces to the wall, and inscribe on the backs, this picture is worth five-hundred pounds, that picture is worth a thousand pounds, and so on.[47]

In this way, Victorian aesthetic philosophy actively collaborated with the cleanliness campaigns, eventually deploring the "Brown-mania" that had celebrated dirty art throughout the eighteenth and early nineteenth centuries. An anonymous reporter in *The Times* insisted that the cleaned paintings in the National Gallery had not been damaged at all, and that contemporary landscape painters, "who are infected by studying dirty pictures to the imitation of them in colours" should be cured by gazing upon "the extraordinary freshness and daylight on the three Claudes."[48] He furthermore counsels the skeptical reader to examine the still unrestored Guidos in the Gallery: "If any other feeling can arise than the most repulsive sensations of human disease in its most loathsome symptoms over the entire skin, they must be insensible to the greatest of charms with which nature has invested feminine beauty" ("Picture Cleaning in the National Gallery" 30). In 1853, Dr. Waagen also rejoiced in the newly cleaned paintings, stating that the public could at last gain proper instruction in the colors of the Old Masters rather than engage in the "unwholesome study of smothered-up pictures."[49] A decade later, Punch finally got around to thanking the new National Gallery trustees, Mr.

Wornum and Mr. Boxall, for their unparalleled act of heroism in the latest round of cleaning:

> They have dared to brave the bray of the noodles and the nincompoops—a very powerful body among the connoisseurs—and have taken the dirt off the national pictures! Not all off, unhappily; but off just enough to give us a relish for the beauty that lies drowned, fathom deep, under Sir George Beaumont's liquorice water, and the later Mr. Seguier's brown varnish. These men have actually had the pluck to dive to the bottom of the filthy brown standing pools, and to bring up the jewels of Rubens and Poussin, and Salvator Rosa, as bright as when they left the hand that set them.[50]

Characterizing the brown varnish of past caretakers as stagnant pools of dirty water, Punch employs the most salient and egregious trope of sanitary reform, suggesting along with many of his contemporaries that aesthetic appreciation and preservation is now the rightful domain of the custodian rather than the connoisseur.

IV. From Soot to Soap

While such suggestive descriptions of picture cleaning seem to credit sanitarians like Edwin Chadwick with mid-Victorian aesthetic reform, Ruskin's charges against the dirty Old Masters could not have been more resoundingly vindicated than they were by the National Gallery controversy of the 1840s. Even his early, abstract accusations of trickery and fraud were confirmed when it was discovered that "the veil of impurity" that had deliberately enshrouded the Old Masters to increase their market value was also used by picture dealers on copies to pass them off as originals. Redgrave cites one such "old master of the cleaning craft" who was among the first to temper his colors with soot, "and then rolling them up, he made them crackle and contract and air of antiquity" (Redgrave 4). Henry Merritt's 1851 *Dirt and Pictures Separated in the Works of the Old Masters* agreed that "the fashion of preserving the genuine productions in a half-invisible state," has made fraud a common practice among art dealers: "Artificial discolourations and layers of dirt are to those creators of the 'modern antique' what night and darkness are to the highwayman and burglar."[51] This brand of fraud is lampooned by Wilkie Collins in his novel *A Rogue's Life,* when struggling artist and rogue hero Frank Softly is offered a job "making" Old Masters for the disreputable picture-dealer, Ishmael Pickup. After being assigned Rembrandt, Softly receives the following advice: "try again and again, and mind you are dark and dirty enough. You have heard a great deal about the light and shade of Rembrandt—remember always that, in your case, light means dusky yellow, and shade dense black."[52] Softly's resulting chiaroscuro promises him great success as a forger, but an unfortunate encounter with "Amsterdam Cleaning Compound" inspires him to seek his fortune in other criminal ventures.

Other mid-Victorian novels feature close associations between artists who work in the style and tones of the Old Masters and disease, filth and crime. Aspiring artist Clive Newcome in Thackeray's 1855 *The Newcomes* runs afoul of sanitary commissioners when he tries to produce a grand historical painting of the battle of Assaye, with the "principal figure in the foreground . . . bestriding the body of a dead cab-horse, which Clive painted, until the landlady and the rest of the lodgers cried out, and for sanitary reasons the knackers removed the slaughtered charger."[53] Mr. Driftwood in the 1854 *Wearyfoot Common* specializes in making Correggio copies for wealthy clients who legitimately possess the originals, but he becomes so good at his craft he eventually takes to passing off his own paintings as Old Master productions.[54] In a filthy studio that smells of meerschaum and mutton chops, Mr. McGilp of the 1868 *Lord Falconberg's Heir* schools his students in the style of Vandyke and Rubens; if we cannot discern his preference for mellow tones from his punny name, we can from the fact that he "could not conceive of cleanliness and genius under the same exterior."[55] And with Mr. Scumble, R. A. presiding at their studio, the "Titian Sketching Club" in the 1866 *Land at Last* face sending-in day for the Exhibition of the British Institution "in a thick fog of tobacco smoke," the paintings virtually indistinguishable from "the discoloured, smoky old walls of the Titians."[56]

It is also the case that the trickery practiced by the black Masters carries more than a hint of necromancy in Elizabeth Lysaght's 1890 *The Veiled Picture, or the Wizard's Legacy,* a novel that begins in Amsterdam with a 1660 burning at the stake of a suspected wizard, and shifts immediately to nineteenth-century England, where a mysterious painting washes up on the beach after a tragic Dutch shipwreck.[57] The painting, in Old Master style, features "only an old man's yellow face and yellow hand appearing from behind the fold of a dingy red curtain" and the inscribed date, 1660. The picture makes its way to London, and eventually to the country home of a rich art collector, who comes to believe it is the work of Hans Vellar, an Amsterdam artist and evil wizard. Everyone who gazes too long at the painting is struck by the same frightful fancy—that the hand in the painting drops the curtain, and the man disappears—and each is struck with illness or the death of a loved one as a result. After a tortuous plot in which the wizard's reincarnation turns up in the guise of the rich collector's half-brother and attempts to poison him, the picture self-combusts and the wizard disappears, apparently for good. But the plot here is less important than the cultural associations that determine the plot: the shape-shifting sublimities described by Anna Jameson are not only unnatural, they are supernatural, a shift in pollution discourse that Douglas suggests is a common cultural response to the danger of unlimited pattern and formlessness.[58] It hardly mattered to advocates of picture cleaning whether the hazy brown varnish on a Salvator Rosa painting had been applied by Beaumont or by the master himself; after the picture-cleaning controversy, the tone itself was associated with foulness, crime and even evil in the minds of many Victorians.

In this way, John Ruskin's intellectualization of the problem of dirty pictures worked in tandem with Chadwick's broader program of civic hygiene to privilege bright color and healthy form over the pestilential tones and degenerate ambiguities favored by previous generations. Although Ruskin was somewhat disillusioned with both Turner and the Pre-Raphaelite Brotherhood in later years, Turner's endemic cleanliness remained central to his understanding of the painter, as exemplified by the *Lectures on Landscape* he delivered at Oxford in 1871. Describing Turner's painting of Eccleston Abbey, Ruskin writes,

> Only a little bit of its stony bed is left; a mill weir thrown across, stays the water in a perfectly clear and delicious pool; to show how clear it is, Turner has put the only piece of playing colour in all the picture into the reflections in this. One cow is white, another white and red, evidently as clean as morning dew can wash their sides. They could not have been so in a country where there was the least coal smoke; so Turner has put a wreath of perfectly white smoke through the trees; and lest that should not be enough to show you they burnt wood, he has made his foreground a piece of copse just lopped, with the new faggots standing up against it; and this still not being enough to give you the idea of perfect cleanliness, he has covered the stones of a river-bed with white clothes laid out to dry; and that not being enough yet, for the river-bed might be clean though nothing else was, he has put a quantity more hanging over the abbey walls.[59]

Perfect environmental cleanliness, and the remembrance of a pre-industrial, wood-burning English countryside is what Turner here symbolizes to Ruskin, each minute, sanitary detail of the landscape standing in direct contrast to the coal cellar of that dirty house where the filthy yellow light and ambiguous shapes of a Rembrandt painting would be best approximated.

Moreover, the early volumes of *Modern Painters* authorized contemporary artists like William Holman Hunt to break from his drawing master's
preference for "dead colouring," and attack the centuries of paralysis that
infected modern artists: "under this miasma" the Pre-Raphaelite painter
explains, "no young man has the faintest chance of developing his art into
a living power, unless he investigates the dogma of his elders with a critical
mind, and dares to face the idea of revolt from their authority."[60] Hunt's auto-
biography of himself and the aesthetic movement he launched records the
young Brotherhood's deliberate choice to abjure "altogether the brown foli-
age, smoky clouds, and dark corners, painting the whole out of doors . . . with
the sunlight brightness of the day itself" (Hunt 62). In the context of ongoing efforts of sanitary reformers throughout the nineteenth century, the Pre-
Raphaelite movement at times seemed to signify the return of health to art,
and by the end of the century the cultural connection between the two movements had so seamlessly coalesced for some art historians like Percy Bate that
they would naturally describe the Brotherhood's aesthetic philosophy entirely
in the discourse of health and cleanliness:

> Neither then nor afterwards did they affirm that there was not much
> healthy and good art after the time of Raphael; but it appeared to them
> that afterwards art was so frequently tainted with the canker of corruption
> that it was only in the earlier work they could find with certainty absolute
> health. Up to a definite point, the tree was healthy: above it, disease began,
> side by side with life, there appeared death.[61]

While William Morris's crusade for environmental hygiene marks one
important articulation of sanitary aesthetics at the end of the nineteenth century, John Everett Millais's entrance into the world of popular advertising
may indicate the more subtle cultural association between Pre-Raphaelite
art and ideologies of health and cleanliness. When Millais sold his painting "Bubbles" to Thomas Barrett in the 1880s, it became the first painting
used to market a mass-produced commodity. The copies were inscribed with
the brand name "Pears" for the purpose of selling a substance once thought
incompatible with the feelings of high art. Soap.

CHAPTER 2

The Sanitary Narrative

Victorian Reform Fiction and the
Putrescence of the Picturesque

You cannot have a landscape by Turner, without a country for him to paint; you cannot have a portrait by Titian without a man to be portrayed. I need not prove to you, I suppose, in these short terms; but in the outcome I can get no soul to believe that the beginning of art is getting our country clean and our people beautiful. I have been ten years trying to get this very plain certainty—I do not say believed—but even thought of, as anything but a monstrous proposition. To get your country clean, and your people lovely;—I assure you, that is a necessary work of art to begin with.

—John Ruskin, "The Relation of Art to Use" (1870)

$\mathcal{I}$n 1860, Ruskin published the first few chapters of *Unto this Last* in the *Cornhill Magazine,* thus inaugurating his well-documented intellectual shift from aesthetics to economics and from paintings to people as the main focus of his lectures and writings. Indeed, there is no mistaking Ruskin's generic transition to political economy: *Unto this Last* opens with an attack on J. S. Mill's assessment of wealth as a stockpile of useful articles, and closes with the now-famous humanist revision of Mill: "there is no wealth but life."[1] Yet it is not the case that Ruskin stopped thinking about art suddenly in 1860 (in fact, the final volume of *Modern Painters* was published in 1862), or that his lofty aesthetic interests simply collapsed beneath the weightier considerations of political economy and social reform. Instead, Ruskin's burgeoning economic philosophy, his political and social theories of labor, wealth, and utility, were actually components of a more expansive aesthetic philosophy that linked the renewal of British art to the regeneration of the British people and their environment. I argued in my previous chapter that Ruskin's most profound contribution to the nineteenth-century cleanliness campaigns was his compelling causal relationship between environmental filth and aesthetic foulness; I will argue in this chapter that what I've termed Ruskin's sanitary aesthetic emerged as a powerful ideological convention of the British novel by mid-century. Perhaps Ruskin himself didn't read much popular fiction, and didn't realize that widely dispersed and self-organizing narratives of aesthetic transformation were collectively adapting traditional marriage plots, traditional reform plots, to his dream of a clean country with lovely people. But by the time Ruskin gave the above 1870 lecture at Oxford University where he bemoaned his perpetual inability to inspire true aesthetic reform, a significant shift in the cultural narrative about art was already emerging. In much mid-Victorian fiction, aesthetic transformation is a dominant mechanism of social reform. The highly educated and exalted taste of the connoisseur is often an inscription of aristocratic excess and cruelty, an aesthetic philosophy associated not only with the polluted tonalities and materials of highly prized paintings, but with filthy working-class people and their environments. Reform is only possible in such novels if the aesthetic indulgences of the property-owning classes are robustly repudiated, making newly sanitary models of beauty the favored modality of social change.

For example, George Eliot's *Middlemarch* (1871–72) is set just before the passing of the 1832 Reform Bill, which also means that its action predates the publication of Chadwick's *Sanitary Report* and Ruskin's *Modern Painters*. This enables Eliot to make certain causal connections between the squalid conditions among working-class peasants on large rural estates in the 1830s and Romantic-era preferences for picturesque landscapes. Embodied by Dorothea's bumbling uncle and guardian, Mr. Brooke, the empty liberalism of the ruling class in *Middlemarch* is explicitly taken to task for locating aesthetic pleasure in communities of dilapidated cottages, starving children, and ragged laborers. Eliot famously writes,

> It is true that an observer, under the softening influence of the fine arts which makes other people's hardships picturesque, might have been delighted with this homestead called Freeman's End: the old house had dormer windows in the dark-red roof, two of the chimneys were choked with ivy, the large porch was blocked off with bundles of sticks, and half the windows were closed with grey worm-eaten shutters about which the jasmine-boughs grew in wild luxuriance; the mouldering garden wall with hollyhocks peeping over it was a perfect study of highly mingled subdued colour, and there was an aged goat (kept doubtless on interesting super-

stitious grounds) lying against the open back-kitchen door. The mossy
thatch of the cow-shed, the broken grey barn-doors, the pauper labourers
in ragged breeches who had nearly finished unloading a wagon of corn into
the barn ready for early threshing; the scanty dairy of cows being tethered
for milking and leaving one half of the shed in brown emptiness . . . all
these objects under the quiet light of a sky marbled with high clouds would
have made a sort of picture which we have all paused over as 'a charming
bit,' touching other sensibilities than those which are stirred by the agricultural interest, with the sad lack of farming capital, as seen constantly in the
newspapers of that time. But these troublesome associations were just now
strongly present to Mr. Brooke, and spoiled the scene for him.[2]

Usually, the starving animals, the dirty laborers, and the neglected yard provide Mr. Brooke with a picturesque scene he can appreciate with high sensibility. Under the coming storm cloud of social and political discontent, however,
the ominous "brown emptiness" of the cow shed is only a filthy forcing bed
for calamities like the typhoid fever that strikes down young Fred Vincy as
he bargains for a horse on the "unsanitary" Houndsley streets (225), and the
cholera epidemic that threatens to swell the population of Lydgate's forthcoming Fever Hospital. In *Middlemarch,* as in so many mid-nineteenth-century
novels, the picturesque is cultural shorthand for filth and disease, and aesthetic transformation is coterminous with the approaching inevitability of
sanitary reform.
     Art is literally filth in the above passage from *Middlemarch,* filth that is
tolerated and even allowed to flourish for the express purpose of aristocratic
ease and enjoyment. While *Middlemarch* is not the only mid-Victorian novel
to dramatize the repudiation of degraded aesthetic pleasure as a precursor to
social reform, it is certainly the most famous; many of the novels I will discuss in this chapter grapple with the philosophical problem of dirty art at the
fringes of what is normally referred to as "literary" fiction. Nevertheless, in a
host of both literary and popular novels published during the mid-Victorian
period, the revival of true art is imagined to be a process of civic purification that triumphs over the filthy and viciously private aesthetic pleasure of
past connoisseurs, instituting artistic reform as a transformation of taste that
privileges people over paintings, much in the way Ruskin described in 1870.
While aesthetic objects, especially paintings, are important material signifiers
in many of these texts, they are less central to the novels than the process of
aesthetic objectification, demonstrated so vividly by Mr. Brooke, that purloins
with impunity "charming bits" of social and economic tragedy for the gratification of elite, educated, and studied visual pleasure. Art objects are often

material icons that must be directly repudiated or exchanged as the price of reform, but the lost icon is displaced by a new aesthetic philosophy rather than by a new object. To be sure, the "healthful" values of Pre-Raphaelite art—bright colors, realist detail, meticulous finish—appear in many of these novels as idiosyncratically preferred aesthetic forms, often stridently opposed to the pestilential yellows and degenerate browns of the earlier Old Masters. But finally, the plots enacted in the novels I discuss in this chapter produce and reproduce a story of sanitation reform that promises more that the banishment of dirt, disease, and immorality from neighborhoods and communities, it promises that sanitary perfection, embodied in a clean country with lovely people, will eventually become, in itself, new cultural aesthetic.

I. Reforming the Picturesque:
Middlemarch and *North and South*

The miasmatic theory of disease, which dominated scientific beliefs about the spread of illness until the advent of germ theories in the 1870s, has long been recognized as a standard shorthand of Victorian reform fiction; a convenient metaphoric chain that links filth, disease, and immorality in a providential plot.[3] Decaying organic matter and the foul smells that emanate from viscous pockets and piles of filth are familiar features of the overpopulated urban environment in particular, providing novels like Dickens's *Bleak House* (1853) and *Our Mutual Friend* (1865) with moral geographies of city life shaped by noxious slums, docks, dust heaps and brickyards.[4] While the miasmatic and metaphoric features of the sanitary narrative are similar in novels with more pastoral settings, ground zero for filth diseases in the country, I would argue, is always the deceptively beautiful impoverished village, the moldering rural farm, or the picturesque cottage. In a variety of these novels published after 1850, the purification of the picturesque is inscribed upon more dominant narratives of character growth and transformation, and the pollution anxiety Mary Douglas theorizes becomes a driving mechanism of the plot. Some of these novels imagine an utopian future where artists will take on the social responsibility of cleanliness and sanitation; others, like *Middlemarch*, remember and reflect upon a dark age when aesthetic philosophy not only blunted moral understanding but promoted physical disease.

One of the many ways we know that reform is coming to Middlemarch is that the definition of beauty has at last become controversial: for example, our heroine and nineteenth-century St. Theresa, Dorothea Brooke, draws plans for model cottages and feverishly promotes her designs to the neighboring gentry, hoping above all "to make the life of poverty beautiful" (29). Her desire to impose a new form of beauty upon working-class existence is in direct contrast with the beauty her uncle Brooke already finds in decayed housing, inadequate food and sickly tenants. Dorothea's drawings, moreover, are not the kind of art most admired by her uncle; he prefers his own collection of Italian engravings and even the more amateurish pages of Will Ladislaw's sketchbook. But such aesthetic pleasure seems poor compensation for social grievances to Dorothea, and as she glances for the first time at both Ladislaw and his sketchbook her words suggest that the coming marriage plot itself may require nothing less than a Ruskinian transformation of aesthetic values: "You know, uncle, I never see the beauty of those pictures which you say are so much praised. They are a language I do not understand" (73). Mr. Brooke good-humouredly blames Dorothea's aesthetic limitations on the fact that she has had "a bad style of teaching" and has taken to reform rather than to fine art; he also regrets that she knows nothing of "*morbidezza,*" the Italian term for delicacy or softness in the representation of flesh (73). But the imported word only italicizes the dislocation of Brooke's values from his environment: when the delicate flesh so idealized by Italian connoisseurs is substituted for the decaying flesh of British peasants, fine art emerges once again as a Romantic fascination with filth.

Conventional arguments about the picturesque have tended to assume that the concept became aesthetically insignificant by the early decades of the nineteenth century, and that the picturesque was largely anachronistic after Regency debates over the enclosure and cultivation of wild wasteland revealed picturesque pleasure to be a taste that England's agricultural interests could no longer afford.[5] But critics like Anne Janowitz and Malcolm Andrews have insisted that aesthetic and cultural preoccupation with the picturesque continued through the nineteenth century. Janowitz, for example, argues that marginalized groups like the Welsh Chartists quite actively appropriated the picturesque as a political tool in their poetry and writing about landscape.[6] Andrews, on the other hand, actually finds the picturesque lurking in the more hegemonic discourse of the built urban environment, pointing out that mid- and late-Victorian architectural writers celebrated the picturesque development of irregular, idiosyncratic London as a sign of British individualism and *laissez-faire* politics.[7] Of course, as Andrews points out, one inevitable effect of *laissez-faire* architecture and city planning is exactly the kind of social neglect demonstrated by Mr. Brooke in *Middlemarch,* and one of the reasons I argue that the long, slow shift in cultural values from the Romantic to the Victorian periods remains visible in fiction through a constant moral revaluation of picturesque pleasure.

Ruskin himself struggled with the word and its powerful implications throughout *Modern Painters,* finally bifurcating the definition in order to pacify his own conflicted conscience. Like "sublimity," the "picturesque" has its high and low manifestations for Ruskin: on the one hand, we have Turner's "consciousness of the pathos in the confessed ruin, which may or may not be beautiful," and on the other hand, we have the Old Masters' "entire denial of all human calamity and care."[8]

> I want the reader to understand thoroughly the opposite element of the noble picturesque; its expression, namely, of suffering, of poverty, of decay, nobly endured by unpretending strength of heart . . . if outward sublimity be sought for by the painter, without any regard for the real nature of the thing, and without any comprehension of the pathos of character hidden beneath, it forms the low school of the surface picturesque. (5–6)

In Victorian writing, the picturesque aesthetic becomes a dangerous anesthetic; an experience of beauty so profound that it actually enfeebles human sympathy, numbs moral judgment, deadens social responsibility. Certainly, this cultural critique of the picturesque did not only appear in Victorian reform novels: Nathaniel Hawthorne's 1860 *The Marble Faun,* for example, suggests that whenever the term "picturesque" is applied to a landscape, its inhabitants are suffering slow and steady genocide: "There is reason to suspect that a people are waning to decay and ruin," he mourns, "the moment that their life becomes fascinating either in the poet's imagination or the painter's eye."[9] But English novels of reform like *Middlemarch* are already caught within the very dilemma exposed by the mid-Victorian problem with the picturesque: the aesthetic power or sheer beauty of the vehicle perpetually risks anaesthetizing the reader against the human calamity struggling for realist representation.

Eliot herself warned against the picturesque perversion of realism in her 1856 *The Natural History of German Life,* where both Dickens and Holman Hunt come under criticism for their prejudices about "the People," as she calls them; the happy, healthy and innocent peasants and laborers that exist in the artistic imagination are sustained by feudal generalizations about the good old days and a form of aesthetic distancing that disguises harsh social relations within the effects of light, color, and tone. "Observe a company of haymakers," Eliot instructs:

> When you see them at a distance, tossing up the forkfuls of hay in the

goldenlight, while the wagon creeps slowly with its increasing burthen over the meadow, and the bright green space which tells of work done gets larger and larger, you pronounce the scene 'smiling' and you think these companions in labour must be as bright and cheerful as the picture to which they give animation. Approach nearer, and you will certainly find. . . . That delicious effervescence of the mind which we call fun, has no equivalent for the northern peasant, except tipsy revelry; the only realm of fancy and imagination for the English clown exists at the bottom of the third quart pot.[10]

At a distance, a connoisseur like Mr. Brooke can access the disinterestedness and leisure of what Pierre Bourdieu has called the "pure gaze," a claim to aristocratic ease and mastery that is normalized and naturalized as an aesthetic impulse.[11] Under Bourdieu's analysis, a preference for the picturesque would mark a form of aesthetic consumption that renders economic exploitation invisible because it disguises itself as a highly personal sensitivity to natural beauty. Indeed, as John Barrell has argued, the "picturesque eye" always masquerades as the natural gaze, offering the highly constructed viewing-position of an educated gentleman as a form of "pure, unmediated vision."[12] The cultural competence required to recognize and value the picturesque becomes, in turn, an extension and ratification of feudal exploitation: picturesque pleasure, for Eliot and Ruskin, for Bourdieu and Barrell, engenders no social involvement or moral outrage, anesthetizing against the dis-ease of social and economic inequity.

Like Eliot and Ruskin, Charles Dickens wanted to reform picturesque pleasure, to rescue the aesthetic beauty of the ruin while becoming mindful of the exploitation that such pleasure endorses and legitimates. After rhapsodizing about the intoxicating charms of Italian travel, he suddenly warns his 1846 readers of *Pictures from Italy* against the desensitizing effects of aesthetic tourism.

But, lovers and hunters of the picturesque, let us not keep too studiously out of view the miserable depravity, degradation, and wretchedness, with which this gay Neapolitan life is inseparably associated! It is not well to find Saint Giles's so repulsive, and the Porta Capuana so attractive. A pair of naked legs and a ragged red scarf, do not make *all* the difference between what is interesting and what is coarse and odious? Painting and poetising for ever, if you will, the beauties of this most beautiful and lovely spot of earth, let us, as our duty, try to associate a new picturesque with some faint recognition of man's destiny and capabilities; more hopeful, I believe, among the ice and snow of the North Pole, than in the sun and bloom of Naples.[13]

Of course, Dickens's literary attempts at imagining a "new picturesque" fell flat for Eliot, who resented Dickens's "miserable fallacy that high morality and refined sentiment can grow out of harsh social relations, ignorance, and want; or that the working classes are in a condition to enter at once into a millennial state of altruism, wherein everyone is caring for everyone else, and no one for himself."[14] The "natural taste" demonstrated by so many of Dickens's uneducated and economically disenfranchised characters, most famously Oliver Twist, certainly informs Eliot's accusation, and testifies to the lingering intellectual power of Shaftesbury and Burke into the nineteenth century. On the other hand, it is clear that the most reform-driven novelists of the mid-Victorian period were troubled by the intellectual dominance of the picturesque as an aesthetic protocol for working-class visibility. With varied and controversial success, Victorian reform writers struggled to represent some lived experience of the People, laboring to reverse the pollution discourse that reserves purity for disinterested and distanced gazes.

More to Eliot's taste might have been Elizabeth Gaskell's 1855 *North and South,* a reform novel most explicitly devoted to reforming the industrial mill owner, Thornton, into a sympathetic paternalist and an appropriate husband for the heroine Margaret Hale. Margaret's own transformation is more subtle here, but just as important: Margaret's marriage plot depends upon her ability to reform her aesthetic values, to realize that her reverence for the picturesque is just as damaging to the working class she wants to help as Thornton's disrespectful and dehumanizing disregard. In the rural village of Helstone at the beginning of the novel, Margaret happily sketches the picturesque poverty of country cottages "before they tumbled down and were no more seen," casually chatting up the almost deaf old man who lives alone under the dark, soggy thatch.[15] But Margaret's relocation to the ugly, filthy, industrialized Milton-Northern, and her inability to anaesthetize herself against the suffering she finds there, causes her to revisit the picturesque Helstone cottagers at the close of the novel with new eyes. Inquiring after Betty Barnes, a former favorite, she listens with horror to a story that the old woman has stolen a neighbor's cat in order to burn it alive, in keeping with an ancient country superstition that the cries of a cat have the power to fulfill the wishes of the executioner (380). Margaret tries to "enlighten" the storyteller, but eventually gives up, and they "thridded their way through many a bosky dell, whose soft green influence could not charm away the shock and the pain in

Margaret's heart caused by a recital of such cruelty; a recital too, the manner of which betrayed such utter want of imagination, and therefore of any sympathy with the suffering animal" (381). The narcotic effects of the pure gaze no longer protect Margaret: instead, she sees the destructive provincialism, the ignorance, and the scientific impoverishment of the rural landscape and People. While revisiting her wealthy country aunt and cousin, moreover, she resents the lofty conversation that once enthralled her, realizing that the dinner guests "talked about art in a merely sensuous way, dwelling on outside effects, instead of allowing themselves to learn what it has to teach" (397).

This Ruskinian realization about art in the novel is also accompanied by an interesting transformation of cleanliness and its moral meanings, as Margaret discovers when she visits the home of John's mother and spends some time alone in the drawing room where a taste for ornament and color is preserved against all odds.

> The walls were pink and gold: the pattern on the carpet represented bunches of flowers on a light ground, but it was carefully covered up in the center by a linen drugget, glazed and colorless. The window-curtains were lace; each chair and sofa had its own particular veil of netting or knitting. Great alabaster groups occupied every flat surface, safe from dust under their glass shades. . . . Everything reflected light, nothing absorbed it. The whole of the room had a painfully spotted, spangled, speckled look about it that impressed Margaret so unpleasantly that she was hardly conscious of the peculiar cleanliness required to keep everything so white and pure in such an atmosphere, or of the trouble that must be willingly expended to secure that effect of icy, snowy discomfort. Everywhere she looked there was evidence of care and labour, but not care and labour to procure ease, to help on habits of tranquil home employment; solely to ornament, and then to preserve ornament from dirt or destruction. (112)

In Thornton's rarely visited drawing room, cleanliness is not only dedicated to enshrining the vulgar taste of the industrial class, it further severs the objects of industrial production from their human origins, rendering alabaster figures and lace curtains even colder and more lifeless than before. Ornamental objects beyond the scope of human use even seem to reintroduce dirt and disease at the heart of inanimate cleanliness: as the "painfully spotted" look of the drawing room unpleasantly indicates, this cleanliness has nothing to do with health or with beauty. At Margaret's simple house, by contrast, the daily struggle for cleanliness is dedicated to keeping alive the frail human inhabitants, preserving, and sometimes failing to preserve, the warmth, health and vitality of tenuous human existence. With this reassessment of cleanliness, dirt's definition is too refined: the filthiness of the struggling industrial classes becomes progressive and productive in *North and South,* a sign of labor that is democratic and inherently valuable, while the filthiness of picturesque rural environments is regressive, superstitious, unproductive and finally illusory. Marjorie Garson has pointed out that exposure to Margaret awakens John Thornton's higher aesthetic feeling, teaching him that good taste is a reflection of "emotional and intellectual receptivity, domestic comfort, and genuine hospitality."[16] But it is important to recognize that Margaret's aesthetic values have also undergone significant transformation, and that the marriage of John Thornton and Margaret Hale becomes, in itself, the new aesthetic that replaces the diseased standards of both bourgeois vulgarity and aristocratic sensuality. In providing what Catherine Gallagher has famously termed a closing "tableau of reconciliation" between social classes, economic interests, and intellectual philosophies, their union consecrates a new and more harmonious society in the shape of Ruskin's sanitary aesthetic.

II. Prevention and Progress: The Socialist Aesthetic

The social reconciliation provided by the marriage plot in *North and South* is one example of the kind of reform often promised by mid-Victorian sanitary fiction: a genre that gave narrative structure and reformist teleology to an aesthetic of social "perfectibility" that surfaced in the social sciences as early as the 1840s. From their earliest days, sanitary practitioners had imagined hygiene and health to be the primary engine of social harmony, unity and progress. For Edwin Chadwick and William Farr in the 1840s and 50s, this meant eliminating pockets of fever and filth in the aggregate social body; for Benjamin Ward Richardson and Alfred Carpenter in the 1870s and 1880s, it meant using environmental and domestic sanitation to eliminate the very possibility of disease in an individual human body, thus achieving a state of physical perfection that would render future medical interventions completely unnecessary. In 1879, for example, Dr. Richardson predicted that by the year 2050, humankind would finally achieve its natural lifespan of 100 years.[17] In "Salutland," his imagined utopian community, people will be "happy, powerful and beautiful" because everybody knows the basic sanitary laws and the modern principles of preventive medicine. In Salutland, Richardson rhapsodizes, there will be no center of government, no capitol, no gender inequity, no standing army, no legal system, and no medical profession: instead, "common health and common wealth—for health and wealth are one—will make us a model and perfected people" (12). At the 1883 Glasgow Health Congress Dr. Alfred Carpenter was almost as optimistic when he declared that "everything is preventable," not only smallpox, cholera, and diphtheria, but consumption, cancer and deformity too.[18] Disregarding even entrenched Victorian assumptions about economic and biological determinism, and still resisting the rising tide of germ theory that would later turn sanitation into a physiological tool, Carpenter expressed a plain and positivist faith in the long-term effects of environmental cleanliness: "The sanitarian does not believe in the permanence of hereditary evils" (405).

By 1880, sanitarians had fully adopted as mission statement a phrase that now seems little more than homespun cliché: prevention is better than cure. Moreover, prevention itself was a concept that expanded the intellectual importance of sanitary reform into discourses and disciplines far removed from its original Chadwickian ethos. For philosopher and activist Edward Carpenter, in his 1889 *Civilisation: Its Cause and Cure,* the possibility of "prevention" could convert health into a positive attribute rather than a degraded concept, "a negative thing."[19] Currently, Carpenter explained, to be *not* gouty or *not* rheumatic was "the very limit of our impoverished understanding of health" (11). What needed to be recognized was that there a direct correlation between the social body and the individual body, and that in both models, health manifests itself as a simple unity of parts, while disease signified a loss of natural wholeness.

> For as in the body disease arises from a loss of physical unity of parts, which constitutes health and so takes the form of warfare or discord between the various parts . . . so in our modern life we find the unity gone which constitutes a true society, and in its place warfare in classes and individuals, abnormal development of some to the detriment of other, and consumption of organisms by masses of social parasites. (2)

Of course, "civilization" itself is a negative stage of human society for Carpenter, a term that reflects not progress and enlightenment, but the current state of human discord, debilitation and disease. For society to cure itself, Carpenter argues, nature must again become the home of man, private property must disappear, and the "great, positive force of Health" must become, as it was for the ancient Greeks, an endemic aesthetic truth (20). The Greeks produced the greatest works of art because they valued health over all other human attributes and because they had no concept or consciousness of sin (10). "Which all means cleanness," Carpenter explains, "The unity of our nature being restored, the instinct of bodily cleanness, *both* within and without, which is a marked characteristic of the animals, will again characterize mankind—only now instead of a blind instinct it will be a conscious, joyous one; dirt being only disorder and obstruction" (38).

While the Hellenic inspiration of Carpenter's vision would obviously dismay Ruskin's fervent Christian medievalism, this last passage from *Civilisation* could be easily mistaken for an extract from *Modern Painters*. For English sanitarians and social reformers writing at the end of the century—from Carpenter to William Morris to Havelock Ellis—harmony, unity and proportion were the very definition of health physically and socially, and within this discourse of communion is the same aesthetic philosophy at work in Ruskin's directive to "get your country clean and your people lovely." "Socialism is an all-embracing theory of life," explained William Morris in 1891, "it has an ethic and a religion of its own, so also it has an aesthetic . . . to the Socialist, anything made by a man is a work of art."[20] In his aptly titled "The Socialist Ideal in Art," Morris continues,

> To the Commercialist, things are divided into art and not art. The Commercialist sees that in the great mass of civilized human labor there is no pretence to art, and thinks that this is natural, inevitable, and on the whole desirable. The Socialist, on the contrary, sees in this obvious lack of art a disease peculiar to modern civilization and hurtful to humanity; and furthermore believes it to be a disease which can be remedied . . . the great mass of effective art, that which pervades all life, must be the result of harmonious cooperation of neighbors. And a rich man has no neighbors—nothing but rivals and parasites. (63–67)

The "socialist ideal in art" for both Morris and Carpenter is socialism itself: a socialism imagined as wholeness, health, and cleanliness, a model of human existence that both produces and embodies Art. Commercialism, by contrast, is disease and dirt, fragmentation and filth, not just because it infects the environment, but because it degrades humanity. In this context, sanitation is material as well as political, a transformation of the socioeconomic order that will simultaneously purify man and the state. "The great positive force of Health, and the power which it has to expel disease from its neighborhood . . . will be realized when the more squalid elements of our present day civilization have passed away," Carpenter insists.[21]

Obviously, the intellectual legacy I am trying to trace here from Ruskin to Morris to Richardson to Carpenter and beyond is often recognized as a relatively radical strain of social criticism; a school of protest that rises from a desire for change rather than stasis, for revolution rather than restraint. Compared to the close of *North and South,* for example, socialist reform promises the eradication of the industrialist, like a stamping out of some pestilent disease, rather than his happy rehabilitation through marriage. But an interesting facet of the new socialist aesthetic that developed in the late nineteenth century is that it fits neatly inside a much larger, longer history of aesthetic philosophy that is anything but radical. As Terry Eagleton has described in his intellectual history of the aesthetic, traditional eighteenth-century philosophy, from Shaftesbury to Adam Smith, made the graceful and harmonious movements of a virtuous social order the very definition of art; for Edmund Burke, famously, beauty was a social quality that inspired us with necessary "sentiments of tenderness and affection" toward other persons, and a willingness to enter into personal relationships with them.[22] Indeed, as Eagleton reveals, this strain of aesthetic philosophy shows art to be central to the work of political hegemony, and thus power, the class system, and the economic hierarchy. "The beautiful is just the social order lived out on the body, the way it strikes the eye and stirs the heart," he writes. "The socially disruptive, by contrast, is as instantly offensive as a foul smell. . . . The maladroit or aesthetically disproportioned thus signals in its modest way, a certain crisis in political power" (38–42).

It seems appropriate that the opposite of beauty, harmony, and art, is for Eagleton, as it is for Ruskin, Gaskell, Carpenter and so many other Victorian writers, the foul odor of sanitary disaster. By averting such disaster, I argue, the fictional sanitarian also averts political crisis, reifying the aesthetic by remaking the known world at the close of each and every volume. Well into the twentieth-century, a familiar teleology surfaces in a variety of novels: dirty art produces disease, the dirty artist or connoisseur must be disciplined, and the fetishized art object or the filthy theory of the picturesque is subsequently exchanged for a sanitary philosophy derived as much from Ruskin as from more certified sanitarians. Importantly, the ideological work accomplished by the sanitary fictions I discuss throughout *The Sanitary Arts* often seems liberal, seems reformist, seems revolutionary. But the aesthetic objectives of sanitation reform also work against disruption and social upheaval, repeatedly offering hegemony as a form of harmony, and continuity as the essence of beauty. In most sanitary fiction of the period, the moneyed classes emerge well-lessoned, but relatively unscathed and, in fact, much more popular. The marriage plot usually provides both pedagogical apparatus and harmonious social reconciliation, as it does so smoothly in *North and South,* softening the rich industrialist in order to assimilate him into a happier, healthier social order. What is most radical, what is most revolutionary, about such novels is finally their ideological alchemy: they so

successfully transform the lowness and banality of sanitation reform (stinking sewers and pipes, filthy ditches and dung heaps) into a sophisticated aesthetic, effectively translating dirt into art for the sake of political power and
social hegemony. Sanitary novels are efficient vehicles of the kind of culture
most famously described by Matthew Arnold in *Culture and Anarchy,* providing balance, regulation and harmony, instead of the vulgarity of social agitation and political opposition. "But there is of culture another view," Arnold
explains,

> in which all the love of our neighbor, the impulses towards action, help,
> and beneficence, the desire for removing human error, clearing human
> confusion, and diminishing human misery, the noble aspiration to leave
> the world better and happier than we found it—motives eminently such as
> are called social—come in as part of the grounds of culture, and the main
> and pre-eminent part. Culture . . . is a study of perfection.[23]

Culture, for Arnold, is both a process and an institution, simultaneously the
"removing," "clearing" and "diminishing" work of re-form, and the harmonious aesthetic form of perfect social order.

III. Sanitary Fictions and Fictional Sanitarians

By arguing that the emergence of the sanitary aesthetic signals a conservative
brand of power, I am not suggesting that the earnest socialism of, say, William Morris, was anything less than earnest or socialist, or that the realism
of George Eliot didn't strive to represent, in some irreproachable way, the
lived experience of the People. But as we know, even progressive aesthetics
are ambivalently and unreliably political, and as Eagleton points out, "lived
experience, which can offer a powerful critique of Enlightenment rationality,
can also be the very homeland of conservative ideology" (60). Sanitary narratives, I would argue, were ideologically powerful because they demonstrated
public hygiene operating impersonally, impartially, collaborating with aesthetic philosophy to reconcile a hierarchical and divided society. I will be
discussing the increasingly less progressive implications of public and even
"social" hygiene in the final chapters of *The Sanitary Arts,* specifically in the
context of some early-twentieth-century sanitary fictions. But in order to
rehearse the broad connections between mid-Victorian sanitary reform and
late-Victorian eugenic philosophy, it is useful here to remember how early in
the nineteenth-century aesthetic preference for the picturesque began to be

linked to physiological and psychological degeneration. Ruskin, for example, in his 1860 *Elements of Drawing*, insisted that "colour power is a great sign of mental health in nations; when they are in a state of intellectual decline, their colouring always gets dull."[24] For this reason, individual artists must keep in good physical and mental health: as Ruskin warns fledgling painters, "your power of colouring will depend much on your state of health and balance of mind; when you are fatigued or ill, you will not see colours well" (235). While his logic is circular, Ruskin succinctly links bad health with bad art: illness and exhaustion causes diseased vision, and diseased vision, in turn, is a sign of immorality and even insanity. As we have seen, Ruskin's doctrine of cleanliness and health sharply reverses the powerful eighteenth-century association between muted colors, soft tones and an evolved "natural" sensibility, and this reversal, in turn, was popularized through fictional reflections on color, taste, and the moral sentiments.

In Averil Beaumont's intriguingly titled *Magdalen Wynard, or The Provocations of a Pre-Raphaelite* (1872), Ruskin's aesthetic diagnosis is echoed when Bernard Longley, our painter-hero, asserts early in the novel that "an exclusive love of semi-tones in colour would betoken weakness, mental and physical, just as much as perpetual preference of the minor key on music; for depend upon it, the perfect man likes a full chord of colour, boldly struck."[25] Longley argues further that "bodily weakness" and ill health prevented both Keats and Shelley from having "perfect appreciation of colour" in their poetry (133). This self-proclaimed Pre-Raphaelite successfully "cultivate[s] literature, health, and art" for a good portion of the novel, devoting himself "to the study of Ruskin, and the question of the Old Style versus pre-Raphaelitism" (28). But while walking through Dorminster on his way to sketch the cathedral, Bernard begins to be distracted by "a dreadful place" just around the corner, a dirty by-street where ragged children play and filthy mothers gather on stoops, and he is soon driven to a hill outside the city for a more aesthetic and less aromatic view of the poisoned river and polluted streets.

> The flitting to and fro of the sunshine, from the steaming pool, along the walls along the walls and rag-patched windows and indescribable meanness of the tottering, decrepit houses which formed the end of the water lane, was lovely to see, but would have required the spirit of self-sacrifice and endurance of a martyr to paint. On the high ground and from a distance all was perfect. The smoke of the city lay heavily along the course of the valley, warm in the afternoon light . . . the bridges were indistinct blurs upon the sheen of the river, while, over all, upon its platform of rock, rose the great shade of the cathedral, its massive towers refusing one sparkle of

light, and losing no whit of their keenness of outline from the drifted mist
of the world below. (217)

Bernard is so fascinated by the scene that he is moved to begin a large, cum-
brous painting, and hires a local man, "Cracky Charlie," to cart his paints and
painterly apparatus to and from the hillside so that he can be free to enjoy
the distanced and "unencumbered" pleasure of watching the light change and
the shadows shift (228). But eventually Cracky Charlie is stricken with cholera and dies, and Bernard realizes that his detached "pure gaze" is to blame.
Overcome with regret for abandoning his healthy Pre-Raphaelite principles,
his moral commitment to clear details rather than hazy effects, Bernard gives
up painting entirely and dedicates himself to nursing the poor of his community through what proves to be a cholera epidemic.

One likely reason that the miasmatic theory of disease was so slow to disappear in the late nineteenth century is that this kind of association between
sanitation and salvation, purification and perfection was too ideologically
entrenched and attractive in Victorian culture.[26] The germ theory of disease,
on the other hand, as it was pursued by a variety of bacteriologists through
the last decades of the nineteenth century, found no fundamental relationship
between dirt, disease and immorality, and the microorganisms discovered
in all human and animal life seemed disappointingly indifferent to schemes
for sanitary perfectibility and moral improvement. Instead, throughout the
end of the Victorian period, sanitary fictions like *Provocations of a Pre-
Raphaelite* continued to pursue social transformation through the eradication of the fever nest, the poisoned village, the dilapidated cottage, the dirty
peasant. Sanitary reform may have prescribed social behaviors and put in
place intrusive and oppressive regulations ranging from the Poor Laws to the
Contagious Diseases Acts, from slum clearances to home visitations.[27] But it
advanced these goals under the banner of aesthetic perfectibility, imagining
progressive, utopian communities like the one found in B. W. Richardson's
1876 *Hygeia: A City of Health,* where a healthful civilization is a beautiful civilization, and disease and social degradations unknown.

> As in the highest development of the fine arts the sculptor and painter
> place before us the finest imaginative types of strength, grace and beauty,
> so the silent artist civilisation, approaches nearer and nearer to perfection,
> and by evolution of form and mind develop what is practically a new order
> of physical and mental build.[28]

Richardson, an ardent anti-contagionist, here foresees the rebirth of Greek
culture in England, as "artist civilisation" begins creating healthier, stronger,

more beautiful British bodies, foreshadowing as well the path that sanitary prevention would follow in the late nineteenth century as it moved from environmental to biological to even eugenic advocacy.

A similar story of sanitary transformation can be found in Florence Caddy's 1878 *Artist and Amateur, or The Surface of Life,* a novel that explores the development of two female artists, Flora Potts and Elma Dean. Elma, an upper-class woman who runs away to London to pursue her art studies, has an eager but undisciplined appreciation of color that paralyzes her ability to paint well: there is so much color in the world, Elma explains, "I am literally borne down by quantity, and can do nothing."[29] Her old friend, Flora, gives her a home in London and some necessary guidance; Flora is the daughter of a master-craftsman, and has been trained in South Kensington art schools, most notably by a Morris-like sage Raymond Dalvey, whose domestic setting is characterized by its Venetian colors and medieval accoutrements. Elma realizes that Dalvey's colours unfold "as Nature unfolds hers," when she watches his wife bring "into the room a colouring of tea-rose in her face and dress that harmonized perfectly with the bluish-velvet pile carpet, on which was a waving, watery, reedy pattern, designed by Mr. Dalvey himself, in soft tints of pale grey and sea-green" (123). When Flora introduces Elma as an artist with "vaporous and vague" ideals who desires to go to Italy to study, Dalvey chides her by stating that "an artist's home is his own country . . . look not to Italy, daughter, it is rather a grave . . . their history is over; reverence the holy shrines, but worship no dead relics" (123).

Both female artists do travel abroad, however, when Flora gains a Ruskinian commission to make drawings of ancient buildings in France and Italy "before they are restored beyond all recognition" (206). Passing through Milan, Flora explains to her companion why she must avert her gaze from a prominent Renaissance cathedral: "This is one of the buildings I am not to draw. I am told to shun the Renaissance like a pestilence and even pure northern Gothic is not part of my present contract" (157–158). Flora is eventually tempted to sketch outside her contract, and develops an appropriately infectious fever, however, upon recovery, she is able to explain the aesthetic lesson implicit in her experience: "I am sorry my illness came on when I was working at something outside my commission. I was told not to draw classic temples, and I was caught at play" (222). A similar fate is reserved for the more aesthetically wayward Elma: in France, Elma insists upon painting late into the damp, misty evening, "because it always needs a little mist to generalize details" (210). In response, Flora tries to warn Elma that her fortune is health rather than wealth: "If you go on expending health beyond the strength that is given you for daily use, it is like spending your capital . . . dear Elma, take care of your health, for health means your art, and you are rich in many gifts" (210). The two women separate after this incident, and Elma struggles to make her way to Florence in the early stages of an illness that necessitates her rescue by St. Bernard dogs in the Swiss Alps.

What must be clear about these sanitary narratives so far is that they display an ideological clarity that makes any potential marriage plot morally legible. If art is bad, health is good; if aesthetic knowledge is a symptom of selfishness, vanity, and degradation, sanitary knowledge is a sign of altruism, personal responsibility, and social progress. At the end of *Artist and Amateur,* Flora marries her art, but Elma marries a man little seen since the beginning of the novel, a man who manages to speak with Elma about both Ruskin's "tenderness of colour" and the realities of rural poverty in the same conversation (52). The narrator tells us that Elma's future husband, a wealthy and somewhat mysterious agent of international finance, is characterized by his "health, prolonged by temperance and active employment, bearing up against the enervating influence of hot climates," and the way his "mental food" is "taken according to strict hygienic principles . . . assimilated and digested without effort, reviving the soul for its work in the service of its possessor" (98). As a character, Henry Wentworth is ill-developed and belated; as an ideological vehicle, however, he is delineated to perfection, demonstrating just enough sanitary commitment to permanently purify Elma's diseased aesthetic proclivities, and to reconcile art and health for future generations of citizens.

A sanitary reconciliation enacted through the marriage plot may move the heroine from illness to health, as it does in *Artist and Amateur,* or it may force her to choose between men who represent radical sanitary alternatives and social philosophies. Gillian Lattimer, in Rhoda Broughton's *Second Thoughts* (1880), is courted by painter and poet Francis Chaloner, an aesthete who favors sickness, dislocation and unwholesomeness as artistic objectives.[30] When Gillian critiques the morbid nature of his art, he replies "gently but firmly, 'there is nothing so beautiful as disease. The beauty of the pearl is greater than that of any other jewel, because it is the beauty of disease'" (189). After mistaking a female figure in his painting entitled "Amor Dolorosus" for a cholera victim, Gillian becomes more interested in rival suitor Dr. Burnet, and begins visiting sick children in Kings' Hospital out of interest in his vocation; ironically, a particularly pathetic sickbed scene eventually allows the marriage plot to commence on more healthful grounds. While Broughton's novel is less interested in environmental reform than the other texts I discuss above, the inadequate healthfulness of human forms in late-Victorian, especially late-Pre-Raphaelite, "aestheticism" was widely debated in sanitary circles as well: as Edward Cookworthy Robins declared to his audience at the

1886 meeting of the Sanitary Institute, in a paper called "The Artistic Side of Sanitary Science,"

> There has lately sprung up a taste in Art that can only be postulated as a taste for disease—a leaning towards the outward expressions of decrepitude and decay. . . . In one school, at least, of the art movement, we find woebegone women, ill limp and unwholesome. They look thin, weak and weary; their complexions are not those of health, and their attitudes are of a long-enduring debility. . . . The unfitness of the association is condemnatory of its artistic character. It is as inartistic as it is insanitary.[31]

While I will be pursuing the sanitary status of human figures in art in a later chapter, it is worth noting here how thoroughly pollution anxiety had permeated aesthetic discourse at the end of the nineteenth century, and how, when it comes to a novel like *Second Thoughts,* it can provide sufficient ideological agency for a marriage plot. In *Second Thoughts,* Gillian Lattimer is merely asked to favor a suitor who is a doctor over a suitor who is a painter in order to protest the unwholesomeness of *amor dolorosus,* embracing cleanliness over filth and health over illness. But it is much more common in sanitary fictions for the female character to enforce hygiene and health through scientific knowledge or ethical principles by marrying and converting a dirty artist or connoisseur. Women were natural sanitarians, according to B. W. Richardson, because the domestic sphere is the best laboratory for healthy families and cleanly nations; moreover, sanitation is an art rather than a science, a standard aesthetic responsibility of middle-class housekeeping.

> I would with all my strength suggest to women that to be practitioners of the preventive art of medicine; to hold in their hands the key to health; to stand at the thresholds of their homes and say to disease, "Into this place you shall not come, it is not fitted to receive you, it is free only to health, a barrier to disease."[32]

Certainly Florence Nightingale's sanitary campaigns in Scutari during the 1850s make Richardson's assertions in the 1880s less surprising. In *Notes on Nursing,* Nightingale insists that medicine and pathology are distinct disciplines, and that every mother and governess should learn enough about the prior (cleanliness, ventilation and diet) to significantly diminish the need for the latter (primarily surgery).[33] By the mid-Victorian period, in fact, disease prevention was a domestic purview, and women were practitioners of a form of cleansing and revival that would extend ideologically from the domestic to the national. As both Nancy Tomes and Alison Bashford have argued, more-over, while bacteriology increasingly interested doctors and surgeons in the 1870s and 80s, sanitation, hygiene, and cleanliness remained the primary dis-course of nursing, and thus became an increasingly female program through the end of the century.[34] In fiction, heroines forge new equivalences between the sanitary and the beautiful in a variety of ways, always using the marriage plot to impose final harmony on the supposedly competing claims of science and art. In Charlotte Mary Yonge's *Astray: A Tale of a Country Town* (1886), for example, Frida Wood is an orphan, an heiress, and a painter, who dreams of traveling to Italy for art study until Burton King reorients her vocation.[35] King has moved to Emery St. Lawrence with his family under a mysterious cloud of disgrace: it emerges that he endured seven years of penal servitude for the crime of forgery, a sentence that interrupted his medical training and derailed a promising career. It also happens that Emery St. Lawrence was once viewed as a second Bath, but a typhoid epidemic due to defective drain-age gave it a bad reputation that frightened off potential visitors. King pre-tends he knows nothing of medicine while secretly doctoring residents for diphtheria and scarlatina (scarlet fever) in Gridiron Lane, a working-class slum, and lobbying simultaneously as a concerned citizen for a new conva-lescent hospital. The community practitioners, Dr. Blackstone and his son, are suspicious about King and hostile about plans for a new hospital; they dislike innovation, dismiss sanitary efforts, and fear the presence of "nurs-ing sisters" in the community (176). Even when the water in six of the seven wells in Gridiron is found to be undrinkable, the Blackstones refuse to help King, as he begins to dig an Artesian well while finishing construction on a new mission room in the working-class neighborhood. Inevitably, summer brings unbearable heat and repulsive smells to Gridiron Lane; the children begin to sicken and eventually to die, and finally King comes out of hiding to treat them. His best helpmeet during the new typhoid epidemic is his beloved Frida, who designed and executed the large, delicate frescoes on the walls of the Mission Room just in time for it to receive patients. Here, she "nurses admirably" throughout the epidemic, while "her pale paintings make the sick feel better" (358). After the Blackstones leave town, and King becomes the chief practitioner of the new hospital, Frida marries King and continues to use her art as a form of nursing itself, a fundamental component of a holistic healing process.

In George Halse's *Graham Aspen, Painter* (1889), our eponymous artist is described as "another [P]ygmalion" who devotes "abnormal" energy to the realization of an ideal study of a beautiful woman he has supposedly never met; eventually, however, we learn it is a picture of his dead mother.[36] As might be expected, Graham's obsession with this painting as well as other "sublime" images of death and decay renders his mind morbid, his body sickly, and his colors "false." Dr. Eustace, himself an amateur artist, warns Graham that occupation with death "emasculates his mental facilities and his body pays for it. Hence, the inability at times to pursue the art you love" (57). Indeed, Graham begins to decline rapidly when his body demonstrates an intrinsic lack of harmony and vitality by failing to properly digest food (152). The heroine, Hester, is so moved by watching Graham faint in Dr. Eustace's office that she becomes a nurse; however, the two don't actually meet until some time later when she intrudes upon a picture he is painting of "dead trees in a wood," and his assistant Starkey wisely suggests that Graham add her to it. Hester's healthy, living image gradually displaces Graham's dead mother's ghostly presence, and the marriage plot ultimately coalesces around a project that formally recognizes the new healthfulness of Graham's art when Graham inherits a famous health farm long-celebrated for excellent drainage system, fine air, and pure water. Aided by Dr. Eustace's desire to employ some capital "in the interests of science and an equal portion in the advancement of British Art—the two fields of study which divide my attachment," painter and nurse transform Flinders Farm into a famous art-school where enfeebled British painting will be cleansed and strengthened (283).

> Flinders is the solution. It is a famous health resort. In conjunction with your friend Starkie, make it an equally famous art resort—and here my purse comes in. Reconstruct and adapt the place as an art-school in the truest sense. Let your aim be the highest; tolerate no mediocrity; allow no trifling with art; stamp out all meretriciousness; show that it should be pursued seriously, if at all. Let your motto be Nature, and your first and last canon, Truth . . . resolve that everything done under your sway shall be thorough, and you will render the art of your country a great service. (283)

A year later, a newspaper proudly reports that the creative arts have been reborn at the health farm: "Under these two guiding forces, Flinders in unique and destined to be famous as the Alma Mater of a great revival in British Art" (291).

Finally, in George Gissing's 1890 *The Emancipated*, the aesthetic awakening of a formerly puritanical widow, Miriam Elgar, reaches its natural apogee in Italy, where she falls in love with and eventually marries a British artist named Mallard. We know these two are destined for the altar when they dramatically dislike each other at the outset: Mallard resents Miriam's narrow asceticism, while Miriam deplores Mallard's socially purposeless aestheticism.

The highest moral life for Miriam, as Mallard scornfully suggests, would be something like "the life of a hospital nurse, or a sister of mercy" (94), a vocation significantly at odds with his pursuit of personal pleasure through painting, and his disgust at Miriam's prim suggestion that his art should be "useful" or should "serve mankind" (95).[37] Mallard is likewise scornful of the repressive cultural force represented by Miriam's religion, which he explains to his friend, Spence, is the bourgeois, domestic and especially "Philistine point of view":

> We become more and more prudish as what we call civilisation advances. It is a hateful fact that, from the domestic point of view there exists no difference between the noblest things in art and poetry, and the obscenities which are prosecuted. . . . If ever I marry, *amico mio,* my wife shall learn to make more than a theoretical distinction between what is art and what is grossness. If ever I have children, they shall be taught from the first a natural morality, and not the conventional. If I can afford good casts of noble statues, they shall stand freely about my house. . . . If a daughter of mine cannot describe to me the points of difference between the Venus of the Capitol and that of the Medici, she shall be bidden to use her eyes and her brains better. I'll have no contemptible prudery in my house! (329)

As Arnold had infamously warned in *Culture and Anarchy,* most religion was incapable of "transforming vice and hideousness;" because Hebraic religions believe sin is perpetually thwarting man's path to perfection, only Culture, that mechanism of "sweetness and light," can help us achieve the harmonious expansion of human nature that Hellenic cultures nurtured through aesthetics.[38] A shade of Arnold is here channeled by Gissing in order to isolate the ideological conflict between Miriam and Mallard as clash between the Hebraic and the Hellenic, and to forge a solution that represents an appropriate transformation of sin into sweetness, and religion into a socially conscious aesthetics. Prior to emancipation, Miriam had promised a large sum of money for the construction of a new Puritan chapel in her village; however, once Mallard gives her a new way of "looking at a thing" (322) Miriam is transformed by art and can no longer honor her pledge. Miriam and her soon-to-be husband together decide to reallocate that money from the propagation of religious oppression to the construction of public baths for the working poor. Hellenic culture meets sanitary culture in the reconciliation that concludes *The Emancipated,* and the closure negotiated by the marriage plot is consecrated by the aesthetic. The house in Roehampton that Miriam and Mallard share after their marriage is "sacred to love and art," and their first visitor is struck by how "the air seemed purer than that of any other house she entered; to breathe it made her heart beat more hopefully, gave her a keener relish of life" (446). Indeed, the work of aesthetic transformation in so many sanitary fictions gives narrative form to Arnold's Hellenic model of perfectibility, offering through the marriage of art and science, through the marriage of working and upper classes, through the marriage plot itself, a "tableau of reconciliation" that can stand in for Culture. Importantly, the objectives of sanitary fiction also warded off the problem of *laissez faire* politics and the vulgarity of "doing as one likes": such anarchy, as it was called by Arnold, would be as dangerous as revolution and as ugly as the reality of harsh social relations. Only art joined with social responsibility, only aesthetics joined with ascetics, could revive Culture at a time of so much environmental ugliness and social degradation.

I've been arguing throughout this chapter that sanitary fictions repeatedly sought to liberate Victorian aesthetics from the putrescence of the picturesque. Such liberation inevitably seems less triumphant when the work of sanitation gets defined as an effort to conserve power rather than disperse it, inspiring the rich landowners and selfish artists to discipline their wayward aesthetic inclinations and turn beauty into a political tool in the service of a more graceful and harmonious society. Sanitary fictions, in general, are not like to close on a note of interrogation; they re-form through rehabilitation, often nursing the diseased social hierarchy back to health and power. But the fact that I see sanitary fictions as formally coercive, demonstrative in the long view of socioeconomic power and class hegemony, makes me no less aware, in the still longer view, that these novels are also stridently oppositional, chafing against a tradition of aesthetic power and social oppression that had dominated intellectual discourse from the eighteenth-century Age of Enlightenment. Inconsistently and imperfectly ideological, the sanitary fictions I've written about in this chapter and will continue to write about in *The Sanitary Arts,* always expose the relentlessly political work of aesthetic discourse, even at the very moment of radical recapitulation to conservative ideology. As Caroline Levine points out, one helpful objective of "new" formalist methodologies might be "not to isolate forms, to bind them to intentions, or to choose between them, but to recognize their challenges to each other."[39] I would modify Levine's point to the extent that though forms themselves are constantly changing, we *can* actually isolate intentions that are quite different from effects, and can attribute a certain degree of self-organization to the effects that emerge from collaborations between discourses. At the very least, Ruskin's intentional articulation of a sanitary aesthetic became much more entrenched and controversial in Victorian culture than he gave himself credit for in 1870; in a variety of aesthetic contexts, cleanliness and health came to embody the highest cultural values, and the future of the British people seemed to distill itself into a deceptively simple question asked most succinctly and earnestly by William Morris: "So, which shall we have, art or dirt?" Dorothea Brooke's unrequited desire to make the life of poverty beautiful may be, in the final analysis, a troubling aesthetic goal, but its formal challenge to dominant discourse and social power could not have been articulated more clearly.

CHAPTER 3

Victorian Dust Traps

The sky, with the sun in it, does not usually give the impression of being dimly lighted through a circular hole; but you may observe a very similar effect any day in your coal cellar. The light is not Rembrandtesque, usually, in a clean house; but it is presently obtainable of that quality in a dirty one. . . . [I]t is the aim of the best painters to paint the noblest things they can see by sunlight. It was the aim of Rembrandt to paint the foulest things he could see—by rushlight.

—John Ruskin, "The Cestus of Aglaia" (1865)

*A*n important aspect of the argument I have been making in *The Sanitary Arts* is that, by mid-century, the connection between art and dirt was topographically obvious. For reformers like Edwin Chadwick, art was dirty because its cherished environments were dirty: Venice, that revered paradise of aesthetic culture, was "pestilential and foul" in Chadwick's assessment, and the art it contained and inspired must necessarily be degraded and contagious.[1] Famous self-help authority Samuel Smiles even counseled his readers to shun aesthetic education in their quest for upward mobility, using a similar sanitary geography to argue that any belief in art as socially and individually improving was demonstrably false. If aesthetic beauty had moral value, Smiles wryly observes in his 1871 *Character*, "Paris ought to contain a population of the wisest and best human beings," and Rome would not be so "inexpressibly foul."[2] For the rising British middle class, Smiles recommends soap and water instead of aesthetic tourism, insisting that "a little common education in cleanliness is much more improving, as well as more wholesome, than any amount of education in art" (Smiles 263). And in the less didactically obvious world of fiction, aesthetic travel is often scorned and even reviled by writers who learned from early sanitarians that the pleasures of the pictur-

esque were often immoral and sometimes deadly. As Flora Potts and Elma
Dean finally learn in *Artist and Amateur,* the picturesque pleasures of Italian
travel undermine both artistic and bodily health.

Yet mapping the unsanitary status of distant European capitals was not
the primary geographical effect of the sanitary idea. As Peter Stallybrass and
Allon White have influentially argued, Victorian reformers like Chadwick
and Henry Mayhew were instrumental in the invention of more local geographies, especially the ideological mapping of London for the Victorian middle
class.[3] By locating, exploring, and evocatively describing stinking slums, sewers, cesspools and other so-called "fever nests" for the fastidious bourgeois
reader, Chadwick, Mayhew and other reformers engineered a city plan that
drew imaginary safe, sanitary borders around middle-class shopping districts,
neighborhoods, and finally, around the apex of cleanliness, the middle-class
home. While critics like Mary Poovey, Nancy Armstrong and Catherine Gallagher have written extensively on the concept of the middle-class home as
a self-contained moral universe, it is also the case that in the second half of
the nineteenth century, Victorian domestic space was under increased pressure to appear hygienically inviolable, impermeable, and unassailable.[4] For
the bourgeois citizen, the domestic sphere was not only a haven in a heartless
world: it was, as Stallybrass and White argue, a snug, hermetically sealed zone
of middle-class comfort and smug, scopophilic pleasure in the filthiness that
resided just around the corner.

Miasmatic theories of bad air, foul smells, and spontaneous generation
continued to dominate sanitary discourse in the 1870s and 80s, but as germ
theories entered circulation the impenetrable Victorian home became an
increasingly anxious fantasy rather than a reliable domestic construct. Sanitary geographies of the city turned inward, eventually producing analogous
geographies of the over-decorated, architecturally busy Victorian interior.
Even purpose-built environments could contain pockets of potential contamination and illness; in fact, the architectural flourishes and decorative fittings
so identified with mid-Victorian style became sites of suspicion and fear as
the nineteenth century waned. In these new domestic geographies, I argue,
the decorative "dust trap" rivaled the urban fever nest as a primary locus of
pollution anxiety, emerging as a contested site of cultural value and meaning
in a variety of Victorian texts. Dust has a complicated cultural history, as Kate
Flint persuasively demonstrated in her writing about the paradoxical phenomenon of the airborne dust mote. When particles of dirt were illuminated
by sunlight or other atmospheric conditions, Victorians could simultaneously
experience the transformative beauty and the contaminating agency of dust.
Dust specks, as Flint thus explains, were both powerful literary metaphors

and a "meeting point for the intersection of science, vision, and imagination."[5] For Victorian home decorators and house wives that meeting point presented a set of practical challenges, as a beautiful home, decorated in the favorite styles of an aesthetically eager middle class, almost always proved to be a sanitary disaster. Even innocuous-sounding instructional manuals like the 1882 "How to Hang Pictures" approach home decoration as an inevitably contradictory and at times irresolvable set of choices for amateur householders, explaining that style and science do not often harmonize in the Victorian home: "If we hang pictures to slope downward, there would be a shelf above for porcelain, terra cotta, and the like, or condemned for being a 'dust trap' according as one were bitten with the aesthetic or the sanitary mania."[6]

Sanitary "maniacs" not only condemned the nooks, crannies, tunnels, dark rooms, narrow hallways, and turrets cherished by Gothic revivalists, they also dismissed the favored features of Aesthetic decoration—dados, decorative carving, shelving, cornices, tapestries, curtains and carpets—as "dust traps" or, in other words, "the forcing beds for disease germs."[7] Inside the dust trap an aesthetic philosophy became a material household canker; a site of sensory and physiological crisis, where the opposing claims of art and hygiene collided with potentially dangerous effects. More genteel addresses eventually ran afoul of sanitary regulators, and the decorative artist and architect joined the painter and fine artist as the suspected enemies of health, hygiene and cleanliness. By century's end, this chapter concludes, the transition to a sleeker, more seamless Modernism in British art and architecture looked less like a purely aesthetic revolution than the collaborative effects of the Victorian cleanliness campaigns.

I. Sanitation and Decoration

Perhaps because London had few pastoral pleasures to offer, its artists were often accused of finding beauty in the urban features it did have in abundance: soot, smoke, fog, architectural decay, wastewater, mud, and ordinary dirt. "The London atmosphere is never free from moisture or mist," architect William White mourned in an article called "Undrained London: A Fog Factory" that appeared in an 1882 issue of *The Builder;* "David Roberts painted it, and I am credibly informed that Mr. Ruskin admires it."[8] In the same issue of *The Builder,* Sir Frederick Leighton felt compelled to deny such charges in his own essay, "An Artist's View of the Smoke Question." The "smoke pest fastens upon us artists just as it does upon the rest of you," Leighton insisted, "we wheeze, we cough, we choke, and occasionally we fairly flicker out like the rest of you."[9] Like Wyke Bayliss and other late-century artists, Leighton was convinced that art could only be produced in clean countries and cities, and that the revival of true art in England would require its own version of sanitary reform. "Are you going to help us against this great enemy?" Bayliss demanded of his audience of sanitary engineers, "Are you going to clarify the air of London, Liverpool, and Manchester, and the other dark places of the Earth? . . . If you will enable is to see London, I promise you that Art shall make it beautiful to look upon."[10] Indeed, by the last decades of the nineteenth century, the urban sensibility of many Victorian artists had adapted itself to the sanitary aesthetic, and Bayliss joined the likes of Ruskin and William Morris in calling for a transformation of England into an environmental utopia, that aesthetic "City of Hygiea" as it was called by Richardson in 1876.[11]

As we already know, Ruskin's sanitation of fine art first required a recognition and refusal of the aesthetic values represented by the Renaissance Old Masters. The Old Masters were dangerous and degraded because the pictorial worlds they revered—sunless, filthy, environmentally compromised—threatened to contaminate the aesthetic values of British painting. Certainly the yellow-brown tones of the dirty Old Masters could only have been inspired by the most unsavory, unhealthy shades of local color, and, as we can see in the quotation that serves as the epigraph to this chapter, for Ruskin these colors were clearly indicative of a domestic setting especially reviled by the Victorian middle class: the dirty house. While Ruskin's "Rembrandtesque" house is a distinctively graphic and specifically middle-class variation on the fever nest, it existed not only as a descriptive metaphor. Mellowed by time, warmed by a fine golden tone, paintings by the "brown" and even "black" Renaissance masters imposed a formidable aesthetic standard on both pictorial art and the still-life of home decoration favored by late-Victorian aestheticism. Although Ruskin is often identified as the founder of the aesthetic movement, aestheticism generally favored art that had the power to make life not more moral but more beautiful, with Walter Pater's notion of "art for art's sake" standing as the unofficial motto of Aesthetic practitioners. While Pater never mentions Ruskin in his idiosyncratic, solipsistic aesthetic manifesto, *The Renaissance,* Ruskin's distaste for the pagan darkness and moral indifference of the fifteenth century is critiqued and rejected on every page.[12] As Talia Schaffer and Kathy Alexis Psomiades explain, "aestheticism's interest in artifice, intense experience, the mixing of beauty and strangeness, and the desire to experience life as an art" easily yielded an artistic concept of decadence, "with its fascination with the unnatural, death, decay, the body, and the exotic other."[13] Not only did Pater's theories revive aesthetic interest in the Renaissance, they reanimated some of the dirty interests Ruskin had found so appalling in art criticism written at the end of the eighteenth century, especially the notion that beauty could be found in the contemplation of dirt, disease, or even death. The child Florian in Pater's famous aesthetic narrative, "The Child in the House," has the enlightened soul of an epicure, and "does not hate the fog" that nightly rises from the city streets because "it is false to suppose that a child's sense of beauty is dependent on any choiceness, or special fineness, in the objects which present themselves to it."[14] Much like the Romantic idea of sublimity, aesthetic and decadent philosophy valued art for its ability to allow the viewer to achieve a personal transcendence untrammeled by moral, social, or even sanitary feelings.

For Ruskin and Morris, art ceased to be beautiful when it ceased to be useful; Pater, on the other hand, had no use for use. Art, for Pater, was "always striving to be independent of the mere intelligence, to become a matter of pure perception, to get rid of its responsibilities to its subject or material" (*The Renaissance* 88). Consequently, at its most decadent, the aesthetic design for living was highly ornamental, artificial, and above all Rembrandtesque. Dirty browns, muddy yellows, and livid greens were favorite shades for household decoration, and these unsanitary colors had corresponding human hues; because the most exquisite feelings were usually sensations of sorrow, fatigue, or pain, sickly, sallow complexions were considered more expressive of aesthetic "intensity" than the robust faces of health. As Mr. Chaloner, the villain of Broughton's satiric *Second Thoughts* explains, in barely exaggerated Paterian language, "There is nothing so beautiful as the passionate pulsations of pain!"[15] Obviously Victorian sanitarians had little patience with the decorative choices of the aesthetically inclined. "Most houses in London are dark naturally and helplessly," Mrs. Florence Caddy explains in her 1881 novel and home design guide *Lares and Penates, or The Background of Life,* "People generally regret this, but some affect darkness and even increase it to gain 'tone' and 'repose;' which are often euphemisms for dirt and idleness."[16] As the narrator of *Lares and Penates* visits a series of aesthetically noteworthy houses, she creates a sanitary map of London and its suburbs: at Alford House near the South Kensington Museum, she satisfactorily notes bright lights and colors, but in South Hampstead, the "younger rival" of South Kensington, Mrs. Caddy finds red brick houses clustered like "carbuncles," and in the home of Belinda Brassy, she discovers colors like "a symphony in boiled vegetables," and "spinach in an advanced state of decomposition" (Caddy 172). Conversely, at the suburban house of sanitary architect and engineer, Mr. Newbroom, the narrator is able to inspect an alternative background for life. "We don't allow any dust here," said Mrs. Newbroom, "None of your matted paint and embossed papers—all of them dust-traps" (Caddy 244). But while Mr. Newbroom's house is light, bright, and polished to a high gloss, our reporter admits that something more intangible and less sanitary may be missing:

> The beds were curtainless, of course, and the floors, equally of course, were uncarpeted. The partequeterie floors were waxed to icy slipperyness; the very rugs only stood still by being buttoned to the legs of the bed. . . . Life in this house may not be beautiful—it is not, indeed—but it is cleanly. It is scarcely even comfortable; the air is too freely changed, and too much according to rule, not allowing human nature to indulge a weakness, one petted sin. It is no grovelling, dust-coloured life, but one of perpetual stimulant, a mental pepper. (Caddy 254)

In Mr. Newbroom's house, cleanliness has defeated beauty, and constant circulation has banished stillness and repose. "But what would the disciples of the tone school say to you?" our narrator inquires of the architect, "Poets and Artists enjoy the peacefulness of dust." "Were I an independent man," Newbroom replies, "I should call them a pack of savages . . . it is modern sanitary science versus dust, or choked knowledge . . . and your art work is most of it a dust-trap" (Caddy 243–46).

The dusty corners of Victorian middle-class houses were thus important nodes of sanitary and aesthetic controversy, simultaneously places of artistic imagination and filthy accumulation. This ideological battle is distinctly visible in Charlotte Mary Yonge's 1873 *The Pillars of the House,* where an apparently simple argument about wallpaper is transformed by sanitary rhetoric into a controversy about dust traps. Of the orphaned Underwood siblings, two—Cherry and Edgar—are painters, trained by Romantic-era art criticism to appreciate the dark sublimities of Renaissance art. Wilmet, their practical elder sister and housekeeper, has just repapered the parlor in a pattern her brother calls "Philistine"; Edgar deplores the domestic incarceration of sister Cherry "among the eternal abortive efforts of that gilded trellis to close upon those blue dahlias, crimson lilacs, and laburnums growing upwards, tied with huge ragged magenta ribbons."[17] Edgar, a fledgling Bohemian, and Cherry instead wax rhapsodic about the old wallpaper "which could only be traced by curious researches in dark corners," and the color which was "soft, deepening off in clouds, and bars, sunsets and stormclouds, to make stories about." "Where it was most faded and grimy!" Wilmet replies in Ruskinian recognition of aesthetic pretensions, "It is all affectation not to be glad to have clean walls." "Clean!" cried Edgar. "Defend me from the clean!"[18]

By the 1880s, due in part to evolving ideas about germs, it was apparent that sanitation consisted of more than adequate plumbing and good ventilation; cleanliness was an aesthetic and architectural decision that had converted the ephemera of taste into the science of health. Hefty instructional manuals appeared throughout the decade, containing design tips that could have been penned by Mr. Newbroom himself. Architect Robert Edis's contribution to the 1883 volume *Our Homes and How to Make Them Healthy* was called "Internal Decoration," and it contains the clearest call for a modern collaboration between decoration and sanitation:

> For many years, we have been content to cover the whole floor surface of the rooms with carpets, under which dirt and filth naturally accumulated, to exclude light and air by heavy fluffy curtains, to form resting places for blacks and dust by the use of internal Venetian blinds, and to fill our rooms with lumbering old-fashioned furniture, with flat or sunken tops, which formed dirt and dust traps, rarely cleaned out. We have covered our walls with papers absolutely deleterious to bodily health, and have had but little regard to the mental effect of jarring colours and patterns, or the nervous irritability which is almost unknowingly is excited by the use of badly designed furniture, incongruous and staring decoration, and vulgar anachronisms in household taste, all of which, I believe exercise to an important degree an influence equally damaging to our mental as bad drainage and improper ventilation do to our bodily health.[19]

According to Edis, old-fashioned colors and contours could produce both physical and mental disease; indeed, anachronism itself was a trap where much filth could fester. Joint Art and Health Exhibitions began to be held all over England, with artists, scientists, and doctors together hosting discussions on "Healthy Furniture and Decoration," "Dress in Its Relation to Health and Climate," and "The Hygenic Value of Colour in the Dwelling." Moreover, architects, engineers, and furniture designers like Phillip Webb, Norman Shaw, and E. W. Godwin joined Edis in an attempt to invent the "Healthy House," a modern living environment that eliminated architectural nooks, decorative crannies, and the dust-trap anachronism.

Edis's 1881 lecture, "On Sanitation in Decoration," followed a William Morris doctrine of utility in furnishing, advising that

> everything in the House should be made useful; all ledges and unnecessary dust spaces should be carefully avoided, and everything so arranged that may be cleaned with as little labour or trouble as possible. All furniture which has superfluous carving or moulding should be avoided, and simplicity and utility should take the place of excessive ornamentation. . . .

There is no reason why we should convert our homes into pest houses by a style of furnishing which renders accumulations of filth not only likely but positively inevitable.[20]

At the same conference, Dr. Alfred S. Carpenter agreed, adding that "carpets, curtains, and comforts of all kinds retained the debris from our skin and our pulmonary membranes," and that "the excreta from our sweat glands are allowed to settle on our uncleaned windows, on out of the way cornices, useless ledges, and so-called architectural and upholstering ornaments."[21] Such decorative dust traps were perceived as the hiding places of diseases from typhus to measles to scarlet fever; as the editor of *Our Homes and How to Make Them Healthy*, Shirley Forster Murphy, explained in his introduction, poisonous disease particles could live indefinitely in the beautiful borders of the Victorian home. "It may be enclosed in woolen materials, it may be concealed in adhesive material, on the walls, in the ceilings, on the floors . . . it may be a solid particle, and dried up as mere dust, it retains its poisonous properties."[22] Murphy goes on to tell story after story about people who bought new houses in suburbs and soon died from design-related pulmonary disease. This wasn't surprising to architects Percival Gordon Smith and Keith Downes Young, who devoted their own chapter in Murphy's anthology to the modern practice of wallpapering rooms with papers and pastes "almost entirely composed of vegetable substances . . . and, frequently, not of the purest description" adding that "the readiness with which a mass of half a dozen layers decays and ultimately becomes putrid is easily understood."[23]

It may be the case that some of the anxiety about hidden pockets of putrescence in the Victorian home stemmed from a desire to prevent the middle classes from encroaching upon decorative styles previously reserved for the upper classes. Improvements in mechanical reproduction made rich tapestries and flocked wallpapers much more accessible to homeowners on a budget; however, as Rhoda and Agnes Garret advised in their 1877 *Suggestions for Home Decoration,* even if a middle-class family could afford to purchase such furnishings and fittings, they would not be able to afford their sanitary upkeep. "Now nothing compensates in a house for dirtiness," the sanitary sisters warned, "and for moderate incomes it is therefore better to have the walls and ceilings treated in such a manner that they may take their turn to be cleaned and done up without any very serious outlay."[24] Indeed, it is clear that many Victorian home decoration guides were meant to harness the potentially wayward tastes of untrained middle-class domestic designers, especially in the choice of wallpapers, and that the pedagogical mechanism used to produce aesthetic taste was often sanitation reform. Even if a threat to the body could not actually be discovered in deleterious dyes or rotting glue, a threat to the mind was always immanent if an individual was forced to perpetually contemplate the horrors of bad design. "When we choose wallpapers," advised William White, FSA, "those that are the most beautiful in form and colour are to be preferred. We should, however, satisfy ourselves that the patterns on the papers with which our rooms are hung have not a look of motion. Nothing is more distressing than to be in a room where the pattern of the paper seems always to be moving like a drop of dirty water under the microscope."[25]

Interestingly, germ theory surfaces here in the rhetorical image of water under a microscope, but only long enough to provide a suitably ugly and disturbing simile for unhygienic wallpaper patterns. It is also an image that allows White to introduce that other aspect of health perpetually threatened by dirty art: psychological health. Edis too discouraged the choice of strongly repetitive or monotonous patterns in wallpaper on the grounds that "such patterns would be a source of infinite torture and annoyance in times of sickness and sleeplessness, would materially add to our discomfort and nervous irritability, and after a time would have a nightmare effect upon the brain."[26] Badly designed wallpaper causes sensory crisis and literally makes you sick, so the Garret sisters add that a good choice of pattern is especially important for the bedroom of an invalid: "select a paper that has an all-overish pattern that cannot be tortured into geometrical figures by the occupant of the chamber, who, especially in hours of sickness, is well-nigh driven to distraction by counting over and over again the dots and lines with endless repetition before his aching eyes" (Garrett and Garrett 69). With this kind of advice, mental hygiene became a new frontier of cleanliness for aesthetic principles to discipline through design.

II. Architectural Anachronism: The Haunted House

In the context of such testimony, it is impossible to resist revisiting Charlotte Perkins Gilman's 1892 "The Yellow Wallpaper" as neither ghost story nor feminist protest, but as a psychological revolt against bad design. Our already depressed American protagonist is initially struck by the "repellent, almost revolting" color of the wallpaper in the upstairs room she is placed for postpartum "rest" by her doctor-husband: she describes "a smouldering, unclean yellow, strangely faded by the slow-turning sunlight. It is a dull yet lurid orange in some places, a sickly sulphur tint in others."[27] Our heroine also tells us she knows something "of the principle of design," and that not only is the

furniture in her room "inharmonious," but the wallpaper is "committing every
artistic sin" by not adhering to "the laws of radiation, or alternation, or repetition, or symmetry, or anything else that I ever heard of" (Gilman 9). Gradually the wallpaper begins to torment her already strained nerves. She sees
morbid images (broken necks, bulbous, unblinking eyes) in the paper, and
eventually fancies the ugly trellis design to be a prison or cage, from which a
creeping woman is trying to escape. While this "debased Romanesque" wallpaper has been read as a metaphor for patriarchy and as an icon of psychological entrapment, it is also the case that within the nineteenth-century concept
of the healthy home, this wallpaper is a sanitary menace. Although the protagonist is ostensibly assigned this room at the top of the house because it is
the most healthy, the sulphurous paper not only stains the clothing of all who
go near it, it gives off the "subtlest, most enduring odor" in damp weather, an
odor the heroine can only identify as "like the color of the paper! A yellow
smell" (Gilman 15). Even though she cannot identify the exact smell given
off by the rotting wallpaper, a sanitary investigator of the miasmatic school
would be more interested in the fact of the smell itself: "When you perceive a
bad smell," explains Florence Stacpoole in her 1905 tract *A Healthy Home and
How to Keep It*, "something unclean, and perhaps poisonous actually touches
you."[28]

Importantly, the house featured in "The Yellow Wallpaper" is a colonial
mansion, an old, hereditary estate "empty for years" that the middle-class
Doctor has been able to lease for his wife's recovery because it is mysteriously cheap. The protagonist wonders briefly if it is haunted at the beginning
of her stay, and perhaps the answer to her question from the perspective of
sanitary design is yes. The presence of unclean spirits in many fictional Victorian homes may, in fact, have more to do with anxieties about domestic contamination that were unevenly circulating at the time, than with any cultural
interest in the supernatural or the occult for its own sake. Sharon Marcus has
already noted that the Victorian ideology of the home as an "impenetrable,
self-contained structure" was galvanized by public health warnings about
overcrowding, and has argued that ghost stories proliferated in the late nineteenth century because anxieties about "mixed" lodging houses and semi-
detached villas suggested that even newly built middle-class residences were
already too populated with "souls."[29] Marcus adds, "in many stories, illness
and death follow as consequences of seeing a ghost" (Marcus 125), and while
this is certainly true, I would argue that overcrowding is just one public health
anxiety that might be written into such fatal Victorian ghost stories. As I have
already mentioned, one of the most controversial aspects of germ theory was
its denial of the miasmatic, or spontaneous generation of disease, the intellec-

tual bedrock of environmental sanitation efforts prior to Pasteur's discovery of microbes in the 1860s. Progressive scientist John Tyndall explained in his 1883 book *Essays on the Floating Matter in the Air* that previous generations of sanitarians "believed epidemic diseases arose spontaneously in crowded hospitals and ill-smelling drains. According to them, the contagia of epidemic disease are formed *de novo* in a putrescent atmosphere."[30] Transmissible by air and detectable by smell, disease was believed to be generated *de novo* by organic dirt and decay, and therefore could be banished by the systematic application of principles of hygiene and cleanliness.

As I have discussed, such sanitary optimism was difficult to extinguish. Through the last decades of the nineteenth century, germ theory met with enthusiastic repudiation from anti-contagionist doctors like B. W. Richardson, on the grounds that "no one has ever seen a germ."[31] Disease was still a matter of matter for Richardson, most particularly that matter out of place still accumulating so foully inside overlarge middle-class houses with unused rooms and untrodden passageways.

> In many private houses, houses even of the well-to-do and wealthy, streams of devitalized air are nursed with the utmost care. There is the lumber-room of the house in which all kinds of incongruous things are hidden away and excluded from light and air. There are dark understairs closets in which cast-off clothes, charged with organic debris of the body, are let rest for days and even weeks together. There are bedrooms overstocked with furniture, the floors covered with heavy carpets in which are collected pound upon pounds of organic dust. There are dressing rooms in which are stowed-away old shoes and well-packed drawers of well-worn clothes. (*Diseases of Modern Life* 211)

While Richardson attempted to keep the medical gaze on diseased houses rather than people, his descriptions of unused clothing and furniture are haunted by human traces, invisible particles of absent breath and departed bodies. Festering in spare rooms of wealthy houses, the detritus of material human life found a spectral and dangerous existence, making it especially interesting that Tyndall also used a definitively gothic discourse to describe the superstitious beliefs of elder sanitarians: prior to Pasteur, he explains, "they believed in the existence of a deleterious medium, rendered epidemic by some occult and mysterious influence which was attributed the cause of disease" (Tyndall 18). Given that miasmatic, *de novo* beliefs about illness were widely referred to as "occult" theories of disease, it is strongly possible that the haunted houses flourishing in mid- to late-Victorian literature borrow from an already sensationalized discourse of disease to invest older models of gothic horror with a new sanitary hysteria.

Certainly that hysteria is more than evident in William Bardwell's 1873 book *What a House Should Be, versus Death in the House*. Here we are warned that "the pabulum of disease lies festering in unremoved heaps" inside even the wealthiest, single-family homes, and that the untimely deaths of whole families in a single residence are less mysterious than most people suppose.[32]

> Look again how the members of families in certain streets gradually disappear, until a forlorn survivor is left to transport his pining frame to another quarter, and give room to a fresh family supply, which in turn feeds the domestic demon—an unhealthy home. If you care to examine the component parts of this monster, you will find prominent the fatal soil pipe, the water closet, the sink and rotting boards, and tainted wall papers, the dust-bin, filled with decomposing vegetable and animal matters, or defective and trapped drains; all or any of which send up deadly emanations to poison the air in the house. (Bardwell 5)

A home may indeed be cursed, Bardwell warns, and as an architect and sanitary engineer, he is quick to locate the domestic demon in the "fatal" bowels of the Victorian house. Nooks and crannies, bins and toilets, wet apertures and decaying decorations, are deadly from a sanitary rather than supernatural perspective, causing a house itself to spring to life as a vengeful monster. Less impervious to environmental influences than middle-class inhabitants assumed, houses themselves respired like fiendish organisms; indeed, according to fellow architect William White, "almost every dwelling house" in London was constantly giving off and taking in the city's poisonous vapors (White, "Undrained London: A Fog Factory" 367).

Given this gothic architectural discourse, it seems likely that the unclean spirits of many unlucky, abandoned and rotting nineteenth-century haunted houses in fiction are essentially the foul emanations of the dirty decorating styles associated with upper-class waste and bourgeois excess: indeed, as one Captain Arrows declares to the new owners of Myst Court in A. L. O. E.'s 1876 novel *Haunted Rooms*, "It appears to be a law of nature that whatever is useless becomes actually noxious. . . . That closed chamber, into which the sun never shines, will tend to make the dwelling less healthy, as well as less cheerful."[33] But after we learn that the haunted room at Myst Court has been sealed by codicil ever since old Uncle Myers died of hydrophobia inside of it, we suspect that organic decomposition is also, somehow, to blame. Sealed-up rooms and stagnant air become prime sites of *de novo* infection, disease, hysteria, and madness in nineteenth-century fiction, but in working out the material source of these troubles, the supernatural surfaces repeatedly as a narratological vehicle and red herring. In J. E. Murdock's 1887 *The Shadow Hunter: The Tragic Story of a Haunted Home,* Miss Tryphena Sabine inherits the ancient family mansion of her former (rejected) suitor, an old eccentric named Mr. Jerrald. From the moment she crosses the threshold, she is seized with "unaccountable" shuddering; the house is in a state of general dilapidation, it smells moldy, and most of the rooms are sealed up. Soon after their arrival, Tryphena and her sister Flo begin hearing dripping noises, and seeing gauzy vapors and spots of blood. Both women get nervous, irritable, and eventually ill, and a doctor is called in for consultation. Dr. Trapmore is not superstitious, and is less interested in the bloody floating head Tryphena claims she sees than in an apparently bricked-up part of the wall, which he advises her to tear down. His advice goes unheeded, Flo and Tryphena become sicker and finally die, and Dr. Trapmore inherits the haunted estate. The first thing he does is tear down that suspicious false wall, and he discovers a sealed-off room at the center of the house from which emanates an odor "peculiarly sickening and foetid."[34] The aptly named Trapmore discovers that the "place was a charnel house" with two dead bodies festering in the very spot Mr. Jerrald had bludgeoned and decapitated them. At the end of the tale, Trapmore decides that the only way to purify the house is to raze it, and the Doctor accomplishes sanitation and exorcism simultaneously.

Wilkie Collins's 1878 story "The Haunted Hotel" also features foul smells that emanate from an ancient family mansion, but this haunted house is a damp, moldy Venetian palace with a bloody history of Inquisition-era crimes.[35] The palace is destined to be turned into a lavish hotel by a group of English speculators when Lord Mountbarry, his new wife, the former Countess Narona, and her brother, the Baron Rivar, rent it for several months. Lord Mountbarry dies suddenly while in residence, the Baron and the Countess emigrate to America, and though a series of plot twists the remaining members of the Mountbarry extended family are the first guests in the new hotel. The only two rooms in the hotel that have escaped renovation are the bedchamber where Lord Mountbarry died, and the Baron's bedroom directly above. These rooms are the most luxurious in the hotel, with original fittings and sumptuous antique furnishings, but each Mountbarry family member who attempts to sleep in the dead man's room fails to rest comfortably. First Henry Westwick loses both sleep and appetite to the room, and decides that something in the room must be "unhealthy." Mrs. Norbury, Henry's sister, falls asleep but has frightful dreams that feature her dead brother: "she saw him starving in a loathsome prison; she saw him pursued by assassins, and dying under their knives; she saw him drowning in immeasurable depths of dark water; she saw him in a bed on fire, burning to death in the flames; she saw him tempted by a shadowy creature to drink, and dying of a poisonous draught" (Collins, "The Haunted Hotel" 172). Mrs. Norbury moves upstairs to the former bedroom of Baron Rivar, but is pursued by the same nightmares. The hotel Manager changes the number on the dead man's room, but Francis Westwick, another Mountbarry brother, is driven from it by an offensive odor. Finally, Agnes, the dead Lord's jilted lover, wakes in the night to a vision of a bloody head floating in the air above her bed, and a sickening smell that penetrates the entire room. Henry Westwick opens an investigation, and discovers that Baron Rivar's room contains an ornate mantelpiece with a hidden cavity; the doors of the cavity spring open when the heads of two sculptured Caryatides are pressed. Inside the cavity is the source of the foul odors: a partially decomposed human head, eventually identified by false teeth as Lord Mountbarry's. Like the mansion in *The Shadow Hunter,* the Palace Hotel is a charnel house; Henry discovers that the rest of Lord Mountbarry's body was mutilated and hastened to decomposition by chemicals in the Baron's vaults, and that the unclean spirits that haunt the palace are the putrid gases of organic decay.

Importantly, the Palace Hotel is haunted by both evil deeds and bad taste: while the hiding-place in the Room of the Caryatides dates from the bloody days of the Inquisition in Venice, the mantelpiece itself is a degenerate design of the eighteenth century "and reveals the corrupt taste of the period in every part of it" (Collins, "The Haunted Hotel" 208). In late-nineteenth-century literature, bad designs of previous centuries habitually appear as hiding-places for a variety of contaminants. Corruption, decay, and disease all fester in the dust trap anachronism, as Jane Ellen Panton, the well-known purveyor of healthy domestic decoration agreed. In her 1893 *Hints for Young Householders,* Panton uses the language of supernatural uncleanliness to describe her memorable visit to the former home of Thomas Carlyle and his wife Jane.

> I penetrated with awe into the dirty, dark chamber of horrors which had been sacred to the master, and I climbed up into the so-called drawing-room, where even the glass in the windows was obscured to hide the view, such as it was: where the drab paper and paint gave me the horrors as I thought of dark November and December afternoons and evenings and thought how much better they might have been had pink or blue replaced the drab; or a cheerful yellow brought sunshine into the nest of murky cobwebs; and when I saw the bedrooms, where the ghastly ghosts of all their sleepless nights seemed still to linger; and as I contemplated them,

and finally descended into their damp, stone-floored awful kitchen; I quite understood why there were so many domestic catastrophes, and so much ill-health, low-spirits, ill-temper, and dyspepsia, for no one could have possibly been well or happy in a house which was arranged and decorated . . . as that one was.[36]

Here, Panton clearly links bad health with the familiar accoutrements of gothic anxiety; dirt and darkness, murky cobwebs, and ghastly ghosts all reveal the Carlyles' mid-Victorian townhouse to be a medieval "chamber of horrors," replete with the dusty decorative anachronisms that are the obvious cause of so much bad temper and disease.

The other important point Panton makes in *Hints for Young Householders* is that houses absorb the personality, the "individuality," even the psychology of the people who have lived there. The sanitary inspector can only test the drains and the dustbins; it is not his task to discover the pedigree of the house, or to determine if it has a healthy record. Panton insists that it is crucial for young home seekers to find out "whether nice, really nice, people have lived there before; for only by such findings can one insure peaceful and healthful possession of it . . . what a bad name may be given to any place where horrid people have been living, and where they have stamped forever their individuality upon it" (Panton 8). This kind of warning is especially instructive within novels that are less explicitly sensational or supernatural, but still stimulate gothic anxiety about the inheritance of old houses that are somehow haunted by past occupants and owners. For example, in Thomas Hardy's 1881 novel *A Laodicean,* Paula Power inherits the ancient De Stancy castle from her father, an enormously influential and wealthy railway engineer, who purchased it from an aristocratic family in economic and moral decline. For our romantic hero, architect George Somerset, Paula represents an exciting new spirit of eclectic modernism coupled with a return to the physical development of the Greeks: she outfits her ancient castle with both a telegraph for rapid communication and a gymnasium for healthful exercise. But Mr. Woodwell, the Baptist minister who keeps trying to baptize Paula according to the deathbed wishes of her father, suspects prolonged residence in the medieval walls of the De Stancys will corrupt the "indomitable energy" of the Power family.[37] Woodwell warns Somerset that "The spirit of old papistical times still lingers in the nooks of those silent walls, like a bad odour in a still atmosphere, dulling the iconoclastic emotions of the true Puritan" (Hardy 64). For Woodwell, the entire castle is a dust trap: the ancient Catholic heritage haunts the De Stancy mansion like an unsanitary smell, collecting in the Gothic chinks and gaps and producing spiritual dullness in the reformed Christian inhabitant.

Indeed, thoroughly modern Paula soon begins to believe that "feudalism is the only true romance of life" (Hardy 92). Moreover, when the dispossessed De Stancy heir begins to court her in an attempt to regain lost family land and monies, Paula is struck by his romantic resemblance to a portrait in her picture gallery, and begins to desire a legitimate place for herself upon the venerable yellow walls.

> As they moved hither and thither, the various expressions of DeStancy's face made themselves picturesquely visible in the unsteady shine of the blaze. In a short time he had drawn near to the painting of the ancestor whom he so greatly resembled. When her quick eyes noted the speck on the face, indicative of inherited traits strongly pronounced, a new and romantic feeling that the DeStancys had stretched out a tentacle from their genealogical tree to seize her by the hand and draw her in to their mass took possession of Paula. (Hardy 189)

The possession of Paula by the unclean feudal spirit of the De Stancy legacy draws her away from her suitor-architect, Somerset, who originally had been hired to restore the castle to its original state; eventually, however, Paula realizes that she has been deceived by false romanticism into a regard for William De Stancy, and returns to her slighted lover. But the strong personality of De Stancy castle still presents a significant threat to the possibilities of modernism, and must be burnt to the ground in the final pages of the novel. Somerset comforts Paula with promises of a new, "eclectic" home on the same ground, and the possibility that her infected mind will yet reflect the "modern spirit" in English life: "You, Paula, will be yourself again, and recover, if you have not already, from the warp given to your mind (according to Woodwell) by the medievalism of that place" (Hardy 431).

III. Architectural Exorcism: The Healthy House

The dust of ages was a deadly feature of ancient mansions, haunting, possessing, and infecting the healthy spirit of modern life. Yet the picturesque dust traps so inevitable in old castles had unfortunately been reproduced in the design of relatively new, suburban middle-class houses; indeed, one sanitary complaint that might be legitimately lodged against John Ruskin was that the critic's impassioned reverence for Gothic architecture had inspired a mid-century revival of dirty medieval eccentricities in new construction. For Ruskin, Gothic architecture was a powerful ecclesiastical testament to medieval faith and joy in individual labor. For mid-Victorian enthusiasts, on the other hand, the Gothic style was perfectly appropriate for shops, warehouses, individual residences, and even pubs. William Bardwell noted that many "model" cottages built for tenants on large estates reflected the designers' "admirations of medieval architecture," and "are irregular in plan and hence irregular in outline, from an idea of being picturesque; and hence all the chimneys are outside, involving loss of heat, and the roof all hips and valleys, and dormer windows requiring constant repair, and exhibiting an utter ignorance of the very first principles of a Healthy House" (Bardwell 8). But of particular concern were the pseudo-Gothic suburban villas that were springing up like our contemporary McMansions on the whims of speculative builders for middle-class families; then, as now, substandard construction materials and shoddy workmanship yielded Romantic decay and picturesque dilapidation much faster than anyone desired. Describing the construction of these suburbs, Robert Edis reported that the plaster was often mixed with trash, road rubble, and a wide variety of accidental impurities, and that the other fittings were similarly contaminated:

> The woodwork is of the trashiest and most flimsy character, unseasoned and utterly unfit for its purpose, so that in a year or two all the joints are shrunk, leaving places for the lodgment of dirt and dust; the paint, and the oil with which it is mixed, of the cheapest and nastiest kind; the size used in the distempering of the walls and ceilings decomposed and stinking; the plumbing work of the cheapest possible character. . . . It is not to be wondered that in such houses there is constant sickness, and a general sense of depression fatal to any sound state of bodily or mental health. ("Internal Decoration" 310)

For Edis, such houses were bound to be filthy regardless of housekeeping efforts. At the 1881 Brighton Health Congress, he asked, "How is it possible to be cleanly or tidy in a house in which the walls are breaking out into patches of damp, the woodwork of the floors or doors opening into yawning cracks, resting places for dirt and dust, which no amount of cleaning should get rid of? How can floors be kept clean where the joints and crevices are filled with decomposing filth?" ("On Sanitation in Decoration" 319).

Under such heightened anxiety about dust traps in both ancient and modern Gothic homes, architects Norman Shaw and E. W. Godwin took on the design and creation of Bedford Park in 1875, an entire sanitary suburb constructed in modified Queen Anne style, without basements, carpets or curtains for the hygienically-conscious but aesthetically-minded middle class.

The community was financed by Jonathan T. Carr, who was closely associated with the new Grosvenor Gallery, and motivated by the idea that the domestic environment could provide ordinary, middle-class lives with backgrounds that were both beautiful *and* cleanly. As sanitary expert Dr. Richardson explained, "Hitherto, it has been generally supposed that perfect sanitary arrangements and substantial construction are inseparable from ugliness. But it is especially claimed for Bedford Park that it is the most conspicuous effort yet made to break the dull dreariness of the ordinary suburban villa."[38] A variety of tasteful William Morris wallpaper designs were available to be installed with cleanly pastes; matting was used instead of carpet, and decorative tile was the preferred substance for most flooring. When stained glass was used, it was used sparingly, and never when it could impede the emission of light. One of the first advertisements for the suburb pronounced it "The Healthiest Place in the World," and proudly described the "gravelly soil" and "the most approved Sanitary arrangements" alongside the encouraging statistic that its "Annual death rate is under 6 per Thousand" (Fletcher 178). Despite its prosaic pedigree, painter Edward Abbey reported that walking into this Chiswick area suburb was just "like walking into a water-colour" (Fletcher 171), and writer Moncure Conway insisted in his 1882 *Travels in South Kensington,* that "the spirit of artistic inspiration had been preserved in this mecca of sanitation, "which had come into existence so swiftly, yet so quietly that the building of it has not scared the nightingale I heard yesterday, nor the sky-larks singing while I write."[39]

Like Abbey and Conway, other proponents of sanitary architecture insisted that a smoother, shinier, seamless design for living was absolutely compatible with artistic inspiration and production; the narrator of *Lares and Penates,* for example, finds the ideal design for a fireplace in the Holland Park home of Pre-Raphaelite painter Lord Leighton: "a single slab of massive milk-white marble, one perfectly plain polished smoothness, with nothing to catch the dust, and no detail to worry eyes needing rest from study of form and colour" (Caddy 57). By continuing to link excessive decorative detail to ocular and psychological distress, supporters of the seamless, fully integrated aesthetic of home design not only banished the dust trap, they banished the fear of "permeability," which Tamar Katz has identified as the defining dilemma of both the Victorian home and the Victorian subject.[40] Moreover, the filthy Romantic concept of "tone" could be permanently divorced from the more desirable domestic and psychological effect of "repose."

But as *The Haunted Hotel, The Shadow Hunter, A Laodicean,* and other works imply, environmental cleanliness also required a veritable exorcism of the psychological depth and architectural space inspired by the concept of sublimity. While praising the cleanliness of Alford House in South Kensington, Caddy's narrator notes its thoughtful architectural design: "there is no loss of space, no bewilderment, as in our pseudo-Jacobean houses, no tracasserie, no labyrinth of shady passages" (Caddy 49). Indeed, E. W. Godwin had associated the revival of past historical periods in architecture with both filth and pre-enlightenment confusion, and had insisted that such architecture made "our modern houses already look weird, as if with forebodings of ghosts and haunted chambers."[41] As Juliet Kinchen argues, "Godwin's modern house was the enemy of secrets and possessions" because its transparency and easy circulation of air and people made gothic anxiety an architectural impossibility.[42] Even Harriet Martineau lobbied for the elimination of decorative dust traps from the modern Victorian home on the grounds that hiding spaces concealed both ancient dust and gothic terror: "we in our tight houses, whose walls have no chinks and no cracks, may better hang our apartments with clean and light and wholesome paper, which harbors no vermin, screens no thieves, and scares no fever patient with night visions of perplexity and horror."[43] In the minds of such Victorian sanitarians, the connection between gothic architecture and psychological disease was clear, and so was its remedy: in order to evict the madwoman from the attic, you had to eliminate the attic. Banishing domestic nooks and crannies gave the pestilence of psychological and sensory distress nowhere to fester.

If we can acknowledge the complicated, collaborative work of sanitation reform and aesthetic development over the long nineteenth century, we can begin to understand, with art historians like Elizabeth Prettejohn, how the "rise" of Modernism is a more complex cultural event than early-twentieth-century art critics like Roger Fry and Clive Bell wanted to suggest. Prettejohn explains that Fry, Bell and other early champions of Modernism, deliberately put forth a rupture narrative of aesthetic development that may still obscure "the historical inheritance of Victorian aestheticism in the wish to effect a dramatic shift in taste."[44] I agree with Prettejohn's point that the history of Modernism is much less sudden and static than many critics, well into the late twentieth century, have implied, but I would add that the shift in taste heralded as a revolutionary remaking of visual and intellectual pleasure was also driven by those less exalted sensory imperatives mobilized by mid-Victorian sanitation reform. As we have seen in this chapter, a bad smell in a beautiful home may be the most powerful and effective agent of aesthetic transformation.

When Mr. Newbroom of Caddy's *Lares and Penates* asks the narrator why she doesn't "write whitewashing up as a fine art," he cogently outlines the effects of aesthetic collaboration with sanitation reform: not only is whitewash the most hygienic varnish for walls and ceilings, "lime has a natural affinity with the acids which cause diseases of body and mind. Let a gouty man try a day's whitewashing and see if it will not draw the acids out of his joints" (Caddy 242). The sickly human body is as fraught with pockets of contamination and disease as the unsanitary house, but the performance of cleansing the latter will also heal the diseases and weaknesses of the former, becoming, in the process, a revolutionary understanding of "modern" art. As germ theories of disease gradually gained public acceptance in the last years of the century, sanitary scrutiny shifted from the environment to the individual, but beauty was still the stated goal of sanitary attention. When beauty is defined in G. K. Chesterton's 1908 cult classic *The Man who was Thursday,* for example, it is a snidely physiological concept, and primarily a synonym for bodily health. In this novel, the poet Gabriel Syme makes his home in Saffron Park, a suburban artistic community modeled on Bedford Park that "never in any definable way produced any art."[45]As the product of a sanitarian mother and an artist father, Syme now believes "our digestion . . . going sacredly and silently right, is the foundation for all poetry. . . . Yes," he exclaims feelingly, "the most poetical thing in the world is not being sick" (Chesterton 12). In this sanitized aesthetic philosophy of early Modernist culture, artistic inspiration is founded upon the healthy body rather than the diseased mind, and the best art is measured by its good effect on human health. But while the dark corners of the Rembrandtesque House had been thoroughly exorcised by the new Modern architectural style, John Ruskin might not have been entirely satisfied with the forms of beauty generated by late-Victorian attentiveness to physiology and material health. "These kidneys are delicious," exclaims an Oscar Wilde–like Mr. Amarynth while feasting on organ meat in R. S. Hichens's 1894 *The Green Carnation.* "They are as poetic as one of Turner's later sunsets, or the curved mouth of the La Giaconda. How Walter Pater would love them."[46]

CHAPTER 4

The Surgical Arts

Aesthesia and Anaesthesia in Late-Victorian Medical Fiction

> To regard all things and principles of things as inconstant modes of fashions has more and more become the tendency of modern thought. Let us begin with that which is without—our physical life. Fix upon it in one of its more exquisite intervals, the moment, for instance, of delicious recoil from the flood of water in summer heat. What is the whole physical life in that moment but a combination of natural elements to which science gives their names? But those elements, phosphorus and lime and delicate fibers, are present not in the human body alone: we detect them in places most remote from it. Our physical life is a perpetual motion of them— the passage of the blood, the waste and repairing of the lenses of the eye, the modification of the tissues of the brain under every ray of light and sound—processes which science reduces to simpler and more elementary forces?
>
> —Walter Pater, *The Renaissance* (1873)

*O*ne of the most striking features of Pater's infamous conclusion to *The Renaissance* is that it begins not with the "inner world of thought and feeling," but with what he terms our "physical life."[1] In any exquisite, isolated moment of bodily sensation, he asks, what is our physical life "if not a combination of those elements to which science gives their names?" Starting with the body, and with the minute elements, currents, and combinations isolated by science, Pater shifts easily into the more familiar passages of *The Renaissance,* where objects lose their realist solidity and become "unstable, flickering, inconsistent" impressions that give aesthetic pleasure in moments of fleeting ecstasy and quicken and multiply the consciousness (151). The perpetual mutability of the human body is, after all, a waxing scientific suspicion by the 1870s: the discovery of the microbe and the invention of bacteriology, the rise of reductionist medicine and medical specialism, the development of antisepsis and anaesthesia, the regulation and regularization of experimental science, all shifted, if gradually, the cultural understanding of the human body from wholes to parts, from stasis to movement, and from a concept of disease as an external invader to be kept at bay through cleanliness and hygiene, to a concept of disease that was always endemic to the factionalized body itself. The increasing instability of the body in scientific discourse, in other words, paves the way for Pater's aesthetic Renaissance: if the perpetual decay and renewal of the human body's various organs and tissues is a physiological fact, if social and bodily perfectibility are biologically impossible, if the God-like status of man is a spiritual myth, then the shapelessness and lack of finish that characterized Pater's art of "impressions" was an enlightened mode of realism that could appeal to the evolutionary philosophy of human life by appealing to the effervescent senses of the fractured individual. "A counted number of pulses only is given to us of a variegated, dramatic life," Pater mused. "How may we see in them all that is to be seen in them by the finest senses?" (152)

This is not to isolate Paterian aesthetics from the more general trend in Modernist philosophy that attempted to return physiological meaning to a word and to an experience that in the original Greek *aisthesis* was rooted in human sensation and perception. Eagleton, in fact, identifies Marx, Nietzsche and Freud as the dominant modern thinkers who returned the body to aesthetic theory, rescuing it from that disinterested Kantian intellectual experience that Bourdieu has called "a pleasure purified of pleasure."[2] But Pater's pleasure is especially important to the story I am trying to tell in this book because it was occasioned by, even authorized by, a scientific understanding of the body that directly clashed with the sanitary aesthetic. With the rise of pathological science through the 1870s and 1880s, an understanding of the human body as a potential site of dissection, anatomy, and surgical penetration threatened to overthrow a vitalist concept of the perfectible body defined by harmony, beauty and physical cleanliness. Always potentially sick, partially shadowed, locked in a perpetual cycle of decay and renewal, the human body that was reimagined by scientific discourse in the late nineteenth century underwrote the decadent body of Paterian aestheticism, the perverse pleasure of ridiculous villains like Broughton's Mr. Chaloner, who locates the highest form of beauty, we will remember, in the "passionate pulsations of pain."[3]

Allison Pease, remarking on the frequent images of death in *The Renaissance,* finds it difficult to imagine a genuine artistic rebirth amongst Pater's scattered corpses, graves, and caskets: the "profound negativity" at the heart of

Pater's writing always manages to subvert his argument for a coming Renaissance.[4] But on the other hand, corpses, graves, and caskets were increasingly
linked with the secrets of life, health, and longevity under the new regime of
pathological science. As Foucault argued, the advent of pathological anatomy
in the nineteenth century marks an epistemic shift in the scientific understanding of life: the declining importance of vitalism and "humourism" in
the scientific interpretation of the body meant that "life is to be distinguished
from the inorganic only at a superficial level. . . . It is profoundly bound up
with death, as to that which threatens to destroy its living force."[5] While the
shift to anatomy and dissection in medicine was not as sudden as Foucault
argues—such procedures had long been practiced by both doctors and scientists—nineteenth-century discoveries in chemistry and biology ensured
that experimental surgeries could be, in Pater's time, undertaken on living
tissue, on humans and animals who were not dead, but who behaved as if
they were dead, during longer, more leisurely operations. Indeed, what seems
especially important to me about Pater, in his specifically physiological context, is that he recuperates the sensational, sensual pleasures of the flesh for
aesthetic philosophy at the very moment a new scientific category of physical experience arises as the very opposite of *aisthesis*. Oliver Wendell Holmes
had coined the term "anaesthesia" back in 1846 to underscore the more than
material significance of the first successful dental surgery performed on a
patient under the influence of ether by American doctor William Morton. In
a letter to Morton, Holmes, writing as Professor of Anatomy and Physiology
at Dartmouth College, heralded ether as a truly great scientific discovery, but
also made it clear that the classification and understanding of surgical sleep
was fundamentally intellectual, even philosophical. Holmes explained,

> The state should, I think, be called anæsthesia. This signifies insensibility,
> more particularly (as used by Linnaus and Cullen) to objects of touch. The
> adjective will be anæsthetic. Thus we might say, the "state of anæsthesia,"
> or the "anæsthetic state." The means employed would be properly called the
> "anti-anæsthetic agent." Perhaps it might be allowable to say "anæsthetic
> agent"; but this admits of question.[6]

While the cultural context and linguistic significance of the word "anaesthesia" has been largely forgotten through the twentieth and twenty-first centuries, it is worth recollecting here that Holmes's word is forged in deliberate
opposition to aesthetics: if "aesthesia" signifies a state of heightened sense perception, "anaesthesia" marks the repression of those senses, a state of the body
characterized by indifference to physical pain or pleasure.

Of course, thirty years separated Holmes's anaesthetic from Pater's aesthetic, but as many historians of science have pointed out, the use of anaesthesia in Great Britain didn't begin to be regularized or even regulated until the 1870s. In fact, Stewart Richards has argued that before 1870 the school of experimental physiology in Great Britain was fairly small, and only began to expand in the last decades of the nineteenth century.[7] After the discovery of germs in the late 1860s and the isolation of anthrax in 1876, the potential results of medical experimentation on living tissue began to outweigh any lingering moral or ethical objections on the part of the scientific establishment. Anaesthesia made it possible for surgeons to undertake longer and more difficult operations in the absence of any personal fear about the pain or anxiety they were inflicting upon a senseless body on the table; in this sense, anaesthesia at least theoretically relieved the surgeon of the subjective burden of empathy and pity as fundamentally as it relieved the patient of consciousness. "A deliberate effort to desensitize oneself from the pain of another was no longer necessary," Susan Buck-Morss explains. "Whereas surgeons earlier had to train themselves to repress empathetic identification with the suffering patient, now they had only to confront an inert, insensate mass that they could tinker with without emotional involvement."[8] While personal revulsion to laboratory medicine persisted, even amongst some doctors, through the end of the nineteenth century and beyond, anaesthesia also dulled the public sense of outrage about the practice of live vivisection considerably, especially after the successful passage of The Cruelty to Animals Act in 1876. Even many opponents of animal experimentation concluded that if there was no pain there could be no cruelty, and thus no moral objection to a form of experimentation that promised so much for the future health and vitality of the human race.[9]

This chapter isn't meant to be an examination of the rise of anaesthesia in medicine, nor a record of the scientific discoveries that made surgery an unremarkable component of mainstream medicine by the dawn of the twentieth century. But anaesthesia, I will argue, helped to reorganize the moral understanding of pleasure and pain, beauty and ugliness, purity and pollution, sympathy and apathy that had authorized and underwritten so much of the traditional aesthetic philosophy I've discussed in previous chapters. The particular threat that anaesthetics posed to traditional aesthetics was no doubt unintended by Oliver Wendell Holmes. But if the distinctions between pleasure and pain, beauty and ugliness, were decided by physiological "pulse" rather than intellectual taste, and could be altered, reversed, confused or manipulated by medical science, the aesthetic and the anaesthetic were hardly oppositional forces at all. In fact, the "pure," disinterested, moral form of aesthetic pleasure so valued by Shaftesbury, Kant, Burke and other eighteenth-century thinkers, the pleasure that repressed the more suspicious feelings of the body in favor of lofty intellectual experience, as Eagleton suggests, might itself "be more accurately described as an anaesthetic" (196). Accordingly, this chapter will explore the so-called revolution in medicine that occurred in the last decades of the nineteenth century as a more protracted cultural controversy about *aisthesis,* an intellectual dispute about the human body that pitted the proponents of sanitary science, or prevention, against the rising forces of laboratory science, or cure.

This cultural debate is vividly illustrated in the sanitary hostility to the incursion of germ theory into debates about illness and epidemic disease, and in the frustration and impatience conversely expressed by contagionists at the continued public focus on miasmatic conditions and environmental fever-nests. In fiction, it is a controversy that is shepherded into an offshoot of what I have been describing as the sanitary narrative; more properly defined as medical fictions, these late-Victorian texts collectively indulge a cultural fantasy about medical perversion within the context of Paterian aestheticism and its decadent obsession with "exquisite" physical and emotional sensation. This brand of medical fiction is less interested in moral reconciliation than the straightforward sanitary narrative; medical fiction instead exposes and exploits moral confusion about the rise of pathology, revealing the shared territory of aesthetics and human health to be not the utopian, evolutionary platform of sanitary perfectibility, but the dystopian, degenerate nightmare of surgical intervention. Prevention is better than cure, in much of this fiction, because it preserves the moral authority of well-regulated public health, the social, even "socialized" medicine of sanitary authorities from Chadwick to B. W. Richardson. But prevention, as we will continue to see, is also about aesthetics, and about the vital, sensible, harmoniously constructed and functioning human body that underwrites those aesthetics. The amoral forces of fragmentation and dismemberment threatened the sanitary beauty of the body, certainly, but they also threatened to inscribe a set of decadent pleasures and pains at the very heart of *aisthesis.*

I. The Anaesthetics of Aesthetics

As I argued in the second chapter, the sanitary narrative provides an ideological clarity that makes the marriage plot morally legible: art is bad, health is good. A heroine like Gillian Lattimer in Broughton's *Second Thoughts* can embrace an entire sanitary philosophy by choosing to marry a cleanly hospital doctor instead of a filthy painter from the Paterian school of aestheticism. But to examine the marriage plot from the perspective of some late-Victorian medical fiction is to encounter a love triangle similar to Broughton's without the happy positivism that manufactures sanitary desire over a convalescent child in King's Hospital. True, Etheleen Stuart, the likely heroine of Roy Tellet's *A Draught of Lethe: The Romance of an Artist* (1891), must choose between a painter and a doctor, but the interests of both men is identically deformed by the late-century rapture over aesthetic decay. Our first glimpse of fair Etheleen is through the eyes of rising British painter, Fitzalan Lindley, who is traveling through southern Germany when he decides to visit a "dead house" in a cemetery.[10] There, on a slab, is the beautiful corpse of a young girl dressed entirely in white, an English girl, who has already served as an attraction for another traveling Englishman that very morning. Fitz is clearly moved and even excited by the senseless body: "If this was death," he marvels, "it was death shorn of all its revolting details—it seemed rather the transfiguration of life by which all material grossness was purged away and an ideal glory was given to the tabernacle of flesh" (Tellet 10). Etheleen, as she is called, has a rope attached to a bell twisted around her right hand, in keeping with the superstitious fear that the seemingly dead body could awaken suddenly and require a different kind of attention; shockingly, the bell begins to ring as Fitz is departing the cemetery, and he rushes back inside to sit with the lifeless body while the doctor is summoned. When Dr. Falck arrives to check the status of the girl, however, he assures Fitz that she is, indeed, actually dead.

We should be alerted to the fact that there is something wrong with Dr. Falck because he arrives in the dead house "lit up in a Rembrandt-like manner" (22). But even if we miss this Ruskinian revulsion, we are impressed almost immediately by his apparently faulty medical training: just as Fitz and Falck are about to screw the lid down on the girl's coffin, her frantic eyes pop open and the love triangle is disturbingly established. In fact, when Fitz realizes later in the novel that he is actually in love with Etheleen, he will realize also that "it was love at first sight; strangest, perhaps of all, it had been love with one to all appearance dead" (121). Elisabeth Bronfen has argued persuasively that images of dead female bodies in fiction and the visual arts are powerful vehicles of sensual aesthetic experience because they articulate "stillness, wholeness, perfection" while presaging "the dissolution of precisely those attributes of beauty."

This image of a feminine corpse presents a concept of beauty which places the work of death into the service of the aesthetic process, for this form of

beauty is contingent on the translation of an animate body into a deani-
mated one. Beauty fascinates not only because it is unnatural, but because
it is precarious. . . . It is not just the translation of the inanimate that
defines the relationship between beauty and death, but also the fact that
this form of beauty, even as it signifies an immaculate, immobile form,
potentially contains its own destruction, its division into parts.[11]

Bronfen's ideas are interesting here because they call attention to an aesthetic discourse of wholeness and perfection challenged, at a most intimate
moment, by the medical desire to fragment, penetrate, and disrupt the vitality of the human body. But when Bronfen suggests that the beautiful female
corpse "places the work of death into the service of the aesthetic process," she
also isolates and describes a particularly resonant translation of the medical-
ized human body into the decadent aesthetic. The Rembrandtesque Dr. Falck,
it seems, has invented the perfect anaesthetic: it is a drug called Worliform
that renders the body passive and ready for the pain of surgery, while allowing the mind to stay active and alert. Dr. Falck was preparing Etheleen for
his own experimental purposes when Fitz accidentally intervened. Now that
she is fully awake, Falck believes his crime will remain undetected because
Worliform has also somehow rendered Etheleen an amnesiac.

Anaesthesia, in other words, becomes the perfect vehicle for aesthesia
in Tellet's novel, an impression reflected by the testimonies of many surgical patients in the Victorian era that reported extremely pleasurable sensations and even "beautiful dreams" during surgical sleep.[12] Ether, in particular,
powerfully "embellished and disguised an operation," stimulating pleasurable
feelings while repressing negative sensations; through anaesthesia, "the ago-
nies of surgery were reconfigured 'into poetry,' and all without pain."[13] This
aesthesia provided by anaesthesia gains even more importance in *A Draught
of Lethe* when Falck attempts to neutralize his rival by appealing to the decadent sensibilities that made the artist fall in love with Etheleen in the dead
house. When Fitz visits the doctor in an attempt to learn the truth about
Etheleen's amnesia, Falck begins to rhapsodize about Worliform's ability to
intensify feelings and cause profound mental stimulation while paralyzing
the flesh. Worliform is essentially Lethe, Falck explains; the mind is active but
the body is pacified for surgery, the sensations of the Lotus-eaters steal over
the patient causing sublime hallucinations and powerful feelings of pleasure.
Fitz ends up begging the nefarious doctor for a dose: he is so happy in his
love for Etheleen that the chance "to intensify my own feelings" is too tempt-
ing for the artist to resist (196). Of course, once Fitz inhales the drug, Falck
drops his mask and begins to prepare his surgical materials. The painter is

saved only at the last minute by a fellow artist who followed Fitz to the doctor's office, and the marriage of an aesthetically chastened Fitz to a living
Etheleen closes Tellet's remarkable story.

Rather than ether, Dr. Falck's Worliform actually resembles curare,
another anaesthetic that was very controversial at mid-century precisely
because it worked to divide the immobile (but still sensitive) body from the
alert mind, and therefore challenged the notion that all seemingly painless
experimental surgery was actually as humane and as moral as its supporters maintained. Decried by vocal opponents of physiological experimentation, or "vivisection," like Mark Twain and Frances Power Cobbe, curare was
described by the surgeons who used it on animals as a drug that paralyzed the
body but had no effect on the sensory nerves. As the eminent French physiologist Claude Bernard infamously revealed in 1864:

> In this motionless body, behind that glazing eye, and with all the appear-
> ance of death, sensitiveness and intelligence persist in their entirety. The
> corpse before us hears and distinguishes all that is done around it. It suffers
> when pinched or irritated; in a word, it still has consciousness and volition,
> but it has lost the instruments which serve to manifest them.[14]

While the above passage was cited frequently in British and American anti-
vivisection materials through the turn of the century, the fact of Curare's
existence was enough to strengthen the widespread cultural suspicion that
experimental surgery could only be carried out by cruel, detached, callous
individuals, doctors who had themselves become numb to the suffering of
their patients. Twain's 1899 letter to the Anti-Vivisection Society of London
cites Bernard's description of Curare in order to disprove the argument that
vivisectors do not "perpetuate cruelty," even in the years since the Cruelty to
Animals Act had forbidden animal surgeries without anaesthesia.[15] Cobbe was
likewise outraged by Bernard's continued use of curare as an anaesthetic long
after his own discovery of the drug's limitations, but more generally incensed
by the callousness to pain and suffering Bernard demonstrates in his also
infamous *Introduction to the Study of Experimental Medicine*. A surgeon or
an experimental scientist, Bernard insists here, is an extraordinary man who
"no longer hears the cry of animals, he no longer sees the blood that flows, he
sees only his idea and perceives only organisms concealing problems which
he intends to solve."[16] Even before anaesthesia gave surgeons the ability to
repress the sensationalized body of the patient during surgery, the truly masterful surgeon, according to Bernard, had already learned to ignore his own

sensory perceptions of bodies in pain. And in repressing both his own body and the body of his patient, the surgeon enjoys a form of detachment and disinterest that, in turn, mimics a perverse form of Kantian *aesthesis*. According to Elie Cyon, another infamous French vivisectionist excoriated by Cobbe, a surgeon who experiences "joyful excitement" and delight when cutting into a living animal is more than a mere scientist, he is an "artist in vivisection":

> The sensation of the physiologist, when from a gruesome wound, full of blood and mangled tissue, he draws forth some delicate nerve-branch and calls back to life a function which was already extinguished—this sensation has much in common with that which inspires a sculptor when he shapes forth fair living forms from a shapeless mass of marble. (45)

The aesthetic pretensions of scientists and vivisectionists enraged Cobbe, who found it especially offensive that Cyon did all of his own sketches for his well-illustrated manual of surgical techniques. Cobbe warns that when physiologists pose as artists, English hospitals, which should be monuments of benevolent philanthropy, charity, and humane medicine, may be better called "Museums of Disease" (Cobbe, *The Modern Rack* 237).

Not everyone at the end of the century was dismayed by the power of the surgical gaze to convert scenes of ugliness and horror into compelling *objets d'art*. "The Science of Beauty," as Avary Holmes-Forbes dubbed it in 1881, assigns beauty to all useful objects, and what might disgust or frighten a common person has different sensual meaning for a scientist:

> Few things can be uglier than the entrails of a fish flung upon the roadside and covered with flies. Should a passing surgeon, however, noticing in it some very extraordinary formation of organism, have brought it away, preserved it in chemicals, sealed it in a jar, and placed it in a museum, the thing would cease to be ugly, and would become an object of interest and value.[17]

The surgical gaze, in other words, has the power to convert even filth into value, and is capable of transforming the most pestilent and insanitary scenes of disease and disaster—"soot, morasses, cesspools"—into something much less revolting, and even, on some levels, agreeable. Furthermore, vision was not the only form of sense perception that could be scientifically recalibrated to recognize value in what was formerly waste. Even the most highly respected natural arbiter of the fair and the foul, our sense of smell, could be anaesthetized against the discomfort of any odor deemed scientifically productive or progressive: "A foul odor is very disgusting, and makes us decidedly hostile to whatever it comes from," Holmes-Forbes explains patiently, but "let the same odour, however, be generated by chemicals in a laboratory, for the purposes of some important experiments, and our disgust is almost annihilated, and the odour becomes much more tolerable" (162).

The hospital, the laboratory and the operating theater were, for late Victorians, crucial sensory switch points; places where the difference between pain and pleasure could be neutralized or reversed, where the moral and social definition of ugliness became transitory, associative, contextual, impressionistic. Indeed, the suspicion that the experimental hospital was a place of aesthetic perversion was well circulated in a variety of late-nineteenth-century anti-vivisection material, including many of those medical fictions I mentioned at the outset of this chapter. Grant Allen, prolific Victorian novelist and science writer, published *Hilda Wade* in 1900, a novel that features a cruel physiologist, Professor Sebastien, at St. Nathaniel's Hospital in London, and his professional nemesis, the intuitive Nurse Wade. Sebastien is perfecting a new anaesthetic called lethodyne that could eventually replace chloroform, and testing it on rabbits and raccoons, sheep and hawks, cats and weasels.[18] When the rabbits, sheep and cats all die, Hilda Wade suggests that lethodyne is poisonous to all "phlegmatic" patients. Only "imaginative, vivid temperaments" will be able to withstand the new anaesthesia, and under this working hypothesis Hilda volunteers to be the first human patient (Allen, *Hilda Wade* 12). She has a tooth successfully extracted under lethodyne, but when Cumberledge, Sebastien's assistant, praises the surgeon's coolness during the procedure, Hilda objects that it isn't coolness, but cruelty; scientists simply want to know the whole truth about the human body, without regard to humanity or philanthropy (14).

> He is a man of high ideals, but without principle. In that respect, he reminds one of the great spirits of the Italian Renaissance—Benvenuto Cellini and so forth—men who could pour for hours with conscientious artistic care over the detail of a hem in a sculptured robe, yet could steal out in the midst of their disinterested toil, to plunge a knife in the back of a rival. (131)

The "disinterested toil" of the artist is certainly on display when Sebastien greenlights further human testing for lethodyne. For example, when a pretty tobacco trimmer is brought in for the removal of a tumor, Sebastien is thrilled: "It is a beautiful case! Beautiful, beautiful! I never saw one so deadly or malignant before. We are indeed in luck's way" (16). The surgical team predicts the patient will die, but proceeds with the operation anyway. Indeed, the outcome of any surgery has nothing to do with the success or failure of any procedure measured in effects: in fact, one surgeon explains his own disinterested toil by asking "How could I preserve my precision and accuracy of hand if I were always bothered by sentimental considerations of the patient's safety?" (16).

Aisthesis, in its original meaning, describes an intensification of our sensory experience. But as Neill Leach argues in *The Anaesthetics of Architecture,* "this flooding of the senses in one domain blots out the reception of impulses in another. The raising of one's consciousness of sensory matters—smell, taste, touch, sound, and appearance—allows a corresponding indifference to descend like a blanket over all else. The process generates its own womb-like sensory cocoon around the individual, a semi-permeable membrane that ensures a state of constant gratification by filtering out all that is undesirable."[19] Heightened aesthetic sensitivity, in other words, is always a form of insensitivity, a suspicion that was wide awake at mid-century when Ruskin, when Dickens, when Eliot criticized the low picturesque as a brutal repression of "harsh social relations." The anaesthetic, in Allen's novel, thus underscores the contradictory force of aesthetic pleasure untethered from morality, utility, or sympathy. Indeed, anaesthesia, in much late-Victorian medical fiction, signals the pure gaze of artistic objectification and empathetic detachment, enabling disease, decay, and, indeed, organ meat, to provide Paterian pleasure because they remind us of our tenuous and unstable physical life.

By the time *Hilda Wade* was published, Grant Allen had been asserting the physiological origin of all aesthetic pleasure for decades, most notably in his 1877 text *Physiological Aesthetics.* Here, just a few years after the publication of Pater's *The Renaissance,* Allen extends the argument for the centrality of the physical life to the appreciation of beauty: rather than celebrating the aesthetic feelings as "something noble or elevated," we must recognize that the senses are a matter of "organ function," and taste a matter of "discrimination in the nerves" (Allen, *Physiological Aesthetics* 39, 48). Allen is no particular lover of fine art, he admits, but that makes him better able to evaluate every aspect of what he calls the more commonplace "aesthetic emotions," and not just the most "fastidious" or intellectual.[20] Our ability to recognize and respond to beauty, he argues, is physical, and rooted in our nervous organization. All pleasures and pains are the result of organic processes, natural or unnatural. "It is the business of Art," he thus reasons, "to combine as many as possible of their pleasurable sensations, and to exclude, so far as lies in its power, all their painful ones; thus producing that synthetic result which we know as the aesthetic thrill" (Allen, *Physiological Aesthetics* 36). For Allen, art must necessarily include and exclude, must indulge and repress, must stimulate the pleasurable material feelings while anaesthetizing the body against weariness, depression, sleeplessness, debility, and, of course, outright physical pain. The body that returns to aesthetic philosophy, at least in this particularly Paterian strand of physiological pleasure, is a fragmented, factionalized organism, a mechanism that must be atomized to be synthesized, and anatomized to be healed.

II. Prevention Is Better Than Cure

In the most obvious, most material of ways, the body, during and after the slow dissemination of germ theory, was increasingly permeable. Microbiology and cellular pathology made the vital human body a set of organs to be separated and tissues to be flayed. But it is especially important here to put this discourse of science-as-fragmentation back into conversation with the discourse of sanitation-as-wholeness, and to locate these oppositional concepts themselves within nineteenth-century aesthetic controversies.[21] First, I'd like to return for a moment to B. W. Richardson's utopian paradise, Salutland, where people are happy, powerful and beautiful because everybody knows basic sanitary laws and understands cleanliness to be the first principle of good health. Among the most interesting features of this future community is that it employs no members of any of the "destroying professions"; in other words, Salutland contains no lawyers, no soldiers, and most importantly, no doctors.[22] Any healer who was concerned only with the symptoms of disease, with the administration of drugs and surgeries, with cure rather than prevention, would be cast out of the "legitimate followers of Aesculapius," and shunned by the community (Richardson, "Salutland" 32).

Salutland's workforce is important to my argument because it demonstrates a split between preventive medicine and curative medicine that divided the medical profession, and helped to prolong the rise and acceptance of germ theories through the end of the nineteenth century. Indeed, Lister proved the existence of microbes in 1865, Koch isolated anthrax bacillus in 1876, and Pasteur discovered the anthrax vaccine in 1881. But through the 1880s and 90s, sanitarians still circulated a mission statement that prevention is better than cure, and insisted that the fundamental laws of diet, exercise and hygiene represented a higher, more evolved form of medical care than surgical and pharmacological interventions. Dr. F. de Chaumont made this line of argument abundantly clear in his speech to the Sanitary Institute in 1880, when he explained that "the highest medicine is that which obviates the use of drugs—the highest surgery that which saves the limb, not that which lops it off. The Greek for Physician . . . signifies 'to avert,' to 'ward off.' It is in this sense that we employ the term medicine, and public or preventive medicine is thus the science that wards off diseases from the community."[23] In sanitary logic, surgery and other curative programs are clearly lower on the evolutionary scale, their continued practice a sign of atavism and cultural degeneration brought on, paradoxically, by the onslaught of industrial civilization. Ten years later, at the Hastings and St.-Leonard's-on-the-Sea Health Congress where Richardson was the presiding officer, Frederick Bagshawe, M.D., stepped up the evolutionary rhetoric of sanitary philosophy: "When we were primitive like quadrupeds, we didn't know much about fevers or ailments . . . and may have stood in need of a surgeon." With the rapid growth of towns and cities under industrialization, Bagshawe explains, "the necessity first for curative medicine, was soon recognized. Still later, for preventive medicine, which has only been fully acknowledged at this late stage of the world's course, and when misery and suffering have taught their lesson."[24]

Sexologist and founding member of the Fabian Society, Havelock Ellis, was similarly disenchanted by "the picture of the world presented to us by the bacteriologist," describing it in 1892 as "undoubtedly somewhat awful, resembling the conception of the medieval Christian. We are surrounded by legions of invisible foes, always ready to take advantage of a false step, the least crevice in our armor," protected only by the medically prescribed act of "swathing ourselves—either literally or metaphorically—in antiseptic cotton wool."[25] For progressives like Ellis, the "discovery" of the germ made disease, once again, a kind of primitive, supernatural belief in the invisible sources of human illness; diseases could not be avoided or prevented under this interpretation, but might mysteriously be removed by "some art, or conjuration, or divination" invented by the new biological science.[26] New discoveries by the bacteriologists would only succeed in making people more hypochondriacal, he argued, more superstitious, and above all, more fearful. While members of the Fabian Society were not, strictly speaking, sanitarians, the Society was an 1884 political offshoot of The Fellowship of the New Life, a group that had united members including Ellis and Edward Carpenter under the ambitious ameliorist goal of "The cultivation of a perfect character in each and all."[27] The Fabian commitment to causes like vegetarianism, pacifism, and universal health care produced a late-Victorian social philosophy that resembled and re-enforced the sanitary philosophy of physicians like B. W. Richardson: harmony, unity and proportion was the very definition of a healthy society for Fabian socialists, while the knife of the surgeon and the drugs of the pharmacist inflicted only disruption, disease and chaos. "To pursue knowledge in this way is to cover ourselves with darkness," exclaimed Carpenter in an anti-vivisection lecture he delivered in 1904. "It is to blind ourselves to the greatest and most health-giving of all knowledge—the sense of our common life and unity with all creatures."[28]

In fact, Carpenter's address to an 1896 meeting of the Humanitarian League of London, specifically warned against the encroachment of reductionist medicine into the human experience of bodies and environments. Everyday life will be at best uncomfortable under the new bacteriology, he surmises, but at worst, daily life will be passed in "a kind of nightmare . . . in the discovery that the air around us is full of billions of microbes; in a terrified study of these messengers of disease, and in a frantic effort to ward them off by inoculations, vaccinations, vivisections, and so forth, without end."[29] Like so many other Victorian crusaders against experimental medicine, the Fabians tapped into a growing cultural prejudice against modern voodoo science, and against those witch doctors who raised ancient, unholy specters of disease in order to test their occult theories and remedies. This return to medical barbarism was cited by a range of sanitarians and socialists as further evidence of late-Victorian cultural degeneration and physical decline: by passively accepting Darwinian ideas of evolution, mankind had abandoned its godlike status in the animal kingdom and voluntarily retreated to superstitious ignorance and simian darkness. "Primitive men attributed disease to magic, spirits of dead men," lamented anti-vivsectionist Dr. Edward Berdoe. And, at the end of the nineteenth century, this "disease demon reappeared in the form of a germ."[30]

Under this assessment of scientific progress, civilization itself was a wasting disease that would eventually enervate the individual and social body. In some of the most dire, devolutionary predictions, human beings would cease to use their muscles and limbs, gradually becoming, according to Carpenter, bald, toothless and even toeless.[31] While this particular claim seems exaggerated, even hysterical, and invites the kind of fear and paranoia to which sanitarians ostensibly objected, it underscores what David Wootton has identified as a long gap, or "delay" between the much-heralded discovery of the germ and the development of most successful medical therapies or cures. He writes, "any history of medicine that focuses on what works immediately brings to the fore these uncomfortable questions about delay, resistance, hostility, and (if we use the word metaphorically) malpractice."[32] In *Civilisation: Its Cause and Cure*, Carpenter asks questions from the midst of that long delay about the swelling ranks of physiologists, bacteriologists, pathologists, and vivisectionists at a moment when disease seemed not in abeyance, but on the increase.

Medical science makes a fetish of disease, and dances round it. It is (as a rule) only seen where disease is; it writes enormous tomes on disease; it induces disease in animals (and even men) for the purpose of studying it; it knows to a marvelous extent, the symptoms of disease, its causes, its goings in and its comings out; its eyes are perpetually fixed on disease (for it) becomes the main fact of the world, and the main object of its worship.[33]

Many historians of science, including Wootten and Bashford, have argued that this kind of suspicion and hostility to medical practitioners rose dramatically during the 1860s, when a rash of deaths in lying-in hospitals and private residences from puerperal fever made it clear that physicians themselves, especially physicians who moved, unwashed, amongst living and dead patients, were somehow contaminating and killing women during labor.[34] But it is also the case that the proliferation of medical specialties, of doctors who focused on parts of patients and bits of bodies, rather than on whole, autonomous persons, was significantly at odds with a philosophy of human life defined by the promise of social and spiritual perfectibility.

Fellow Fabian George Bernard Shaw agreed, arguing in an 1917 article, "What is to be Done with the Doctors?" that medical specialism was commercially motivated, and just as lawyers will distort any legal case they encounter to fit their own field, "so specialists in a particular treatment . . . will try that treatment or operation on all sorts of complaints."[35] Shaw's own infamous specialty surgeon, Cutler Walpole, appears in his 1911 play *The Doctor's Dilemma: A Tragedy;* Dr. Walpole has discovered, with the help of chloroform, that "a man's body's full of bits and scraps of old organs he has no mortal use for," and studied anatomy until he found something "fresh to operate on; and at last he got hold of something he calls the nuciform sac, which he's made quite the fashion."[36] According to Walpole, the nuciform sac is like a physiological fever nest, "full of decaying matter—undigested food and waste products," and patients, especially women with the "hygienic instinct," eagerly line up to have the sac surgically removed (Shaw, *The Doctor's Dilemma* 14–15). In the introduction to this certainly noncanoncial play, Shaw insists that the tragedy of being ill at the current bacteriological phase of human history is that you are subjected to a profession that has normalized cruelty in the search for knowledge, and has done so primarily for money: "It is simply unscientific to allege or believe that doctors do not under existing circumstances perform unnecessary operations and prolong lucrative illnesses" (Shaw, *The Doctor's Dilemma* xv). Moreover, what seems to anger Shaw most pointedly here is that now-familiar concept of surgery as a kind of artistic performance: like

Cobbe, he goes to some length to disparage the experience of surgical *aisthesis* described by vivisectionists like Bernard and Cyon.

> An actor, a painter, a composer, an author, may be as selfish as he likes without reproach from the public if only his art is superb. . . . In sacrificing others to himself he is sacrificing them to the public he gratifies; and the public is quite content with that arrangement. The public actually has an interest in an artist's vices.
>
> It has no such interest in the surgeon's vices. The surgeon's art is exercised at its expense, not for its gratification. We do not go to the operating table as we go to the theatre, the picture gallery, to the concert room, to be entertained and delighted; we go to be tormented and maimed lest a worst thing should befall us. (Shaw, *The Doctor's Dilemma* xxxi)

For Shaw, doctoring was an art only when it devoted itself to keeping people in health rather than curing illness, a kind of holistic sanitary medicine that is disappearing, he fears, under the new bacteriology. Under the new reign of surgical science and reductionist medicine, we can "be as dirty as we please." Our expensive sewerage systems can be dismantled, and nature can once again be allowed to wreak havoc on our water and milk supply. Under the germ theory of disease, Shaw snarked in a 1915 article called "Sanitation vs. Inoculation," we will be able to "enjoy the blessed relief of getting rid of sanitary questions altogether."[37] In other words, cure will render prevention altogether unnecessary.

Physician William Osler expressed his own concerns about specialty doctoring from a medical perspective clearly enough in 1905, when he declared that the "battle against polypharmacy" and specialism was far from over, insisting that doctors needed wider contact with medical men in other fields to correct an "inevitable tendency to a narrow and perverted vision," and to restore a subdivided and atomized organism into "a complex whole."[38] But Fabian texts like Shaw's and Carpenter's are especially interesting because they make explicit what most sanitary literature, including fiction, takes for granted: as I pointed out in the second chapter of *The Sanitary Arts*, there is a direct correlation made in these texts between the social body and the individual body, and in both models health manifests itself as a simple unity of parts while disease signifies "the loss of physical unity which constitutes health and so takes the form of warfare or discord between the various parts."[39] I've already discussed this passage from Carpenter's *Civilisation* as evidence that sanitary philosophy was invested in an understanding of social harmony partly inherited from traditional eighteenth-century aesthetics; in this chapter, however, it is also important to see that Carpenter's words underscore the fact that these aesthetic values were thrown into ideological confusion when germ theory threatened a vitalist concept of health. We may remember that Carpenter's description of social discord in *Civilisation* resembles a medical diagnosis: "in our modern life we find the unity gone which constitutes a true society, and in its place warfare in classes and individuals, abnormal development of some to the detriment of others, and consumption of organisms by masses of social parasites" (2). But medical diagnosis itself is the primary antagonist in *Civilisation;* cellular medicine fractures, fragments, and reduces the body, repressing the whole in favor of parts. Sanitation reform may not be Carpenter's primary or most explicit goal in *Civilisation,* but the holistic remedies promoted by sanitarians for individual and communal cleanliness are identical to Carpenter's solution to the problem of civilization.

> Fresh air and reasonable garments, cleanliness in the full sense of the word, pleasant work and varied exercise, wholesome and abundant food, the healthful play of our secretions and excretions—these are the things that will enable us to resist while others succumb. . . . The key word of our modern methods is not *cure* but *prevention,* and while the task is more complex, it is also far easier. It is to a gigantic system of healthy living, and by a perpetual avoidance of the very beginnings of evil, that our medical science is now leading us.[40]

Leaving aside, if only temporarily, the eugenic implications of preventive medicine in the hands of Fabians like Shaw, Ellis, and Carpenter, it is important to see that what prevention promised was a "gigantic system," a bureaucratic control of health and health discourse that was very much defined against the chaos, confusion, and terror represented by the amoral and seemingly unpredictable germ. The sanitary discourse of wholeness, harmony, and discipline that emerged from late-century preventive theories of medicine also continued to represent a social program as an aesthetic feeling, carried out by public policy and governmental control, certainly, but inspired by the emotional and spiritual love of beauty. Shaw, in fact, was deeply committed to the idea that sanitation was itself the dominant aesthetic mode of Socialism: "We owe almost all our immunity from the ancient plagues to the sanitary engineer, to sunshine and fresh air, and soap and water. And the effect of these . . . is purely aesthetic."[41] Shaw, with the help of his friend Sir Almroth Wright, a leading bacteriologist of the day, apparently even invented a new word to describe this philosophy of sanitation as an aesthetic: Aesthodic.[42]

Importantly, moreover, this Fabian sanitary aesthetic was also invested in preserving the intellectual seat of beauty, the command and control of human beings over lesser organic creatures, the fundamental power of the mind over the body to control the circumstances of existence and the harmonious workings of social life. Announcing "The Need of a Rational and Humane Science" in 1896, Carpenter is clearly envisioning a kind of science directed and restrained by the government, but endorsed and underwritten by Ruskinian, and now Shavian, aesthetics:

> If, on the other hand, the science is approached from a quite different side—from that of the love of health, and the desire to make life lovely, beautiful and pure; if the student is filled not only with this, but with a great belief in the essential power of Man, and his command in creation, to control not only all these little microbes whose name is legion, but through his mind all processes of the body; then it is obvious enough that a whole series of different fact will arise before his eyes and become the subject of his study—facts of sanitation, of the laws of cleanly life, diet, clothing, and so forth, methods of control, and the details and practice of the influence of the mental upon the physical part of man—facts quite real with others, equally important, equally numerous perhaps and complex, but forming a totally different range of science.[43]

Carpenter relies here on the higher intellectual capacity of mankind to subordinate and control the animal pleasures and pains of the physical body. Like Ruskin and profoundly unlike Pater, he equates beauty with health, not just the individual enjoyment of a regular heartbeat and a steady pulse, but an aesthetic pleasure in the laws, methods, and facts that regulate public vitality and produce a harmonious society.

III. *Aisthesis,* Surgery, and Medical Fiction

Without dismissing too wantonly the profound philosophical and cultural differences between Shaftesbury and Kant on the one hand, and Ruskin, Shaw and Carpenter on the other, what is nevertheless important about this particular strand of aesthetic history is the fundamentally social capacity of art: the shared assumption that art has the power to move the collective pleasures of humankind in the service of orderly and ethical behavior. Over the course of the long nineteenth century, moreover, it seems that the byproduct of this aesthetic philosophy, as Buck-Morss and Leach have argued, was a compensatory anaesthetic mode. In any aesthetic theory, there is both indulgence and repression: either the "high" intellectual pleasures of the mind must be privileged or the "low" sensations of the physical body must be gratified. While the sanitary commitment to spiritual, environmental and public health anaesthetized the likes and dislikes, pleasures and pains peculiar to individuals, the new physiology had resuscitated the primacy of bodily feeling in aesthetic experience by making the ephemeral and atomized sensations of human existence the definition of life itself. Ideological conflicts like this one between aesthesia and anaesthesia are particularly provocative in fiction, where whole genres are sometimes invented in order to give philosophical struggles narrative form. If the late-Victorian sanitary narrative simply privileges clean art over dirty art and thus forges a new social order based on aesthetic harmony, the medical narrative fundamentally challenges that social order by challenging the faith in mutual pleasures and collective pains that stabilized and sustained the sanitary aesthetic.

Victorian fiction often dramatizes this philosophical conundrum in the personal conflicts of individual characters that are particularly sensitive to personal pleasure and its social meaning. Cherry Underwood, our heroine and painter from *The Pillars of the House,* reappears in Yonge's 1895 *The Long Vacation;* after a marriage to a now-deceased sculptor, Mr. Grinstead, and a life in the hub of the London art community, Cherry has returned to the bosom of her family, most immediately to nurse her brother Clement through a strange bout of blood poisoning contracted during missionary work in a pestilential village. Cherry is glad that the seaside house they've rented for the invalid is a bit shabby, a bit homely, and contains nothing more than is necessary, cleanly, and comforting: "Don't let us get too dependent on pretty things," Cherry decides. "They demoralize as much or more than ugly ones. I really get confused sometimes as to what is mere lust of the eye, and what is regard for whatever things are lovely. I believe the principle is really in each case to try whether the high object or the gratification of the senses should stand first."[44] The narrative result of Cherry's philosophical struggle in *The Long Vacation* is that she must eventually cope with the problem of how to display a vulgar and physically graphic terra cotta statue of a "Dirty Boy" that was donated to a charity bazaar. She eventually hides it behind an elegant Monkey Puzzle tree, leaving it to Philistine Cousin Marilda to find the contextual "high object" that saves art from lowness and corruption: Marilda offers to buy "Dirty Boy" to decorate a public bath and wash house that her wealthy husband has recently endowed (Yonge, *The Long Vacation* 209).

The Long Vacation solves the problem of vulgar art by cheekily redirecting it to the service of sanitation and the public good; like many sanitary fictions I've discussed in previous chapters, dirty art in Yonge's novel can be neutralized and cleansed in the service of social and human perfectibility. But the crisis represented by physiological pleasure in medical fiction is seldom dispatched so easily or with such sanitary panache. Dr. Edward Berdoe, anti-vivisectionist author of *The Rise and Growth of the Healing Art* also contributed a novel to the genre of medical fiction in 1887 with the pseudonymous publication of *St. Bernard's: The Romance of a Medical Student* by Aescalapius Scalpel. Here, in dark confirmation of all George Bernard Shaw's suspicions, a group of doctors at a large and well-respected London hospital deliberately prolong diseases and perform unnecessary surgeries for the sake of physiological *aisthesis,* indulging decadent sensory feelings through the work of dissection, vivisection, and variously ineffective therapies. Harrowby Elsworth, our hero and junior physician, is given an initial overview of St. Bernard's by the house surgeon, Dr. Wilson, that resembles a guided tour at a museum. Making it clear that the doctors always conspire to operate on dying poor patients simply for the sake of experiment, Wilson first shows Elsworth the room of a girl with a rare and interesting skin condition:

> No active treatment has been yet suggested as it is much too pretty to spoil by any attempt at a cure just yet. Several surgeons are expected to come from other hospitals to see it, so she has an ounce of peppermint water three times a day and full diet, and the cure is postponed till a sufficient number of interested people have seen it. Drawings must be made; the artist to the hospital could not attend for a week to come; then there were photographs to be taken, and it would never do to commence anything so effective as a cure.[45]

In fact, the surgeons at St. Bernard's are all amateur artists themselves who sketch and frame the results of their labors for later edification, and even hire professional artists and photographers to make more appealing, emotionally resonant studies. One doctor is hurrying off to sketch a "beautiful optic neuritis" on a dying woman before it disappears forever; another is blistering patients on purpose to see the impact of lithic acid on the blood, and counseling his students to carefully mount their photographs of the pretty acid crystals with an artistic black circle around the covering glass (Berdoe, *St. Bernard's* 213). A third, Dr. Stanford, forces poor women to undergo gynecological examinations in a medical theater packed with male students in order to give the students "a chance of learning that, for which, they might have paid large sums of money" (290). A fourth, the highly malevolent Dr. Crowe, is described as an "epicure of pain" who prescribes his beautiful Italian wife

chloral at addictive levels, and contemplates her eventual murder as he com-
pletes his rounds (145). Indeed, a patient's term of residence in the hospital
is understood to be just like "an artist's model's visit to a studio," and the callousness to pain displayed by most of the senior doctors at St. Bernard's is
described by our narrator as a reflection of "the true spirit of the artist" (284).

Elsworth is horrified and eventually retreats to Spain, where he travels
through the countryside on a bicycle with a good medicine chest packed with
basic medical appliances. Finding that "healthy life invited healthy thoughts,"
he pursues a cholera epidemic to Granada with little fear for his life: "with the
confidence of God and the wisdom of sanitary precautions which he should
adopt, he decided to do what he could to help the dreadful misery that hung
over the unfortunate city" (255). By chance in Granada he meets the vacation-
ing Mildred Lee, an heiress whose father just happens to be the consulting
physician to St. Bernard's, and who is, of course, soon joined by potential
suitor and would-be wife murderer, Dr. Crowe. Convinced by Elsworth that
"drugs were nothing but a delusion and a sham, and that nothing but nature
and a good nurse were wanted to cure any complaint amenable to treatment,"
Mildred decides, to the disdain of Crowe, to revolutionize the hospitals of
London, first by endowing Nightingale House, a temperance hospital, and
by hiring Elsworth to work there. They marry (but not before the nefarious
surgeon Crowe successfully murders his wife with experimental poison mush-
rooms, proposes to Mildred, and is ultimately fired), and work together to
reinstate sanitary medicine to its status as the only true form of medical art.
"The psychological mania, the drug mania, and the operative furor will pass
away in time like the craze for bleeding," these newlyweds believe, "and it
will ultimately be found that it is perfectly possible to cure the sick and save
the limbs of the injured by merciful, honorable and rational means" (473). Of
course, this interesting conclusion to *St. Bernard's* returns us to the sanitary
narrative, pitting the virtuous and ultimately triumphant forces of sanitation
against both disease and morally reprehensible aesthetic pleasure. But it also
adds another level of ideological struggle to the story, depicting and resolving
an antagonistic relationship between prevention and cure that closely tracks
those contemporary debates in public health circles about the future of medical science.

Many Victorian novels similarly thwart the rise of laboratory medicine
with a swift dose of sanitary prevention.[46] One of best known and cruelest
vivisectionists in Victorian fiction, Wilkie Collins's Dr. Benjulia from the 1883
Heart and Science, is eventually defeated by sensitive physician (and lover of
truth) Ovid Vere, who discovers a manuscript proving that a whole range of
brain and nervous conditions can be cured without experimental medicine,

and consequently, without the practice of vivisection.[47] At the end of the nineteenth century, however, as bacteriology and pathology were gradually normalized, the nightmare of surgical rendition becomes less tractable and less easily ameliorated by cleanliness or a found manuscript; in frightening novels about medical experimentation like Robert Louis Stevenson's *Dr. Jekyll and Mr. Hyde* (1886) and H. G. Wells's *The Island of Dr. Moreau* (1896) reductionist science can no longer simply be banished by the sanitary aesthetic. What we more frequently discover in medical fiction published at the end of the nineteenth century is that the aesthetic has been thoroughly co-opted by the sensualists, and that Paterian physiology has only empowered the decadent pleasures of the mutable body. In Ouida's 1895 *Toxin*, young Sicilian Prince Adrianis falls in love with the Countess Zaranegra in Venice, and initially fears no romantic rivalry from his constant companion, the English doctor Frederic Damer. For a beautiful woman to actually interest Damer, "she must be lying, dead or alive on an operating table" according to Adrianis.[48] The conversation continues:

> "Alive by preference," said Damer, "the dead are little use to us; their nervous system is still like a stopped clock."
>   "A creature must suffer to interest you?"
>   "Certainly." (Ouida 42)

Ouida's Venice here resembles Chadwick's scene of degradation and decay rather than Ruskin's aesthetic paradise: the lagoons are home to ancient crimes and corpses that date from the days when the "white marble of St. Marks had been red with blood" (17), and the house that serves as Damer's laboratory is "obscure and uninviting, standing amidst the clang of coppersmiths' hammers and the stench of iron-foundries . . . befouled, blackened, filled with smoke and clamour, and vileness" (75). Damer has moved to this degraded neighborhood so that he can practice vivisection without the concern that people will hear the anguished cries of dogs coming from his home; he also conveniently dumps "the dead or half-dead mutilated creatures" (92) into the already polluted water when his experiment is complete. Veronica Zaranegra soon discovers she loves Adrianis and fears Damer; she wants to accept Adrianis's advances, but finds that Damer exerts a mysterious magnetic influence that paralyzes and prevents her from doing so. She tries to encourage the doctor to leave on the grounds that his medical vocation must require attention and tending: "Aren't you losing time?" she inquires, reminding us of the image of the stopped clock of the human nervous system. "I never lose time," replied Damer. "A man of science is like an artist; his art is everywhere, wherever natural forms exist" (80).

The importance of the physical life to Damer's brand of *aisthesis* is central to the ideological anxiety of *Toxin,* a novel that is deeply suspicious about the power of the anatomical gaze to find art everywhere, except in harmonious and whole, unified and complete, beauty. Wandering in St. Mark's Square one afternoon, Adrianis is surprised to see Damer contemplating the statuary. "It is too frivolous a scene for you." Adrianis remarks, "Are you longing to dissect the horses of St. Marks?"

Damer smiled slightly.
"I fear I should find their anatomy faulty. I am no artist, or critic either, or I should venture to say that I object to their attitude. Arrested motion is a thing too momentary to perpetuate in metal or stone." (99)

Soon after this exchange, a small child falls into the dark, murky water around St. Marks, water that is fetid with sewage, and, of course, dissected animal carcasses. Adrianis jumps in after him, but Damer knows that the child is already infected with "Boulogne Sore Throat," and that Adrianis will soon catch "what the vulgar call diphtheria" as well (132). No cleansing mechanism or sanitary physician comes to the aid of poor Adrianis, who is sequestered by Damer in a hotel room, and repeatedly inoculated with his so-called cure for the diphtheria virus that is actually just a distilled form of the diphtheria toxin itself. Adrianis dies, and while the novel concludes with a marriage, it is hardly a form of social reconciliation: the deadly Dr. Damer marries a stunned and permanently hypnotized Countess Zaranegra, and the titular "toxin" proves to be a synonym for the irrevocable progress of experimental medicine and the futility and failure of sanitary perfectibility. Art that articulates completion and finish, wholeness without the possibility of decay, is itself dead; while the precarious beauty of the impressionistic body is, for Ouida at least, the future of *aisthesis.*

CHAPTER 5

Aesthetic Anachronisms

Mary Ward's *The Mating of Lydia* and the Persistent Plot of Sanitary Fiction

> The questions of social hygiene, as here understood, go to the heart of life. It is the task of this hygiene not only to remake sewers, but to re-make love, and to do both in the same spirit of human fellowship, to ensure finer individual development and a larger social organization. At one end social hygiene may be regarded as simply the extension of an elementary sanitary code; at the other end it seems to some to have in it the glorious freedom of a new religion. The majority of people, probably, will be content to admit that we have here a scheme of serious social reform which every man and woman will soon be called upon to take some share in.
>
> —Havelock Ellis, *The Task of Social Hygiene* (1913)

*G*iven standard accounts of the sudden "rise" of germ theory in the 1870s, the ideological meaning of the picturesque should certainly be anachronistic by the early years of the twentieth century. The pollution anxiety conveyed so effectively by the dilapidated cottage, the dirty street, and the refuse heap should begin to disappear after germ theory shifts the origin of disease from the environmental to the biological, when the sanitation of a community can no longer promise healthy art or beautiful people. But several times over the course of *The Sanitary Arts* I've pointed to the slow rise and development of any single or singular germ theory of disease; with the help of Alison Bashford, Nancy Tomes, Margaret Pelling, and other historians of science, I've argued that the protracted and uneven assimilation of contagionist discourse in the nineteenth century owes as much to pervasive confusion about the unseen world of microorganisms as it does to an abiding cultural investment in sanitation reform as a moral narrative. In part, this book is an

attempt to shed some light on that long period of overlap between the miasmatic and the bacteriological theories of disease, with particular regard to
the aesthetic promise of perfectibility that sanitation continued to provide
in spite of declining scientific faith in fever nests and filth diseases. Instead
of collapsing under the superior science of germ theory, disappearing as the
misguided obsession of an unenlightened era, I would argue that sanitation
reform actually increased its ideological reach in the era of germ theory. Sanitarians adapted to the new rhetoric of the germ, accommodated the discourse
of the microorganism, and began to seek the fever nest in individual human
bodies as natural extensions of communities, neighborhoods, and houses.
Invested still in social perfectibility and prevention rather than surgical or
pharmacological varieties of "cure," sanitation reformers became interested
in cellular pathology for what it could reveal about the very intimate environments of individual human subjects: "life history, heredity, family and
domestic life, personal habits and customs" were increasingly scrutinized in
the late nineteenth century for different kinds of dirt, dirt that could move
from the individual body to the social body through the biological process of
reproduction.[1]

When we remember that Ruskinian aesthetic revival depended upon
both a cleansed country and a stronger, healthier and more beautiful population, we should be less surprised to realize that the combination of Victorian sanitation reform and the "new" germ theory inspired, in the long, slow
period of scientific hypotheses and ideological overlap, both the doctrine of
social hygiene and the logic of race culture. Perhaps one of the reasons that
germ theory has been celebrated by so many historians as a sudden paradigm
shift in medical knowledge, such a lofty moment of scientific and intellectual
enlightenment, is that the sudden rupture of a revolution can usefully repress
the uncomfortable and even distasteful period of Western development when
sanitarians and other social reformers began to seek the tools of human perfectibility in the ideas of the statistician and the geneticist. While defective
drains and dust traps were less likely to be identified as sources of illness in
the very late years of the nineteenth century, scientists like William Budd and
John Tyndall denied the theory of spontaneous generation by insisting on a
disease etiology that was even closer to home, "Disease," Tyndall explained,
"comes always from a parent stock":

> In cases of epidemic diseases, it is not on bad air and foul drains that the
> attention of the physician of the future will be primarily fixed, but upon
> disease germs, which no bad air or foul drains can create, but which may
> be pushed by foul air into virulent energy of reproduction.[2]

For Tyndall, writing in 1881 as a physicist primarily interested in airborne microorganisms, the use of reproductive rhetoric was, in itself and as Budd had suggested before him, indicative of the inescapable truth of germ theory. Indeed, Budd had noticed that even opponents of germ theory found themselves, late in the century, using words like "propagation," reproduction," and "self-multiplication" to describe the spread of fevers through communities.[3] While Margaret Pelling has usefully pointed out that over-emphasis on the biological associations of words like these by historians has obfuscated rather than clarified their complex historical associations, it seems important to recognize the linguistic contagion of reproductive discourse in late-century sanitary philosophy.[4] The rhetorical accommodation of germ theory, noticed in the 1880s by Budd and Tyndall, marks a gradual shift in sanitary understanding; not the sudden disavowal of spontaneous generation, but the gradual acceptance of supplementary models of prevention that came to understand parentage itself as a potential environmental crisis.

The Sanitary Arts is most directly concerned with germ theory as it relates to developments in sanitation, so this chapter will be less concerned with isolating and articulating the variety of ideas that were circulating about microorganisms from mid-century than it will be in demonstrating what effect that slow shift in scientific acculturation had upon the broader hygiene movement. The introduction of the germ did not simplify or clarify ideas about illness for Victorians; indeed, it complicated entrenched moral, religious, and even aesthetic assumptions about filth, often producing narratives of disease that may seem, to modern readers, etiologically bewildering, strangely anachronistic, and ethically contradictory. This chapter has two interrelated purposes: to explore the development of sanitation reform as it shifted from an environmental to a biological phase in cultural history, and to examine that shift through the persistence of the sanitary plot in British fiction written well after the discovery and general acceptance of microorganisms. Mrs. Humphry (Mary) Ward's The Mating of Lydia is the text I discuss most thoroughly here as a very late sanitary fiction: published in 1913, Ward's novel absorbs many of the most notable features of those mid-Victorian sanitary narratologies I discussed in the second chapter, and it eventually uses the marriage plot as a vehicle to banish environmental degradation, and to inspire a philosophical conversion to a sanitized, socialized aesthetic. But inscribed within the very title of Ward's novel is an acknowledgment of the somewhat refined responsibility carried by that closing tableau of affective reconciliation; if mid-century sanitary fictions cleanse and renew the social order through a harmonious reconciliation of opposites in marriage, late-Victorian and early-twentieth-century novels often emphasize not only marriage, but the biological and reproductive ritual of "mating" as a fundamental component of the new sanitary aesthetic.

I. Sanitary Fictions, Germ Theory, and the New Woman

The overlapping of miasmatic theories and germ theories of disease are particularly interesting when they appear in fiction, and often signal an unwillingness to relinquish the ideological power of the sanitary story to an ambivalent, morally meaningless microorganism. Grant Allen was especially cagey in his novels about the spread of disease, and still invested, as late as the 1890s, in reconciling germ theory with a seemingly anachronistic sanitary aesthetic. Allen's *At Market Value* (1894), for example, is a rather strange story about Arnold Willoughby, the rising Lord Axminster, a young, apparently ugly painter who wants to understand his "market value" in the absence of the class privileges assigned to him at birth. Willoughby reads about an American doctor, Silas Quackenboos, who "undertook to make the plainest faces beautiful, not by mere skin-deep devices, but by the surgical treatment of the human countenance," and hires Quackenboos to reconstruct his face.[5] Newly anonymous and attractive, Willoughby heads off to Venice where he finds an interesting painting companion in Kathleen Hesselgrave, who loves to paint the inconvenient nooks and stagnant corners of Venice: "they're so much more picturesque, after all, than the common things the world admires, and one sees everywhere" (Allen, *At Market Value* I, 67). Kathleen and Willoughby set up their canvases together all over Venice, but while Kathleen paints facing the untrodden streets, quaint old churches, and minor canals, Willoughby focuses his canvas and gaze towards the boats and waves on the open sea. During this long period of aesthetic courtship, Kathleen manages to figure out that Willoughby is the missing Lord Axminster, as does the visiting Canon Valentine, who keeps quiet because his own son will inherit if Willoughby stays lost. While Kathleen's beloved picturesque has been critiqued throughout the novel for being both uncomfortable and insanitary, Canon Valentine is the first to detect disease in Venice's charming dilapidation.

> It is so delightful to see all these beautiful things in company with an artist. But the damp of the lagoons is really too much for my poor old throat . . . as I went along with Miss Hesselgrave to the Academy yesterday, I felt the cold air rise up from the Canal and catch hold and throttle me. . . . Change the air without delay, that's the one safe remedy. And indeed to tell you the truth, Venice is so spoilt, so utterly spoilt since the Austrians left,

that I shan't be sorry to get out of it. Most insanitary town, I call it—most insanitary in every way. (*At Market Value* I, 165)

Given that Canon Valentine dies of typhoid fever by the end of the second volume, one might guess that he was right about Venice and that he paid a standard Victorian price for his aesthetic tourism. But he leaves Italy perfectly healthy, and when, back in England, he complains to Kathleen again about the unsanitary smells of Venice, she rebuffs him with an alternative, more local narrative of the fever nest:

> As to the typhoid, I have my doubts. The sea seems to purify it. Do you know, Canon Valentine, I've spent five winters on end in Venice, and I've never had a personal friend ill with fever; while in England I've had dozens. It isn't always the places that look the dirtiest which turn out, in the long run, to be really most insanitary. And, if it comes to that, what could be worse than those slums we passed on our way out of the close, near the pointed archway, where you cross the river? (II, 10)

Canon Valentine, in turn, aggressively defends these English cottages; they are health and cleanliness epitomized, he asserts, "wholesomeness itself, the last word in sanitation. Nobody ever got ill there, nobody ever died; and he had never even heard of a case of typhoid" (II, 11). The reason the Canon is so offended is that the slums in question are the property of the Dean of Norchester, and currently the subject of a newspaper inquiry into their dubi-.ous sanitary status. Moreover, when a particularly intrepid sanitary inspector confronts him with a glass of suspicious water from Close Wynd, a particu-larly notorious slum by the river, the Canon drinks it without hesitation, and the fatal typhoid is upon him by bedtime. Here, the familiar sanitary narra-tive shifts to a new discourse of disease etiology: "For twenty-one days those insidious little microbes that he swallowed so carelessly lay maturing in their colony in the canon's doomed body. At the end of that time, they swarmed and developed themselves; and even the canon knew in his own heart, unspoken, that it was the Close Wynd water that had given him the typhoid fever" (II, 13). During that period of microbial infestation, Canon Valentine manages to remake his will, leaving two hundred pounds for the sanitary construction of more perfect cottages than the ones "which had proved his destruction" (II, 13), but his hygienic awakening comes too late for himself, his wife, and even Kathleen's mother, all dead of the typhoid within two weeks.

Such a story is perhaps a recuperation of picturesque environments, a geographical reshuffling of the fever nest that the germ theory of disease makes possible by the last decades of the nineteenth century. After all, Kathleen's picturesque Italian paintings sell quite well when she returns to England, and other than a temporary nervous breakdown she appears to suffer no penalty for her own aesthetic preferences. In fact, it is Willoughby who suffers some form of aesthetic retribution in the novel when a surprise shipwreck leaves his right hand crushed and destroys his painting career. While this is probably sanitary punishment for the elective surgical beautification he underwent in the first chapter, it is hardly a deathblow for Willoughby, who becomes a successful translator and is reinstated as Lord Axminster. Moreover, Kathleen and Willoughby marry and move back to the formerly foul city of Venice, where they apparently live happily ever after. This neutralization of the picturesque in the marriage plot gets reflected, of course, in the resolution of the social reform plot as well: microbes are revealed to be the cause of typhoid, not those environments that actually look the dirtiest or smell the most foul. Still, the moral to the story of Canon Valentine's sad demise seems doubly determined by the environmental and the biological, and essentially unresolved by the recuperative money he leaves to the construction of sanitary cottages, but not actually to water purification, in Close Wynd. The Canon is doomed, finally, not only by his religious hypocrisy, but by his inability to give up the Chadwickian-era equation of picturesque environments with biological danger; indeed, his steadfast adherence to the sanitary story blinds him to the new menace of the microorganism. In this way, even after the advent of germ theory, the conventions of sanitary fiction remain visible, propping up the text's moral imperative with a familiar set of aesthetic questions and quandaries.

The novel Allen published the following year, *The Woman Who Did*, eventually became his most infamous work. While this text isn't usually read for what it can tell us about the slow rise of germ theory, its story of female sexual freedom is nevertheless shaped, at least initially, by the familiar narrative conventions of sanitary fiction. When Herminia Barton, a beautiful, healthy, Cambridge-educated "free woman," becomes pregnant with Alan Merrick's child, she refuses to marry him and they flee to Italy for her confinement.[6] Here, Merrick, a barrister, fosters his true vocation, sketching, painting, and studying the early Umbrian painters, and the couple finally settles down in remote, rural Perugia, waiting for Herminia to give birth. Herminia hates Perugia, finds it dismal and disgusting, but Alan loves it: "A Celt in essence, thoroughly Italianate himself, and with a deep love for the picturesque, which often makes men insensible to dirt and discomfort, he expected to Italianise Herminia rapidly" (120). As for Herminia, "The picturesque did not suffice for her. Cleanliness and fresh air were far dearer to her soul than the quaintest street corners, the oddest archways. . . . Dusty, dusty Perugia! O Baby, to be born for the freeing of woman, was it here, was it here you must draw your first breath, in air polluted by the vices of centuries" (121). Most interesting to me about this passage is that the pollution anxiety located in Perugia's picturesque environment retains its moral meaning, but becomes metaphorical rather than physical: Herminia's modern disgust seems to stem as much from Italy's ancient vice and corruption, as it does from Perugia's insanitary dirt and discomfort. Still, Alan's punishment is predictable. After a few weeks in Perugia, Alan develops headaches, looks unwell, and is restless; Herminia asks him to stop painting, fearing the closeness of the streets and the filthiness of his cherished landscape. By the time Herminia calls in a doctor, however, his typhoid fever is pronounced, and he dies before marrying Herminia and conferring legitimacy on his daughter. A traditional Victorian sanitation story, would, as we know, make the moral to this tale aesthetically obvious: pleasure in the picturesque is dangerous, even deadly, and artists who pursue and replicate this selfish aesthetic endanger both the happy family and the harmonious social community. But *The Woman Who Did*, like *At Market Value*, demonstrates an ideological overlap and bifurcated causality common to the period of germ theory's slow rise; as we see, moreover, this period of shifting germ etiology and disease discourse is mirrored in miniature by typhoid's long incubation cycle. First, Alan's doctor explains that his patient's typhoid fever was actually contracted weeks earlier in Florence, where the disease is currently an epidemic. And finally, the narrator describes a chain of events that should sound familiar to readers who remember the relatively recent demise of Canon Valentine.

> Alan had drunk a single glass of water from those polluted springs that supply in part the Tuscan metropolis. For twenty-one days, those victorious microbes had brooded in silence in his poisoned arteries. At the end of that time they swarmed and declared themselves. He was ill with an aggravated form of the deadly disease that still stalks unchecked through unsanitated Europe. (126)

Even for Grant Allen, writing at the dawn of the twentieth century, the picturesque continues to act as a delivery system for so-called filth disease, circulating the invading microbes freely in contaminated environments and unenlightened European capitals. Both of his mid-nineties novels represent the uneven transition between miasmatic and microbial theories of disease production, and the attempt to introduce an amoral and ambivalent agent of death to a narratology still invested in cleansing as a mechanism of social harmony.

It is true that the moral lesson of *The Woman Who Did* is more complicated than the one we see in *At Market Value,* committed as it is to lambasting a society that is still as unwilling to embrace the natural utopianism of gender equality as is it to embrace true cleanliness. Herminia resists the marriage plot repeatedly in her enlightened struggle for freedom and independence, eventually writing a novel with advanced social views that the *Spectator* judges to be genius, but also calls "poisoned": "its very purity makes it dangerous," the reviewer explains, succinctly exposing the contradictory forces of pollution anxiety at a moment of scientific and social upheaval (127). The abject source of both filth and cleanliness, Herminia kills herself when her daughter reenters the established social order, rejecting her mother's hard-fought utopian values in favor of a traditional model of femininity and a life with her moralistic paternal grandfather. While *The Woman Who Did* is certainly a more ideologically strident novel than *At Market Value,* both Allen texts use so-called "New Woman" plots to tell the story of a new social threat, an unprecedented element of chaos and confusion that threatens the straightforward moral connections between sin and disease, immorality and filth. The New Woman, rising at the same moment that germ theory begins to circulate in public discourse, is a threat to any narrative that depends on a closing tableau of affective reconciliation and moral understanding, and given the new sexual and reproductive power demanded by such women, the social and even biological capacity for health and cleanliness was increasingly, and perhaps dangerously, in their hands.

As I've already discussed, the feminization of sanitation is one very interesting effect of germ theory that both Bashford and Tomes examine quite closely; in their view, the most important reason sanitation survived the advent of germ theory as a significant component of medical treatment is that sanitary work was largely relegated to women. Bashford explains that the "sanitarian discourse of health and disease was sustained in the field of nursing knowledge and practice well into the twentieth century. Moreover, the technologies of cleanliness produced by ideas of 'asepsis' allowed for, rather than obliterated, nurses' sanitarian practices."[7] While the rituals of domestic and hospital cleanliness kept women central to the cultural work of hygiene through the early twentieth century, women's role as mate, as mother, as breeder of a hopefully improved race of Britons made them just as important to the new sanitation as they had been to the old. The advent of the New Woman in fiction, a heroine who actively pursued one of the few professions suddenly open to women (usually writing, nursing or painting), and who explicitly questioned her status as reproductive entity, pertinently underscores the way sanitation was reinvented as a specifically female form of labor.

While few novels detail the erratic debut of the microbe as dramatically as the two I discussed by Grant Allen, New Woman fiction, a loosely connected and ambivalently feminist selection of novels written primarily during the 1880s and 1890s, is a genre that consistently demonstrates the shift from sanitary to social forms of hygiene. As Beth Sutton-Ramspeck has persuasively demonstrated in *Raising the Dust: The Literary Housekeeping of Mary Ward, Sarah Grand, and Charlotte Perkins Gilman,* the hygienic aspects of housework, which middle-class women had increasing taken upon themselves in the late nineteenth century, function as a powerful metaphor in New Woman fiction, "sweeping way" old boundaries between public and private, artistic and practical, personal and political.[8] Housekeeping is a subversively empowering image for Sutton-Ramspeck; broadly defined as social activists, literary housekeepers often clean up the public sphere by embracing eugenic marriage and purifying the human species through judicious breeding practices (63). While Sutton-Ramspeck doesn't discuss in detail the broader connections between the mid-Victorian sanitation reform movement and late-Victorian eugenic philosophy, she does make this crucial aspect of New Woman fiction visible in a way that few critics, especially feminist critics, have done, usefully reminding us that the feminist story, like the sanitary story, is much longer and more complicated than historical narratives of enlightenment and liberal progress sometimes imply. The sanitary responsibility granted to (or seized by) New Woman heroines in the late-nineteenth-century novel is the power to remake the world by remaking the aesthetic; through art, through medicine, through eugenic mating, New Woman heroines are tasked (and task themselves) repeatedly with the Ruskinian imperative to get "the country clean and the people lovely." Even when a eugenic program is not the first or final solution to hereditary disease and social ugliness, many New Woman heroines combine their "natural" aesthetic and sanitary talents by working to beautify. the bodies of British citizens.

This is especially true in novels that feature sympathetic female doctors: medical professionals who naturally resist the filthy, reductionist labor of the surgeon, and instead view their vocation as sanitary prevention and perfection for the greater social good. While we've seen this kind of nursing professional well-represented in Grant Allen's *Hilda Wade,* Charles Reade's 1877 *A Woman-Hater* is a relatively early novel about a female doctor, Rhoda Gale, hired by a young, progressive country squire to tend to his community in

Barfordshire. It is beautiful, utopian country, Squire Vizard assures her when she first arrives, and his younger, half-sister Zoe generally agrees: she loves to bring her visitors to one village and one cottage in particular so they can glory in the picturesque. But Zoe has inherited an aesthetic sensibility from her Greek mother, and sees something amiss in the "pasty" faces of the children at Islip: "My sister is a great colorist, and pitches her expectations too high," Vizard explains dismissively. "I daresay their faces are not more pasty than usual; but this is a show place, and looks like a garden, so Zoe wants the boys to be poppies and pansies and the girls roses and lilies."[9] Zoe's friend Miss Dover proposes one facetious solution to the off-color faces of the village children: "Well, you have got a box of colours; we will come up some day and tint all the putty-faces," but Dr. Gale makes it clear that all aesthetic alterations now fall under her medical purview. "Their faces are my business, I'll soon fix them. She didn't say putty-faced, she said pasty" (II, 161).

Dr. Gale's initial inspection of the village reveals many sanitary dangers, from the deleterious green wallpaper in Vizard's own home, to the malarial refuse heap that festers right outside the window of the most picturesque cottage in the village, to her suspicion that the poor children are eating cherry stones to assuage their hunger, thus causing their pallid hues (II, 168). Prevention requires, according to Dr. Gale, a patient and well-trained gaze, a gaze that is not insidiously "pure" as Bourdieu has defined it, not distracted by the aesthetic effects of colors, light and shadows. "You must have eyes, and use them" to investigate predisposing causes and to discover the true sources of illness and deformity that are often masquerading as beauty (II, 225). "The outside roses you admire so much are as delusive as flattery," she insists to a dismayed Zoe Vizard; "their sweetness covers a foul, unwholesome den" (II, 238). But after Dr. Gale requests a microscope from the Squire, it becomes clear that her preventive gaze can be enhanced by scientific technology, and is just as willing to demonize the microbe as the dung heap. The water, Dr. Gale dramatically announces, is filled with "animalcula" that survive and breed in the stomachs of the children, and she produces a set a drawings that transform the picturesque aesthetic of the village into a form of art that "struck terror in gentle bosoms" (II, 230). At first, Vizard objects on the grounds that these hand-drawn creatures are "antediluvian monsters," violations of evolution; Zoe is simply angry because she mistakenly believed her village was an aesthetic paradise (II, 231). Dr. Gale eventually persuades the landowner to dig a new freshwater well and to supply his villagers with healthy milk cows, but only after a lengthy explanation of the various long-term biological effects such microorganisms and others are having on his entire laboring population:

Now, for instance, if the boys at Hillstoke are putty-faced, the boys at Islip have no calves to their legs. That is a sure sign of a deteriorating species. The lower type of savage has next to no calf. The calf is a sign of civilization and due nourishment. This single phenomenon was my cue, and led me to others; and I have examined the mothers and the people of all ages, and I tell you it is a village of starvelings. . . . [T]he race has declined. Only five men over fifty are the appropriate weight and height. By purchasing five cows, you will get rid, in the next generation, of the half-grown, slouching men, the hollow-eyed, narrow-chested, round-backed women and the calf-less boys one sees all over Islip, and restore the stalwart race that filled the villages under your sires, and have left proof of their wholesome food on the tombstones. (II, 242)

As Dr. Gale delineates the biological signs of civilization and savagery for the edification of the gentry, it becomes clear that the goals of sanitary prevention and social perfectibility have become more explicitly imperial and racial. While the picturesque aesthetic is still a problematic site of social disharmony and disease in *A Woman-Hater,* it signals slow physical decline and genetic deformity rather than the threat of any sudden and swift-moving epidemic. The task of the female sanitarian, however, retains its ideological meaning and urgency: sanitary knowledge must purify the community by remaking the aesthetic, teaching the perverse landowning class, in particular, to recognize and appreciate a form of beauty found in healthy environments and beautiful people rather than in the picturesque poison of the decayed village and the degenerated human body. This needful reorientation of the aesthetic gaze is also apparent in the novel's primary love triangle: Zoe loves the beautiful Lord Severne but is beloved by the ugly Lord Uxmoor. Dr. Gale warns Zoe that while Lord Severne is certainly the most beautiful man she has ever seen, her knowledge of physiognomy assures her that he is both too feminine and a liar (III, 3). Indeed, Severne turns out to be a bigamist in the making, and Zoe finally marries Lord Uxmoor after a long depression and illness spent under the care of Dr. Gale. Zoe also sheds, at the end of the novel, her preference for the picturesque, and devotes herself to helping institute new sanitation reforms on her brother's estate. In this way, the preventive gaze can redirect perverse aesthetic pleasure, ensuring the sanitary future of both the biological and social family. The novel ends with a plea for more women doctors, and a gendered understanding of the medical profession that clearly reflects an abiding distrust of male surgical and pharmacological science, and a celebration of female prevention: "The male physician relies on drugs. Medical women are wanted to moderate that delusion; to prevent disease by domestic vigilance, and cure it by well-selected esculents and pure air" (II, 240). The unmarried Dr. Gale "is still all eyes, and notices everything" at the close of the novel (III, 390), but her medical practice is small; instead, she devotes herself primarily to breeding newer and healthier strains of cattle on a small farm on Squire Vizard's estate. Esculents and fresh air are important, even necessary, but by the end of the nineteenth century, sanitarians were, like Dr. Gale, "all eyes," looking for predisposing causes in breeding and bloodlines, rather than in fever nests and dust traps.

II. Biologizing Sanitation

At mid-century, the sanitary story was a popular narrative of social reconciliation and aesthetic harmony. Like the marriage plot itself, sanitation promised a resanctified image of England, free of unchecked epidemics and unattached lovers. By late century, the rise of an alternative and unpredictable model of disease might have threatened the comfortable closure of this realist drama, especially given the rising suspicion at the dawn of the twentieth century that Victorian sanitation reform was generally a failure. By the 1890s, as Teresa Mangum has written, people were generally disappointed that the social reforms of mid-century had so inadequately addressed crime, prostitution and other vices.[10] An unintelligent and unteachable population had failed to respond as expected to the enthusiastic social outreach of the upper and middle classes, and in return liberal do-gooders had become, as Charles Masterman phrased it in 1907, "tired of the poor."[11] Masterman sympathetically summarized this problem in his discussion of *Realities at Home:* "Results seem so inadequate; the material is so stubborn and unpliant; it seems better after all to let things drift and trust piously in a Divine Providence, working all things for good" (5). One specific cultural event had forced these suspicions into more widespread public controversy at the turn of the century: Britain's politically embarrassing performance during the military campaigns against the Boers. The fact that untrained farmers had successfully defended themselves against professional British soldiers for more than two years (1899–1902) prompted an investigation into the state and status of "national efficiency," a phrase that primarily signified an inquiry into the physical and mental fitness of working-class Britons who fought the Empire's battles. The specially formed "Committee on Physical Deterioration" convened in 1903 to review military statistics on the health of potential recruits, and the results "seemed to confirm the existence of a degenerate underclass of the population which formed a residual pool of infection," reflecting studies of the working class by nineteenth-century sociologists like Charles Booth and See-bohm Rowntree, reflecting, too, Charles Reade's fictionalized description of a British race in significant physical decline.[12] While these statistical stud-ies eventually helped put in place nominally progressive policies like school lunch programs, athletic initiatives, and medical examinations for poor chil-dren, many who believed that the British underclass had been degenerat-ing in health and intellect since the early nineteenth century believed also that the mid-Victorian reform movement had completely failed. Middle- and upper-class citizens weren't just tired of the poor, they were dubious about the era of social perfectibility that reformers had promised would be the result of slum clearances, urban sewerage, and public baths.

If, on the one hand, many scientists, doctors, statisticians, and sociolo-gists resented that environmental sanitation had simply failed to transform a degenerated race of working-class city dwellers back into the ruddy, hearty, innately moral peasants of the old agricultural times, many others believed that the mechanisms of mid-Victorian reform had actually created the cur-rent biological crisis by ameliorating the negative social conditions that so usefully preserved the health and strength of the human race. "In the reign of Victoria," Arnold White complained in his 1901 book *Efficiency and Empire*, "hospital, sanitary and poor law machinery for treating avoidable disease, and thus tainting posterity, implies an indifference for our successors incompat-ible with humanity."[13] Even writers who were willing to admit that sanitary sci-ence had achieved much in the prevention of disease and death in the general population argued that its negative effects were actually much more serious: opined George Shee, in 1903 "the causes which are undermining the physique of the nation quite outweigh the results achieved by the progress of medical science."[14]

The groundbreaking text of sanitation reform had been, inarguably, Chadwick's *Sanitary Report,* but for eugenic and proto-eugenic writers of the early twentieth century, the *Sanitary Report* also marked the beginning of the biological deterioration of England. By concerning itself with "only the conditions of life and not life itself," Chadwick's sanitation reform move-ment had wrongly concentrated its cleansing philosophy and apparatus on environments and not people. British sexologist and reformer Havelock Ellis admitted that in the days before Chadwick, people had certainly lived in "unspeakable filth and disease," but sanitation measures and poor law reforms had allowed the weakest specimens of human existence to survive and breed, thus defeating natural selection and generating a "surplus" popu-lation of degenerates.[15] The new era of social reform, in Ellis's opinion, needed to focus on protecting the fit from the unfit, and taking responsibility for the

next generation by encouraging rather than ameliorating the necessary work
of natural selection as it culled the degenerate, the inebriate, and the feeble
from the British gene pool.

> Bad conditions have this compensation that, though they produce an intol-
> erable amount of sordid degradation and misery, they kill off their worst
> victims.
>
> Natural selection, as we say, comes into operation and the more unfit
> are destroyed, the more fit survive . . . our social responsibility is becoming
> a sense of racial responsibility. It is that enlarged sense of responsibility
> which renders possible what we call the regeneration of the race. (39–40)

Certainly Chadwick was an active and opportunistic producer of sanitary discourse in the 1840s, but his power and his primacy as an agent of sanitation
reform declined significantly after the protracted and idiosyncratic collaboration between sanitary philosophy and germ theory. Intent here is separate
from outcome: environmental cleanliness might have been the original goal
of the Sanitary Report, but biological filth was apparently its long-term, generational effect.

Still, even though Chadwick and the mid-Victorian reform initiatives
he helped create were often vilified by late-century scientists, it is crucial to
understand that writers like Ellis didn't want to end the sanitation reform
movement. They wanted to retrospectively recognize environmental sanitation as simply the first stage of what could now be more properly termed
"social hygiene," and extended to prenatal care, infant care, and puericulture.

> Social hygiene, as it will be here understood, may be said to be a develop-
> ment, and even a transformation of what was formerly known as social
> reform. . . . In the first place, it is no longer merely an attempt to deal with
> the conditions under which life is lived, seeking to treat bad conditions as
> they occur, without going to their source, but aims at prevention.[16]

Sanitation appears to have retained its ideological power as a moral vehicle
well into the early twentieth century because it became a new, self-organizing
force of prevention, one that could work in tandem with some aspects of a
very fungible germ theory to promise biological perfectibility for the British
race. Ellis may have been a relative newcomer to sanitary discourse when he
wrote the above words, but it is important that his understanding of the new
phase of social hygiene was widely shared and circulated at the end of the
nineteenth century by many of the same sanitarians who pushed so strongly

for environmental improvements and domestic cleanliness in the old days of the fever nest and the dust trap. As early as the 1879 Croydon gathering of the Sanitary Institute, familiar advocates of Victorian hygiene were beginning to repudiate the growing suspicion that reform efforts had failed by conversely insisting that they simply hadn't gone far enough. Dr. Alfred Carpenter, in his lecture "First Principles of Sanitary Work," staunchly denied that "sanitary science was responsible for the propagation of a weakened race of beings, and was therefore tending to people the earth with a debilitated race."[17] Debilitation and physical decline are not the effect of sanitation reform, he asserted, "but a consequence of neglect of it"; if British "progeny" are taught to obey the laws of God and hygiene, "at the end of three or four generations, there will be a removal of gouty diathesis or the tubercular constitution" (44).

Mid-victorian sanitation hadn't failed, in other words; the concept of environmental prevention was merely beginning to contemplate a new genetic frontier. At the same conference, we may remember, B. W. Richardson was also outlining his plans for the community of "Salutland," an enlightened aesthetic and sanitary utopia where the surgeon has no cause to practice and the drug trade is unnecessary. However, "Salutland" is also a state dictated by certain strict genetic laws, and "intermarriages between people with hereditary taints—insanity, scrofula, cancer, and specific diseases—are forbidden."[18] By 1888, the Chairman of the Bolton meeting of the Sanitary Institute was Douglas Galton, cousin of the rising scientist, Francis, who had coined the term "eugenics" five years earlier. The paper Richardson delivered at this meeting, "Storage of Life as a Sanitary Study," overtly demonstrated how the sanitary debate remained vital after the advent of germ theory; here, Richardson calls the failure to breed human beings in the same way we breed horses and sheep "bad sanitation," adding that because "overpopulation is everywhere producing cripples, our job as sanitarians has now extended to this problem."[19]

> Unless parentage be sound, it is clear, from what has already been said, that long storage of life in an offspring will certainly fail. . . . The question is a sanitary one in the strictest sense of the word, and no argument of a sentimental kind, indicating acknowledged difficulties, ought for a moment to stand in our way. (499)

The interest in proper "mating" as a cornerstone of the new sanitation is clearly inspired by both mid-Victorian utilitarianism and late-Victorian statistical science; by the end of the century, disciples of prevention were not so much interested in wholesale perfectibility, as they were in proportion, averages, and the delicate balance of quality and quantity. Richardson's ideas about the "storage of life," for example, were based on a less than convincing statistical calculation he used to determine the average age of death within a family over several generations, the "life storage" number representing that average. Professor F. de Chaumont similarly used statistical discourse to express anxieties about Britain's imperial power: "If a people's average standard of vitality be lowered," he reasoned at the 1886 York conference of the Sanitary Institute, "then people will assuredly be handicapped in the race of nations by as much as that standard has been lessened."[20] Such dubious statistical thinking may have asked British citizens to forgo sentimental reasons for marriage and to replace the affective model of human reproduction with a clinical method of breeding, but it also imposed a familiar moral narrative upon the newly chaotic science of disease, allowing participants to imagine they were eliminating illness, death, and deformity by controlling heredity itself. "Eugenic love" was also patriotic: "it was the politics of the state mapped onto bodies," Angelique Richardson explains, "the replacement of romance with the rational selection of a reproductive partner in order to better serve the state through breeding."[21] The vagueness and multiplicity of developing germ theories in the late nineteenth century made its lessons rather easy to adapt and appropriate: the microbe simply extended its menacing authority from the dirty home to the degenerate body, often leaving intact the entrenched ideological location of disease within a working-class fever nest. After all, overpopulation and inauspicious breeding were largely blamed on the working classes, and while sterilization would "happily" occur in the natural course of many badly bred families, doctors like J. Russell Reynolds were committed to a concept of sanitation that would help nature function more efficiently.

> There exists in man the power to modify the race to which he belongs; and acting up to his highest light, in all the paths of knowledge to use his art to diminish or destroy that which has within it, at its beginning, the seeds of its own inherent decay, being assured that if he does his work well, nature will internally perform the rest.[22]

While many things are striking about Reynolds's writing, the image of the seeds of decay stands out in particular. This organic, natural, familiar image of germination is common to explanations of germ theory that explain microorganisms as various "seeds" of disease ever-present in air and water, ready to invade and infect susceptible bodies and families.[23] As Tomes explains, after the isolation of anthrax "seeds" in soil samples in the early 1880s the Victorian association between dirt and disease germs actually intensified,[24] allowing both environmental degradation and biological decay to assume responsibility, often simultaneously, for epidemics and physical deformities.

Even Richardson, an ardent opponent of germ theory, insisted that the next generation of sanitary scrutiny should focus on what he called "the seed time of health," in an effort to purify the earliest life of the undeveloped human through the work of the new hygiene: "the new school of sanitarians will take up a new sanitation . . . it involves the problem of the fashioning of the child from the first moment it begins to feed on the universe, by its eyes, its ears, its touch, its taste, its smell."[25] This conscious adaptation to biological science in the discourse of old-fashioned sanitarians like Richardson clearly indicates that germ theory didn't suddenly dethrone miasmatic theories of disease in the last decades of the nineteenth century; on the contrary, germ theory was appropriated by the new school of sanitarians who increasingly believed health and hygiene could penetrate and cleanse the earliest of human environments.

Before I leave Richardson's problem of "fashioning the child" too far behind in this chapter, I want to recall Eagleton's assertion that a sound political regime is one where "subjects conduct themselves gracefully," and social harmony is everywhere shaped through the receptivity of our senses to conduct, to virtue, to beauty:

> What matters is not in the first place art, but this process of refashioning the human subject from the inside, informing its subtlest affections and bodily responses with this law which is not law. It would thus ideally be inconceivable for the subject to violate the injunctions of power as it would be to find a putrid odor enchanting. The understanding knows well enough that we live in conformity to impersonal laws; but in the aesthetic it is as though we can forget about all that—as though it is we who freely fashion the laws to which we subject ourselves.[26]

What is so important about Eagleton's words to *The Sanitary Arts* is that they underscore the close relationship between an intellectual history of the aesthetic as a tool of cultural hegemony and the subtle exploitation of sense perception as the foundation for taste and, therefore, class. From the earliest identifications of fever nests in the urban environment to suspicions that certain bodies were degraded and diseased, sanitarians depended upon the ability of (primarily) the middle-classes to become "*all* eyes": to recognize and be repulsed by mud on streets, in homes, and on bodies, to be sure, but also bad smells, disharmonious shapes, unbalanced limbs, undeveloped muscles.

As we know from Bourdieu, sensory reactions to ugliness seem natural and seem instinctive, but they are actually social and economic distinctions at the very moment of their successful incorporation and reproduction. This version of the aesthetic as cultural agent is especially powerful and persuasive because it allows us to ignore the reality of harsh social relations and economic injustice, providing us instead with an alternative moral narrative, one where the beautiful, harmonious society is more important than the grievances of individuals or even classes of individuals. Statistics organize quantities, qualities, probabilities, averages, but the aesthetic appeals to the conscience, to the senses, to the virtuous necessity for beauty in all aspects of human existence. We are all working toward the "realization of man" as John Simon explained in 1890, "and when sanitary reformers appeal to the conscience of modern civilisation against the mere quantitative waste of human life, their deeper protest is against the heedless extinction of those high and beautiful possibilities of being, against the wanton interception of such powers for good, against the cruel smothering of such capacities for happiness."[27]

"Health is more than mere existence," agreed surgeon C. J. Bond in a collection of essays on the construction of "The Great State" edited by H. G. Wells; health signifies an ability to respond to beauty through all of the body's senses and to shape for oneself a more enlightened, more self-aware existence. "This is no merely modern view," Bond added:

> The citizens of Athens in her best days conceived of the true, the healthy life, as a harmonious development of mental and bodily powers, and as a true adjustment of the man to his environment. Self-realisation meant to the Greek the union of a virtuous soul in a beautiful body, and this was the outcome of the ordered . . . natural faculties under the control of a well-balanced mind.[28]

Like Matthew Arnold, Bond and many other late-Victorian socialists believed that the "sweetness and light" of the Hellenic period provided the best model for social perfectibility, and it was clear that the aesthetic harmony represented by perfect Culture had its roots in much older ideals; we all become artists, as Havelock Ellis argued, when we believe with Lord Shaftesbury that good behavior and social harmony constitute art.[29]

In this context, it is crucial to remember that Richardson's "Seed-Time of Health" was not only to be interpreted as the earliest stage of individual human life, it was also designed to reference that earliest and most perfect stage of human civilization to date— Hellenism. At the opening of that address, he asks his audience to imagine the ancient Greek people and their society in order to conjure an image of utopia that was realized in the past and can therefore be created in the future:

> If these people could be seen in their fair stature and build of body, draped in their loose garments, the eye, like the ear, would be vanquished. Such incomparable beauty! Should a sculptor want a model for a work he would leave for all time, he would find it in them; should a painter want a face for his perfected art, he would find it in them; should a physician want a text for a discourse on the types of health and sanity, he would find it in those types of beauty.[30]

While even the most sensitive human subject couldn't see a microorganism, or depend on his sense of smell to detect the presence of germs, he could still react to disease by reacting to dysgenic types and still recognize health by responding to beauty. And just as sanitary physicians like Grant Allen's Dr. Rhoda Gale were needed to provide concerned citizens with textual descriptions of pasty faces and undeveloped calves, artists must continue to train the "naturally" sensitive to recognize not only undegraded environments but uncompromised forms. Indeed, when social harmony relies so completely on taste as a constitutive mechanism, the role of not only the artist, but the connoisseur, the aesthete, the collector, and the curator become powerful pedagogical positions, common to texts that grapple, often triumphantly, with the problem of harsh social relations. As the textual representative of human sensitivity to beauty, to ugliness, to art and to dirt, the figure of the aesthetic practitioner in so much nineteenth-century literature continues to map the path to perfectibility, negotiating for the middle-class reader an artistic appreciation that kept the political order intact even after the chaos and confusion of germ theory.

III. From the Marriage Plot to *The Mating of Lydia*

Let me begin my discussion of Mrs. Humphry (Mary) Ward's *The Mating of Lydia* with some sanitary boilerplate. As we enter the third volume of that novel, we are invited to contemplate the village of Mainstairs, a filthy, disease-ridden collection of slums on the estate of rich landowner, Mr. Edmund Melrose. Ward writes,

> Over the village rose the low shoulder of a grassy fell, its patches of golden fern glistening under the October sunshine; great sycamores, with their

rounded masses of leaf, hung above the dilapidated roofs . . . and the blue smoke that rose out of the chimneys, together with the few flowers that gleamed in the gardens, the picturesque irregularity of the houses and the general setting of the wood and distant mountain, made of the poisoned village "a subject," on which a wandering artist, who had set up his canvas at the corner of the road, was at that moment, indeed, hard at work. There might be death in those houses; but out of the beauty which sunshine strikes from a ruin, a man, honestly in search of a few pounds, was making what he could.[31]

My larger argument about *The Mating of Lydia* necessarily begins with the ideological labor undertaken by this passage. The dilapidated village, the wandering artist, and the subjection of poverty and working-class desperation to picturesque pleasure are stock ingredients of what I have been identifying as the sanitary narrative: in summary, a series of tropes that mobilize a social revulsion against Romantic aesthetic values in order to plot a version of sanitation reform that could also purify British art. As we have seen, the perversities of the picturesque function as a kind of cultural shorthand for aristocratic detachment and social injustice, and we know that the unwholesome aesthetic pleasure derived from the poisoned village is a kind of sanitary convention that the perambulations of the plot will eventually justify, or even require. For one thing, in *The Mating of Lydia*, Melrose's aesthetic pursuits are the direct cause of the Mainstairs tragedy: Melrose is an insatiable art collector and famous connoisseur, a character who explicitly uses every shred of his income to expand, often illegally, his collection of European art treasures at the expense of his diseased and starving tenants. In the first chapter, which is set "thirty years ago," he imports, as well, a young Italian wife who is the daughter of his dealer in Italian antiquities, a wife who is forced to live in a kind of parallel poverty and isolation at the dilapidated Threlfall Tower estate, where beautiful art and artifacts are stored in all the rooms, but never cataloged, never even unboxed.

Eventually Netta Melrose rebels, stealing a valuable Hermes bronze from among her husband's treasures, and escaping back to Italy with their daughter, Felicia. The remainder of the novel takes place twenty years later, when penniless Netta returns with her child to claim financial assistance from her even more prosperous, even more idiosyncratic estranged husband. The drama of their reappearance is played out against renewed epidemics of diphtheria and scarlet fever at Mainstairs, and Melrose's appointment of fellow antiquarian and minor collector, young Claude Faversham, as his new estate agent and heir apparent. While the eponymous Lydia doesn't enter the novel for several chapters, when she does it is important that she is a landscape painter and a New Woman, and that her potential marriage or mating will be a choice between suitor Faversham, whose perverse aesthetic preferences promise to replicate Melrose's, and Lord Tatham, a rival landowner without aesthetic understanding, who is nevertheless a model paternalist and sanitary overachiever.

Despite the convoluted narrative timeline that first sets us back a generation and then fast-forwards us to a historical moment right at the turn of the century, all of the standard features of mid-Victorian sanitary fiction are in place in *The Mating of Lydia;* indeed, this 1913 novel will eventually use the marriage plot as a vehicle to banish environmental degradation, and to inspire a philosophical conversion to a sanitized, socialized aesthetic. We could easily see this novel as an isolated throw-back to an earlier scientific moment; a sign of Mary Ward's age and old-fashioned devotion to both the social reforms of the mid-Victorian period, and her Uncle Matthew Arnold's formidable commitment to "sweetness and light." But it seems to me that this view prematurely shoehorns *The Mating of Lydia* into an ahistorical sanitary narrative, ignoring Ward's complex and even overdetermined interest in disease etiology and the aesthetic reconciliation marked here by mating rather than marriage, careful breeding rather than injudicious reproduction. The picturesque remains problematic in fiction well beyond its mid-Victorian moment because picturesque revulsion continues to mobilize the discourse of hygiene as an answer to the problem of working-class degradation and degeneration well into the twentieth century. Recognizing the continuity between mid-Victorian sanitary fiction and early-twentieth-century novels like *The Mating of Lydia* may reveal the persistence of certain plots and perversities in British fiction, but it may also expose the evolution of sanitary philosophy as it emerged from its environmental phase and entered upon a biological phase that was much more invested in the prevention of individual illnesses, heredity deformities, and intellectual weaknesses. The repudiation of the picturesque is a crucial ideological linchpin between sanitary and proto-eugenic thinking, I would argue, a trope that captures clearly an abiding effort to naturalize a set of specific social, political and economic problems as an aesthetic controversy.

As we know, by 1913, or at least by 1900, when *The Mating* is probably set, environmental reform had unevenly run its course as a vehicle of social perfectibility. Ward meshes many suspicions about the long-term efficacy of sanitation into the plot of *The Mating of Lydia,* casting the miserable village of Mainstairs as a throwback to unenlightened, insanitary times, and an embarrassment to neighboring landlords who instituted their own reforms in the previous century, and who now fear that Melrose's scandalous treatment of his tenants "brings disgrace on the whole show" (125). Asserting the rights of property, individualism, and the Englishman's liberal prerogative to pursue his own pleasure without regard to social consequence, Melrose defies the Sanitary Inspectors when they attempt to pressure reforms on Mainstairs, decrying the destructive Socialism that constructs hospitals, free libraries, and model cottages for the undeserving Proletariat out of the wealth of the more privileged classes. In fact, personal power and property are the defining features of Melrose's aesthetic identity: as he explains to an increasingly dubious Faversham, his collection of art is the pursuit of a radically private form of pleasure, an outgrowth, in fact, of the gaming habits of his youth. "In my view the object of everybody should be to live as acutely as possible—to get as many sensations, as many pleasant reactions as possible, out of the day" (276).

In this sense, the poisoned village is an ideological touchstone that points backward to mid-Victorian sanitation reform and simultaneously to its Modernist failure: the picturesque effects of decay and death in Mainstairs are an anachronistic byproduct of Melrose's much more contemporary participation in the principles of aestheticism, an investment in "art for art' sake" that ensures the purest of all possible gazes. Boxed up in a private house, Melrose's treasures are radically decontextualized and dehistoricized; atomized and unseen, they are the essence of private property and individual pleasure. To unbox and catalog these art treasures, as Faversham would like to do, would represent the contamination of context, of public narrative, and of civic responsibility. Instead, Melrose woos Faversham with the tactile pleasures of private aesthetic experiences, coming to Faversham's bedside while the beautiful boy recuperates from a bicycling accident, bringing him rare gems and antiquities to languidly stroke and turn over while the collector tells stories of his aesthetic exploits.

Indeed, in protracted defiance of its own title, the primary seduction in *The Mating of Lydia* seems to be the one undertaken by Melrose of Claude: each beautiful object revealed to the younger connoisseur tempts him to repress his lingering conscience and burgeoning love for Lydia and stay within the secluded sensations of Threlfall Tower. It also evinces a sterile form of taste that is deeply at odds with the aesthetic articulated by Shaftesbury and Kant; as Allison Pease has argued, traditional aesthetic enjoyment is deeply personal, but it also establishes a baseline theory of the beautiful that is communal, and socially constitutive.[32] Purely personal gratification is merely the foundation of the "agreeable" in Kantian philosophy, and this private form of consumption, Pease explains, is pornographic rather than aesthetic (20). Claude is also perversely attracted to Melrose's power and Nietzschean assertions of radical autonomy and liberty; when Lydia criticizes his fealty to

Melrose, Claude admits "his morality is abnormal, but his will and brain are superb" (406). Furthermore, Melrose pays Faversham an exorbitant amount of money—3000 pounds per year—to "manage" his estates, and Claude, at thirty, has determined not to marry until he has amassed enough capital to live easily, even well. Another complication to the traditional marriage plot presents itself when Lydia decides that she herself will never marry; in accordance with the New Woman spirit of equality and independence, Lydia wants above all things platonic friendships with men. Lydia also struggles, like Claude, with painterly pornographic pleasures that could finally eclipse her lingering social responsibility and civic consciousness: "she was, before everything, one of those persons who thrill under the appeal of beauty to such a degree that often threatens or suspends practical energy. Save for conscience in her, she could have lived from day to day just for the moments of delight, the changes in light and shade, in color and form, that this beautiful world continually presents to senses as keen as hers" (59).

Lydia's keen enjoyment of her own highly developed sensations, her love of the effects of shifting lights on color and form, threatens to import all the past perversities of the picturesque under the new reign of Impressionism. In fact, Lydia is much influenced here by the contemporary painter Delorme, who periodically visits the Tatham homestead of Duddon Castle and proclaims himself "Whistler's lawful and only successor. Pattern and harmony possessed him; finish was only made for fools, and the story-teller in art was an unclean thing" (246). This repudiation of Ruskinian realism temporarily reverses the pollution anxiety of aesthetic discourse: haziness, mistiness, and the blurred effects of distance repress the unclean story in favor of the pure gaze. Delorme does little actual painting in the novel, but he visits Duddon frequently enough to represent, along with Melrose, the unraveling of traditional aesthetic philosophy, especially the coupling of morality and beauty that once allowed the mechanism of social cleanliness to promise human perfectibility and artistic harmony. "'There is no relation whatever between art and morality,' Delorme smoked pugnaciously, 'The greater the artist, generally speaking, the worse the man'" (247). Cleanliness, for the Impressionist, has other associations, and many of them demonstrate that the aesthetic perspective on social perfectibility is now a racial rather than a sanitary narrative. Contemplating a visiting Tatham cousin, Delorme "perceived in him the sure signs of a decadence which was rapidly drawing the English aristocratic class into the limbo of things that were," and takes the opportunity to languidly suggest that a marriage between the beautiful, robust and healthy Lydia and the less impressive heir Lord Harry will be just the thing to energize the Tatham bloodline. Defensively, Cousin Tatham replies the family's blood is pure: "You'd find if you looked into it that we descended very straight. There's been no carelessness." To which Delorme responds, "Carelessness, as you call it, is the only hope for a family nowadays. A strong blood—that's what you want—a blood that will stand this modern life—and you'll never get it by mating in and in" (225).

It seems important that this dysgenic analysis is the special purview of the modern painter in *The Mating of Lydia,* important too that this avatar for Whistler is here given his own embodied version of Ruskin to fully flesh out the shift that has taken place in aesthetic philosophy. Cyril Boden is a fellow of All Souls, an advanced radical and art critic who is "quaintly Ruskinian in matters of art, believing that all art should appeal to ethical or poetical emotion" (246). Boden and Delorme nakedly generate all of the animus of Ruskin v. Whistler in their arguments about art, morality, and civic responsibility; as Delorme sneeringly summarizes his rival, "Boden admires a painter because he is a good man and pays his washing bills . . . his very colors are virtues and his pictures must be masterpieces because he subscribes to the Dogs' Home or doesn't beat his wife" (246). When Boden insists, moreover, that all great painters have felt emotional connections to the "multitude," Delorme replies that the "multitude is a brute beast" (248). The stigmatizing and taxing of wealth by the Socialists is, for the great painter, another violation of natural selection because he believes with Melrose that democracy is also dysgenic: "Wealth is only materialized intelligence!" he thunders at the quaint Ruskinian, while the activist is busy ferreting out the Sanitary Authorities to make a complaint about the "horrible insanitary hole" he passed on his walk that morning.

As we might expect, Boden makes the most noise about Mainstairs in *The Mating of Lydia,* visiting the village repeatedly to learn the individual, unclean stories of the inhabitants, and what he learns does seem to confirm that there is something of a population crisis among the working classes, who are sorting out their own principles of natural selection without regard to the perceived racial needs of England. Like *Middlemarch, The Mating of Lydia* is set in the midst of an agricultural depression that has sent the strongest and ablest inhabitants of Mainstairs to "great Canadian spaces beyond the Western seas" (57). Left behind are the women, the sick, the young, the intemperate, and the feeble; while widespread "blood poisoning" after childbirth has killed off many women already "weakened by the long effects of filthy conditions," at least thirty children have died in the past year, and a "paralysis" that sets in after diphtheria is widespread among the surviving children (325). The deeply entrenched ideology of the fever nest here appears intact well after the development of germ theory, but a new despair about physical degeneracy and biological decline accompanies the sanitary narrative. While the novel keeps some distance between the reader and most of the individual working-class bodies, Boden frequently manages to bring one particular poor family under the reader's gaze. John Brand inherited a small farm from his father, but his "dull brain" has no management sense; he drinks, he gambles, and he spends himself into a debt that exposes him to Melrose, who, because of a small legal dispute, surreptitiously pressures the bank to foreclose on the farmer. Brand has a similarly dim wife and two sons, but the elder, stronger, more intelligent sibling has left for Quebec, leaving only Will Brand to help support the declining fortunes of his parents. Will is a strangely clumsy boy who, at twenty, is generally regarded as "queer" and "feeble-witted," best known in the neighborhood for putting on white sheets and frightening young lovers in the gloaming.

Only his parents know that Will is also capable of fits of rage, a pertinent aspect of his dysgenic profile when it comes to the resolution of Ward's somewhat convoluted plot. Late in the novel, Melrose is murdered in his own art gallery, shot in the chest after a confrontation with Claude, who has finally broken off their arrangement for the sake of Lydia. Claude suspects there was somebody else in the gallery during their argument because he senses movement behind a new Nattier portrait from Paris, a portrait that is subsequently found face-down on the ground next to Melrose's corpse. It is fitting that the affected and artificial work of Louis XV's court painter provides a decorous disguise for the working-class degenerate with a gun; also fitting that the exposure of Will Brand as the murderer is only accomplished by Cyril Boden, who knows each family in Mainstairs personally, and who finds out that the boy hated Melrose and ran off after his death. The villagers warn Boden that Will may never be caught: the strange, intellectually stunted boy has unusually sharp survival skills, as if the decline in human characteristics in the feeble working classes has yielded compensatory animal instincts. Boden reports that Will knows to avoid the railroad and stick to the fells, and that the villagers "tell the most extraordinary tales of his knowledge of the mountains—especially in the snow and wild weather. They say that shepherds who have lost sheep constantly go to him for help" (468). When Will finally appears to Boden after five winter months on his own in the mountains, he is a

> tottering and ghastly figure. Distress—mortal fatigue—breathed from the haggard emaciation of face and limbs. Round the shoulders was folded a sack, from which the dregs of some red dipping mixture it had once

contained had dripped over the youth's chest and legs, his tattered clothes and broken boots, in streams of what, to Boden's startled eyes, looked like blood. (480–81)

Hunted by human civilization and animalized by his brutal environment, Will speaks to Boden long enough to confess to the murder before jumping from a cliff into the foaming river below. Interestingly, however, when the jury inspects the obviously injured corpse at the inquest, what they see is a body "botched by Nature in the flesh" (484), confirming the novel's repeated assumption that Melrose's environmental crime against Mainstairs has been biologically altering and deforming its inhabitants. Mainstairs has always seemed "bloodstained" and a place of outright "murder" to Claude, but he likewise identifies Melrose's crime as a generational unmaking of the human condition:

Had Melrose, out of his immense income, spent a couple of thousand pounds a year on the village at any time during the preceding years, a score of death would have been saved, and the physical degeneracy of a whole population would have been prevented. (327)

While the picturesque village in *The Mating of Lydia* may be an inscription of Ward's scientific confusion or even an ideological red herring, it might also be the springboard for a new sanitary narrative that requires biological cleanliness to underwrite the next stage of social perfectibility. On the other hand, when it comes to the question of judicious mating in Ward's novel, the answer is provided not by the modern Mr. Delorme, but by the anachronistic Mr. Boden. Boden has perpetually mourned the greedy modern preoccupation with wealth that prevents men like Claude Faversham from wanting to marry; indeed, both Claude and Lydia are segments of the British population that so-called "positive eugenicists" believed should be encouraged to mate and breed in racially invigorating numbers. Delorme's favored aristocratic bachelor, Lord Tatham, is consigned, somewhat punitively it seems, to a marriage with Melrose's dispossessed daughter, a girl of twenty-two who looks sixteen because her malnourished body is a symbolic inscription of her father's paternalist failures, the deformity of an entire community legible in her small frame and unusually large head. Disenchanted with fortune and with Melrose's deadly aesthetic, Claude reinstates Felicia's rightful inheritance, asking only to retain residency at Threlfall Tower, and permission to enact a form of sanitation that will eradicate the perversities of the pornographic gaze. His greatest pleasure since Melrose's death has been the unboxing and the cataloging of the art treasures, discovering in each hidden archive the exquisite work of the living human mind reaching out "through the centuries" to touch the lives of future generations (494). If dirt is matter out of place, Claude's catalog will be, in itself, cleansing; but his proposal to both Lydia and the new Lord and Lady Tatham is to return the story to Melrose's art, to create a public record and context for aesthetic experience in the new century.

> What would she think, he asked her, of a great Museum for the north—a center for students—none of your brick and iron monstrosities, rising amid slums, but a beautiful house showing its beautiful possessions to all who came; and set amid the streams and hills? And in one wing of it, perhaps curator's rooms—where Lydia, the dear lover of nature and art, might reign and work—fitly housed? (494).

Fortunately, Lydia has undergone her own aesthetic transformation by the end of the novel. Disillusioned with Delorme, she finds that helping Boden minister to the poor children in Mainstairs has deprived her of the pure gaze: "she, who had plumed herself on the poised mind, the mastered senses," can no longer lose herself in beauty, and she abandons her maiden life with little reluctance to marry Claude and help him curate and convert the myopic pleasures of aestheticism back into a space of social harmony and economic reconciliation, "a House Beautiful, indeed, for the whole north of England" (504).

Finally, the sanitary narrative is on familiar ground: deviant aesthetic philosophies are repudiated, and art is cleansed and revived within the public space of the museum. This enlightenment fantasy of social progress through cultural reform might be the most anachronistic aspect of *The Mating of Lydia*, underscoring Ward's fundamental conservatism and her unwillingness, finally, to do anything more in her novel than consolidate vast wealth in the hands of a liberal, through dubiously fertile, aristocratic couple. But our Ruskinian hero, Mr. Boden, appears to reject the passive aesthetic program of social improvement designed by Claude Faversham; in the closing passage of the novel, Boden's eyes "kindle" when he thinks of the power that could be harnessed by Claude and Lydia in order to truly "turn the ground," "restore the waste places," and "enrich" England's garden. "Curator!—stuff! If he won't own that estate, make him govern it, and play the man! Disinterested power!—with such a wife and such a friend? Could a man ask better of the gods! Now is your moment. Rural England turns to you, its natural leaders, to shape it afresh! Shirk—refuse—at your peril!" (512). The agricultural metaphors and the discourse of returning fertility make of Claude and Lydia a new middle-class resource for political power, their aesthetic philosophy of public access and sympathy working to create a healthier and more harmonious society. The smooth, graceful functioning of a beautiful culture may no longer be a matter of blood, of class, and the accidental privileges of birth, but it is a matter of conscious, careful and "natural" breeding.

CHAPTER 6

Intensive Culture

John Ruskin, Sarah Grand, and the Aesthetics of Eugenics

> Our first duty then, is not to mend the arts—you cannot mend a cripple. But it is rather to mend the parents who bring forth this cripple—to mend Life itself, and above all Man.
>
> —Anthony Mario Ludovici, *Nietzsche and Art* (1912)

I. Eugenealogies

The previous chapters of *The Sanitary Arts* have worked to undo a series of standard narratives about aesthetic revolutions and scientific discoveries, demonstrating, above all, the ideological complexity and interdisciplinary context of such seemingly straightforward epistemologies. This sixth chapter begins, accordingly, with a conventional story that should already be on shaky ground, given the late-Victorian shift in sanitary attention from the environmental to the biological, from places to people as the epicenter of social cleanliness and aesthetic perfectibility. The standard narrative for the rise of eugenic theories in nineteenth-century England begins, predictably enough, with Sir Francis Galton, and in short goes something like this. In the 1870s, Galton developed a methodology he termed the science of biometrics, which eventually spawned the field of statistics, which, in turn, became a mechanism for measuring and mapping the basic principles of human heredity. In 1883, Galton coined the term eugenics in his book, *Inquiries into Human Faculty and Its Development*, as a concise referent for the "science of improving stock" though both "judicious mating" and the increased breeding of the most "suitable races and strains of blood."[1] Galton's work inspired not only Karl Pearson's statistical mathematics, but Havelock Ellis's sexology, Edward

Carpenter's theories of civilization, the War Office's pursuit of imperial and bureaucratic "efficiency." The Fabian Society, and, most uncomfortably, the late-Victorian feminist purity campaigns and novels like the two by Sarah Grand I will discuss here: *Adnam's Orchard* (1912) and *The Winged Victory* (1916).

This chapter does not intend to deny this distilled and depressingly dystopic narrative. The specter of Sir Francis Galton as the father of a eugenic reform movement that continued to inspire theories, philosophies and novels right up until the second world war (and even beyond) provides a pseudo-scientific teleology with an appropriately mad scientist; a necessary Dr. Frankenstein for another story of medical depravity and human improvement. But within late-nineteenth and early-twentieth-century eugenic discourse itself, I have found an interesting and common tendency to repress the scientist in favor of a more gracious and genial figure, and in doing so to deny the inhumanity and, indeed, the very ugliness of statistical thinking. In Karl Pearson's 1891 *The Grammar of Science,* for example, we find that eugenic methodology depends not on statistical mathematics, but on aesthetic judgment. "All great scientists," he insists, "have, in a certain sense, been great artists; the man with no imagination may collect facts, but he cannot make great discoveries."[2] Moreover, because "our aesthetic judgment demands harmony between the representation and the represented . . . science is more artistic than modern art" (17). Harmony, as we have seen in the previous chapter, was endemic to the language of preventive medicine as it emerged from mid-Victorian sanitation reform, and referenced a scientific method that understood human perfectibility to be an aesthetic project. As early as 1876, B. W. Richardson was urging sanitarians to extend their goals of preventive medicine into the province of the "unborn," promising that his coming city of Hygeia would be populated by a new order of human beings sculpted, in effect, by the Art of scientific progress and sanitary perfection. Just as "in the highest development of the fine arts the sculptor and painter place before us the finest imaginative types of strength, grace and beauty, so the silent artist, civilization, approaches nearer and nearer to perfection, and by evolution of form and mind develops what is practically a new order of physical and mental build."[3]

What is so striking about eugenic discourse as it emerges from the sanitary reform movement is that it invents itself through aesthetic discourse, recasting the suspicious scientist as a judicious artist, and translating the project of racial regeneration into an aesthetic cultivation thoroughly in keeping with natural selection and the survival of the fittest. The German doctor Heinrich Lehmann had dubbed these aesthetic practitioners "hygienic physicians," and had argued that their intervention was necessary to revive modern art by allowing a harmonious (rather than "dysaemic") conception of the world to shape the future of mankind.[4] "Ugly men are not influenced by beauty," he explained, in the 1901 translation of his book *Natural Hygiene*, effectively dismissing environmental reform as an inadequate instrument of aesthetic improvement.[5] Beauty is once again the disinterested goal of the new cleanliness campaigns at the turn of the century, and even when eugenicists begin suggesting more aggressive approaches to race culture than sewerage and slum removal, they are advocating social warfare in the decorous guise of aesthetic perfectibility. "One might wear any passion out of a family by culture, as skilful gardeners blot a color out of a tulip that hurts its beauty," Havelock Ellis explains in his 1921 tract *Eugenics Made Plain*. "We are only today beginning to accept seriously the great principle they embody, and to apply it earnestly for the heightening of man's physical and spiritual beauty."[6]

Of course, one could look outside the sanitation reform movement to find aesthetics and science so paired, and one could also look farther back in Victorian intellectual history for an argument that Science was really Art in disguise. Even before germ theory turned sanitary attention from the environmental to the biological, Herbert Spencer's famous synthetic philosophy was already paving the way for science to be understood as the key to aesthetic progress and human perfectibility: in his 1860 *Education: Intellectual, Moral, Physical* he cited the Pre-Raphaelite painters as obvious evidence that the highest art of every kind is founded on scientific knowledge.[7] But by the end of the century, in the hands of racialists and statisticians, Spencer's positivist synthesis of science and art enabled eugenics to emerge as an aesthetic imperative rather than a scientific experiment; a way to ameliorate ugliness and impose harmony on degenerate bodies, degenerate families, degenerate nations. Once it was retrofitted as aesthetic philosophy, moreover, eugenics required a story of origins that began not with science but with beauty, bypassing Sir Francis Galton, Benjamin Ward Richardson and even Herbert Spencer, in order to espouse a parentage that began instead with John Ruskin. In a wide variety of eugenic materials published at the turn of the century, Ruskin is invoked as both totem and touchstone, authorizing a brand of racialism that looks like liberal enlightenment and civic virtue.

Dr. Caleb Saleeby's 1909 *Parenthood and Race Culture*, for instance, opens by dismissing the unfortunate idea that eugenics is actually a subset of mathematics; for Saleeby, eugenics is both a science and a religion based on the laws of life, and as a religion it "proposes to rebuild the living foundations of Empire. To this end," Saleeby writes, we shall preach a new imperialism, warning England to beware lest her veins become choked with yellow dirt, and demanding over all her legislative chambers there be carved the golden words, "'there is no Wealth but Life'"[8] (33). While Ruskin's 1862 *Unto This Last* provides the motto for racial hygiene Ruskin's other writings provide the methods, and Saleeby quotes liberally from the economic texts of his new sanitary Moses, emphasizing most particularly those passages from the 1867 *Time and Tide* that focus on environmental reforms, and, yes, on a kind of social conditioning that would improve the stock of the British nation. Eugenics "finds abundant warrant and support in Ruskin's own wonderful writings," effuses Saleeby, and some of the sentences,

> require to be read and remembered by the majority of our present advisers. He says . . . "Make your nations consist of knaves, and as Emerson said long ago, it is but the case of any other vermin—the more the worse. . . . The French and British public may and will, with many other publics, be at last brought . . . to see farther that a nation's real strength and happiness do not depend upon properties and territories, nor on machinery for their defence, but on their getting such territory as they *have,* well-filled with none but respectable persons, which is a way of infinitely enlarging one's territory, feasible to every potentate." (109–10)

Just as eugenics becomes a new imperial strategy for Saleeby, Ruskin becomes indispensable reading for rising genetic imperialists, and Saleeby closes his text by recommending not just *Time and Tide* and *Unto This Last,* but *Munera Pulveris* (1872) as "some of the most forcible and wisest things to be written on race-culture, and its absolutely fundamental relation to morality, patriotism, and true economics" (320).

Robert Reid Rentoul uses *Unto This Last* similarly in his sensationally titled *Race Culture or Race Suicide? A Plea for the Unborn* (1906), deploying "There is no wealth but life" as a seemingly obvious epigraph to a chapter called "Some Causes of National Deterioration and Degeneracy: The Use of Abortion Drugs, Etc." Rentoul is also happy to extend Ruskin's quotation for another line, concluding with the utilitarian refinement to Ruskin's poetical redefinition of wealth as life: "The country is the richest which nourishes the greatest number of noble and happy human beings."[9] Throughout his text, Rentoul employs a set of architectural metaphors that might aim to provide an appropriate rhetorical home for Ruskin's dislodged eugenic sentiments. Children begotten by the diseased, by idiots, imbeciles or epileptics, by the insane and by the deformed, have been "jerry built" by unlicensed and unregulated designers, parents too degenerate and "backward" to be entrusted with the sacred duties of race culture: "As Empire builders," Rentoul explains, "they are decidedly jerry" (29). A few chapters later, Rentoul turns again to Ruskin for a vivid illustration of race culture at its strongest and most promising (if not its most English), citing Ruskin's retelling of the ancient story of the barbaric Queen who was reproved by another Queen for her lack of jewelry. "She replied by sending for her seven strong sons, manly in health and grace, and presented them with the short but immortal speech—These are *my* jewels" (65).

Somehow, the citation of "There is no Wealth but Life" became a proto-col for eugenic writers in the early twentieth century, providing an unim-peachable epigraph for chapters on eugenic marriage and the limitation of offspring in books like Anna Mary Galbraith's 1920 *The Family and the New Democracy: A Study in Social Hygiene*. It also surfaces as a token of shared philosophy for eugenic writers who casually use the phrase to authorize a form of race culture that seems jarringly disconnected from Ruskin's Vic-torian contexts. In "The Science and Practice of Eugenics; or Race Culture" (1912), Dr. Meyer Solomon speaks of fostering and treasuring the best types of humanity, and passing a brighter light on to future generations: "Since we believe with Ruskin that 'there is no wealth but life' . . . no stone should be left unturned to arrive at the means of producing the best type of men and women, and of purifying, bettering, and advancing the race."[10] Again, in *The Mothercraft Manual* (1922), Mary Lillian Read imagines a similar audience of devout racial Ruskinites when she happily heralds the dawn of a eugenic moment where the elimination of all causes of criminality and imbecility is finally possible: "'There is no Wealth but Life,' we are realizing with Ruskin."[11]

But as ubiquitous as Ruskin's famous phrase becomes in early-twentieth-century eugenic discourse, it is also the case that Ruskin texts in general are perpetually at the service of eugenic writers. Other lines from *Unto This Last* are also popular, as Scott Nearing demonstrates in *The Super Race: An Ameri-can Problem* (1912) when he heralds the coming Nietzschean superhero with Ruskin's assurance that "there is as yet no ascertained limit to the nobleness of person and mind which the human creature may attain."[12] But Nearing also harnesses *Time and Tide* to his racial argument, using Ruskin to summarize the self-evident value of what he terms "Positive Eugenics": "As Mr. Ruskin so well observes—'It is a matter of no final concern, to any parent, whether he shall have two children or four; but matter of quite final concern whether those he has shall or shall not deserve to be hanged'" (33). Even *The Stones of Venice* resounds with eugenic wisdom for advocates of race culture in the early decades of the twentieth century, providing a slogany advertisement in a volume of *The Bookman* magazine for Helen Baker's forthcoming *Race Improvement, or Eugenics* (1912): "Eugenics means an answer to a cry that

Ruskin heard, "rising from all our cities . . . that we manufacture everything there except men."[13]

Certainly Ruskin had turned a disciplinary corner when the words and works that most interest these eugenicists were composed. Generically speaking, *Unto This Last, Time and Tide* and *Munera Pulveris* are works of political economy rather than art criticism, and as such do not necessarily signal a definitively aesthetic agenda within eugenic writing. But when these texts were written, in the 1860s and 1870s, Ruskin's status as an aesthetic authority had not fundamentally changed, and I would argue that the principles often identified as eugenic advocacy in his economic writings are actually aesthetic principles adapted for political use. I argued in the first chapter of *The Sanitary Arts* that Ruskin's unique participation in mid-Victorian sanitation reform helped to transform cleanliness into an aesthetic value; I am arguing in this last chapter that as the sanitation reform movement gradually evolved into the eugenics movement, aesthetic philosophy remained an endemic and exploited component of the discourse of hygiene. As we know, Saleeby, Rentoul or any other eugenicist could just have easily turned to Ruskin's aesthetic writings for an impassioned argument about promoting physical health and cleanliness in the working classes; human health and vitality was, for Ruskin, a fundamental prerequisite for the return of beauty and art to England. "The Relation of Art to Use," was a lecture originally delivered at Oxford University in 1870, well before Galton coined the term "eugenics," but it certainly provides another kind of example of what passes for Ruskin's investment in race culture. In this lecture, which I've already cited in a much earlier context, Ruskin bemoans his ongoing inability to inspire environmental change in England, or to convince fellow artists and critics that aesthetic reform was vitally linked to personal and national cleanliness:

> You cannot have a landscape by Turner, without a country for him to paint; you cannot have a portrait by Titian without a man to be portrayed. I need not prove to you, I suppose, in these short terms; but in the outcome I can get no soul to believe that the beginning of art is getting our country clean and our people beautiful. I have been ten years trying to get this very plain certainty—I do not say believed—but even thought of, as anything but a monstrous proposition. To get your country clean, and your people lovely—I assure you, that is a necessary work of art to being with.[14]

To be perfectly clear, I am not arguing that Ruskin's despair about the environmental state of England in the 1870s constitutes the origins of eugenic thinking. But just as Ruskin's focus on clean landscapes and clean people as the necessary path to national aesthetic reform is an important manifestation of the broader Victorian cleanliness campaigns, the wanton appropriation of Ruskin by eugenic writers is also an appropriation of his aesthetic advocacy and reputation, an espousal that makes the curious aesthetic pretensions of Karl Pearson and Havelock Ellis intellectually legible. Indeed, the resuscitation of Ruskin as the unwitting father of eugenics seems inevitable if eugenics is understood as an outgrowth of a much more broadly defined hygiene movement that perpetually articulated itself as an aesthetic philosophy.

II. The Nietzschean Aesthetic

I began this chapter by suggesting that social scientists adopted Ruskin in order to disguise or to disarm the fundamental inhumanity of their eugenic project, but it is also the case that they may have been using Ruskin's moral authority to revive flagging public interest in hygiene as the path to both national and imperial perfectibility for Great Britain. For writers like George Shee, we will remember, the physical appearance of working-class bodies was a troubling material index of Britain's waning imperial power, and he also cited Ruskin to plead for more expansive sanitary initiatives like universal military training for boys; after all, Shee argued, in the language of our versatile Victorian reformer, wealth had no more accurate measure than in the "greatest number of happy and healthy men and women."[15] This kind of eugenic advocacy for physical education, like eugenic support for prenatal care, nutritional programs, and milk purification, was dubbed "positive" eugenics by writers like Caleb Saleeby, an obstetrician fundamentally concerned with the production of healthy British babies and children. Most eugenic writers at the turn of the century agreed that sanitation reforms of the mid-Victorian period had exacerbated the current problem of racial degeneration by interfering with natural selection and preserving a fundamentally unhealthy population of individuals for the breeding of an ever-declining British race. Saleeby's philosophy of "eugenic reconciliation," however, insisted that genetic modifications were only ethically possible *before* the conception of a child actually occurred, and thus any eugenic program must require the humanitarian care and preservation of all living children regardless of race or medical condition.[16] It is true, Saleeby admits, that "indiscriminate humanitarianism" has too long mistaken sentiment for morality, but an ethic of care, of compassion, and of love is perfectly compatible with a eugenic insistence that infirm individuals should not be allowed to propagate their infirmities (30).

On the other side of the spectrum, according to Saleeby, were a group of racialists who didn't even deserve eugenic nomenclature; these theorists believed the regeneration of the race necessitated the sacrifice of morality, and, indeed, the sacrifice of degenerate populations to the revitalized work of natural selection.

> On the other side of the eugenicists stand those whom we may for short call Nietzscheans. They see one-half of the truth of natural selection; they see that through struggle and internecine war, species have hitherto maintained themselves or ascended. They declare that all improvement of the environment, or at any rate all humanitarian effort, tends to abrogate the struggle for existence, and even, as is only too often true, to select unworth and let worth go to the wall. This school then declares that infant mortality is a blessing and charity an unmitigated curse. In short, that we must go back as quickly as possible to the order of the beast. (31)

Nietzsche, who declared morality irrelevant, even pernicious, who blamed racial deterioration on democracy, and who theorized that a dominating race of overmen could only arise from "terrible and violent beginnings," certainly severed what it meant to be human from what it meant to be humane, and put into circulation, at the end of the nineteenth century, a metaphysical justification of birth, blood, and the biological will to power.[17] Nietzsche's own admonitions and exhortations about breeding are, of course, never vulgarly associated with an outright doctrine of eugenics; Nietzsche despises both science and social science as reductionist schemes that contribute to the smallness of man by insisting on man's fragmentation rather than fully synthesized wholeness. But "Nietzschean" is still a particularly apt term for the casual regret expressed by Havelock Ellis, for example, when he notes in 1921 that bad environmental conditions are no longer bad enough to kill off the "unfit" in requisite numbers.[18] "Nietzschean" also suits Karl Pearson quite well when the statistician dismisses the humanitarian impulse altogether as, in fact, a pitiful misapprehension of what it means to be human: "It is a false view of human solidarity, a weak humanitarianism, not a true humanism, which regrets that a capable and stalwart race of white men should replace a dark-skinned tribe which can neither utilize its land for the full benefit of mankind, nor contribute its quota to the common stock of human knowledge."[19]

These discursive skirmishes over "true" humanism and "indiscriminate" humanitarianism in eugenic thinking are, I would suggest, an important attempt to trademark humanity itself in the service of race culture. Like the appeal to aesthetics, an appeal to humanism works to naturalize eugenic theory, making a preference for healthy bodies and Anglo-Saxon features seem like a matter of endemic good taste rather than a sign of class revulsion or racial dis-taste. As Bourdieu clarifies, "What is at stake in aesthetic discourse and in an attempted imposition of a definition of the genuinely human, is nothing less than the monopoly of humanity. Art is called upon to make the difference between humans and nonhumans" (491). Indeed, with the help of Bourdieu it becomes clear that the widespread use of John Ruskin within turn–of–the–century eugenic writing humanized the dismal science of race culture by making eugenic advocacy seem like a highly evolved natural preference or "pure taste" for healthy, strong bodies. Furthermore, Bourdieu's analysis of the political function of taste in the construction of a cultural aristocracy sheds interesting light on the aesthetic case that Saleeby, Pearson and Ellis so fervently pursue for race culture and biologism. When Pearson claims that eugenics is an obvious outgrowth of aesthetic philosophy, when Ellis claims that genetic manipulation is the pursuit of beauty, the poor and working-class subjects of social reform disappear from ethical consideration and even human classification. That "pure gaze" of the connoisseur displaces the scientific gaze of the statistician, and the master race reimposes a cultural aristocracy based on natural taste. "This claim to aristocracy is less likely to be contested than any other," Bourdieu concludes, "because the relation of the 'pure' 'disinterested' disposition to the conditions which make it possible, i.e. the material conditions of existence which are rarest because most freed from economic necessity, has every chance of passing unnoticed" (56).

Accordingly, when Nietzsche rhetorically inquires in *The Will to Power* how a stronger, healthier species could emerge from the current degenerate stage of European democracy, he answers in the familiar discourse of aesthetic philosophy that human regeneration requires, above all, taste: "Classical taste: this means will to simplification, strengthening, to visible happiness, to the terrible, to the courage of psychological nakedness . . . one must be faced with the choice of perishing or prevailing" (465). Only as a matter of taste—the healthy preference for pleasure over pain, for beauty over ugliness, for wholeness over fragmentation—could human evolution be pursued as a biological project, necessitating the judicious breeding of human life not in the service of pitiful, reductionist Science but as the very essence of Art. The aesthetic capacity, as Eagleton reminds us, was a physiological instinct for Nietzsche. Taste is purified to the degree that the race is strengthened; the strongest type of man, the "synthetic" man, would have the power to create a race "with its own sphere of life, with an excess of strength for beauty, bravery, culture, manners, to the highest peak of the spirit . . . beyond good and evil; a hothouse for strange and choice plants" (478). The beautiful is perfect symmetry, power and physical capacity, while the ugly is characterized by bodily degeneration and imperfection: "the ugly limps, the ugly stumbles: antithesis to the divine frivolity of the dancer" (427).

Eugenic writers, I would argue, install Ruskin as Nietzsche's opposite, casting two formidable figures in nineteenth-century aesthetic philosophy as the conflicting forces within a single debate about race culture. While Ruskin's fervent commitment to social perfectibility, moral improvement, and religious faith make his differences from Nietzsche almost too obvious, it is important to realize that both Ruskin and Nietzsche believe beautiful, healthy human bodies in hygienic environments are the very essence of art. Nietzsche's art and beauty, however, is the domain of the racially elite, the physiologically enlightened, the graceful; his political order consists of a perfected biological aristocracy that rules and controls the degenerate herd. The intellectual legacy revitalized by Nietzsche was not lost on Havelock Ellis, who drew a relatively straight line from the aesthetics of Lord Shaftesbury to modern metaphysics in his 1923 *The Dance of Life*. Shaftesbury believed, of course, that virtue was defined by a love of order and beauty in society; by extension, when we learn to act we are "learning to become artists."[20] Less interested in virtue as a social characteristic, Nietzsche nevertheless believes, in Ellis's turn of phrase, that "every man is a work of art he makes himself" (280). Ellis, the former Fabian, here speaks with pity and even derision about "the ambitious moral reformer" who refuses to understand the essential ambiguity, the indefiniteness, of aesthetic morality (282): "To take 'art' and 'morals' and 'religion' and stir them up, however vigorously, into an indigestible plum-pudding, as Ruskin used to do, is no longer possible" (316). Our understanding of true and living art, according to Ellis, could no longer be so narrowed and debased by an image of "Moses with the Ten Commandments": aesthetic beauty produces physiological pleasure and material comfort, while ugliness, like plum pudding, "interferes with digestion . . . disturbs the nervous system, impairs the forces of life" (328). Simply and succinctly put, good art imparts health, and, in fact, *is* health; bad art, on the other hand, makes you sick and, in fact, *is* sickness. Regardless of one's taste for realism, for morality, for religion, for plum pudding, the potential physiological power of art expressed by Ellis makes Ruskin seem like the inadvertent father of eugenics after all.

III. Realism, Repose, and the Reclamation of the Picturesque

In hindsight, from the lofty distance of this sixth chapter, Ward's *The Mating of Lydia* can be revisited as less of a battle between Ruskin and Whistler, and more as a struggle between Ruskin and Nietzsche, or a clash between the "positive" eugenic programs that will encourage judicious mating, and the "negative" programs that more actively assist nature in her project of natural selection. While Mr. Boden is the explicit representative of Ruskinian values in the text, the Nietzschean is also well-delineated in the vociferously anti-Socialist, anti-democratic, morally indifferent slumlord and aesthete, Edmund Melrose. As the narrator explains, the only public matter that ever concerns Melrose is that "his own class began to show a lamentable want of power" in the putting down and keeping down of the "proletariat" (84). Melrose's attractiveness, as Faversham explains, is his superb will and brain, an attractiveness that makes his moral abnormalities somehow less alarming. His *laissez faire* attitude towards Mainstairs, moreover, his hostility to sanitary reform and social perfectibility, as we will remember, are underwritten by a radically individualist, wholly physiological, philosophy of aesthetic pleasure that also cagily identifies the fretful interventions of social reformers as the mere effects of degenerate taste.

> In my view the object of everybody should be to *live,* as acutely as possible—to get as many sensations, as many pleasant reactions as possible—out of the day. Some people get their sensations—or say they do—out of fussing about the poor. . . . I make no apology whatever for my existence. (276)

When Melrose is shot in his art gallery, when Boden gives his closural blessing to the newly mated couple in the House Beautiful, what we get, of course, is a triumph of Ruskinian morality over solely sensual, sensational pleasure. Lydia's "poised mind and mastered senses" (332), like Faversham's sole ownership and enjoyment of a private art collection, must yield to the sanitary aesthetic, and the moral imperative of public health must displace the seductive power of the pure gaze. But more than social reconciliation, this mating plot reflects Saleeby's "eugenic reconciliation," where "we must have the worthy and only the worthy to be the parents of the future."[21]

By the twentieth century, as Dan Stone has argued, "biologism" was no longer a progressive ideology, no longer a useful democratic bulwark against social and economic hierarchies.[22] Biologism was an ideological tool of the right wing by the time Ruskin was drafted into its service; as Nietzsche had effectively demonstrated, the biological privileging of strength, health and racial purity could be radically individualistic, and could effectively revitalize the latent Victorian doctrines of liberalism and self-determination that fear of dirt and disease had temporarily stifled. The social and sanitary reforms of the mid-nineteenth century had long been seen as a plenary contradic-

tion of the entrenched British habit of 'doing as one likes.' Frances Power
Cobbe's 1882 *The Peak in Darien,* for example, had decried the widespread
public "Hygeiolatry" that had permitted the passage of Compulsory Vaccination Acts and Contagious Disease Acts as innovations in British legislation
that had sacrificed individual rights to a dubious new authority: "Health of
the body has been accorded the importance which the—real or supposed—
interests of the soul alone commanded two centuries ago," Cobbe explained,
"and the tyranny of the priesthood of Hygeia threatens to be as high-handed
as ever was that of the Churches of Rome or Geneva."[23] This kind of assessment of bureaucratic control of the body, of a state-dictated physiology that
could wrest the concept of heath away from moral and religious meanings,
was a discerning perspective at the end of the nineteenth century, but it was
typically answered with dripping sarcasm about sentimental notions of the
"liberty of the subject" by sanitarians. Frederick Bagshawe suggested in 1889,
"it might be thought that sentiment was not worth much when linked with
loathsome disease, or liberty of much value to a dead or disabled subject."[24]
But the bodily health that Nietzsche promised had nothing to do with public
sewers or bathhouses, with compulsory vaccination or housing authorities;
Nietszche's biologism was, of course, the natural aesthetic instinct and privilege of an exalted racial type. Indeed, if the dead and the disabled were never
subjects to begin with, were not fully human under the biological laws of
harmony and perfection that determined humanity, then their liberty was a
democratic fiction, a perverse and profound Socialist lie.

The most radically conservative popularizer of Nietzsche in England
was probably Anthony Ludovici, an early-twentieth-century eugenicist
who found in the German metaphysician a triumphant argument against
the great scourge of racial miscegenation that had degraded the European
type. For Ludovici, a former art critic and connoisseur, the most important
thing about *The Will to Power* was that it was essentially an aesthetic handbook; at the opening of his 1911 book *Nietzsche and Art,* he insists that the
principles found in *The Will to Power* will be the basis of a "new valuation"
in art, especially as it pertains to British art and criticism.[25] According to
Nietzsche, explains Ludovici, democracy implies a desire to please and a dis-
inclination to assume power that "contradicts the very essence of Art" (17).
Under democracy, art becomes realistic and relativistic, illustrative of poverty, lassitude, exhaustion and degeneracy; by definition, democratic art is
ugly and can excite no interest or passion in man other than a self-hatred
caused by the exhibited decline of his type. Nietzsche's "Ruler art," by contrast, acknowledges that true beauty is biological and can exist only within
the confines of a specific Ruler race:

The ruler artist is he who, elated by his own health and love of Life, says "Yea" to his own type and proclaims his faith or confidence in it, against all other types; and who, in doing so, determines or accentuates the values of that type. . . . By the beauty which his soul reflects upon the selected men he represents in his works, he establishes an order of rank among his people, and puts each in his place. (137)

In privileging order over chaos, system over anarchy, hierarchy over democracy, the ruler artist harnesses a program of classification to his aesthetic that clearly works, as Mary Douglas has theorized, as a cleansing apparatus. Pollution discourse emerges, we will remember from the first chapter, when form has been attacked, when the facts revealed by realism are "ugly, bare and dissatisfying" (71). What was needed instead, what was provided by the Ruler artist, was "a scheme for life, a picture for life, in which all the naked facts and truths could be given some place and some human significance—in fact, some order and arrangement, whereby they would become the chattels of the human spirit, and no longer subjects of independent existence and awful strangeness" (71).

At a distance, this zeal for organization and classification, order and arrangement, might even resemble Ruskinian methodology, the sanitizing impulse to put matter back in place. But the beauty revealed by Ruskin's system of arrangement was the highly wrought detail and truthful drama of everyday life, the "unclean story" of harsh social relations. In Nietzsche, in Ludovici, and in a whole tradition of conservative, anti-democratic aesthetic theory, order and arrangement were the mechanisms that repressed detail in favor of what Shaftesbury called social harmony and what modern writers called good health.

We are acquainted with the irascible nerve-patient when he pours his curses on the head of a noisy child; and in his case we are only too ready to suspect a morbid condition for the body. But when we see in ourselves, or our young friends, or our brothers . . . when still in their teens, a sort of gasping enthusiasm before a landscape, a peasant child, or a sunset; when they show an inability to bide their time, and remain inactive in the presence of what they consider beautiful, we immediately conclude from their conduct, not that they have little command of themselves, but that they must of necessity have strong artistic natures. . . . [I]t is only in our age that this neurotic touchiness could possibly be mistaken for strength and vigor; and yet there are hundreds of this kind among the painters and sculptors of the day. (38–39)

Importantly, what separates the ruler artist from this "pathological usurper" appears to be his inaction, and his disinterested, impassive contemplation of the picturesque, his ability to achieve peace and repose from a scene fraught with moral and ethical difficulties. To be moved to realist representation or moral action by a landscape or a peasant child is evidence of physiological degeneracy, whereas true aesthetic power masters and commands the scene, imposes an order and arrangement based on personal feelings of racial vigor and biological privilege.

Less exorcised than Ludovici about the racial problem of miscegenation, and speaking in defense of modern Post-Impressionist painting rather than in objection to its decadence, Bloomsbury art critic Roger Fry still expressed a similar aesthetic concern about the potentially destabilizing emotional experience of material life.

> The more poignant emotions of actual life have, I think, a kind of numbing effect analogous to the paralyzing influence of fear in some animals; but even if this experience is generally not admitted, all will admit that the need for responsive action in us hurries us along and prevents us from ever realizing fully what the emotion is we feel, from coordinating it perfectly with our other states.[26]

Again, the need for action in response to a scene, a situation, or a landscape prevents true emotional understanding, actually anaesthetizing our highest, most potentially harmonious aesthetic pleasures. The true artist, for Fry, translates pure sensation into an emotion that can be given back to us in forms and colors, and we are thus spared any need for action or response. This ability to blend the sensational and the emotional, the scientific and the intellectual, is only possible for the truly "generalizing intellect"; when generalization is the goal, "the mind is held in delighted equilibrium by the contemplation of the inevitable relation of all the parts to the whole, so that no need exists to make reference to what is outside the unity, and this becomes for the time being the universe."[27] Inevitably, this best, most synthesizing, most revitalizing Modern art would not appeal to "ordinary man," Fry admitted: "In proportion as art becomes purer the number of people to whom it appeals gets less."[28]

In other words, the transvaluation of pollution discourse over the long nineteenth century continues, in a wide variety of anti-democratic aesthetic writing, to be a reclassification of those controversial sensations provided by the picturesque. In the Romantic aesthetic philosophy of Hazlitt, Burke, and Shaftesbury, haziness, blurriness, and generalization were the revered agents of personal, imaginative sublimity, the warm brown tones and dark backgrounds of Renaissance painting providing a free space of intellectual exploration and experience that moved aristocratic morals in the service of enhanced and elegant social relations. By the end of the nineteenth century, after laboratory science had appropriated the ideological space of fragmentation, pessimism, and materialism, detail was demonized once again as a fretful shattering of the harmonizing aesthetic instinct into anatomy, pathology, and the profound ugliness of social and economic reality. In the assessment of James Hinton, a surgeon, homeopath, and mystic who deeply influenced Havelock Ellis and the Fellowship of New Life, realist detail even defeated and degraded the cherished Victorian belief that the beautiful was always morally useful, because detail was a slavish abasement before things rather than ideas: "While the painter is endeavoring to accurately represent certain things which come before him, he is serving those things. When he is sacrificing those things to fulfill the claims of other things, he is not serving them, but using them."[29] The imagination, Hinton explained, must sacrifice detail for the sake of higher beauty, and for this reason, he argued, as Nietzsche might, that such synthetic thinking itself should be understood as an Art.

Another philosopher who significantly shaped the aesthetic ideas of Havelock Ellis as well as Nietzsche was the Neo-Kantian Frederick Albert Lange, whose book *The History of Materialism* first appeared in the middle of the materialist 1860s, when science was just beginning to measure the limits of human knowledge by the scope and capacity of the senses.[30] Here, Lange argues that the highest and noblest functions of the human mind work constantly to supplement the low realities of physical life with an ideal world of its own creation, an optimistic image of life that is harmonious in form and free from deformity and perversion. The problem with realism and scientific detail is that it is depressing, degrading to the human spirit and ruinous to art, and Lange illustrates the problem by walking his reader up a hillside to contemplate a view.

> When from some elevated point we regard a landscape our whole nature is attuned to ascribe to it beauty and perfection. We must first destroy the powerful unity of the picture by analysis, in order to remember that in those huts, peacefully resting on the mountain slope, there dwell careworn men; that behind that little sheltered window perhaps some sufferer is enduring the most terrible torments; that beneath the murmuring summits of the distant forest, birds of prey are rending their quivering prey; that in the silvery waves of the river a thousand tiny creatures, scarcely born to life, are finding a cruel death. To our sweeping glance the withered branches

of the trees, the blighted cornfields, the sun-scorched meadows, are only shadows in a picture which delights our eye and cheers our heart. . . . Thus the world appears to the optimistic philosopher. He praises the harmony which he himself has introduced into it." (338)

Under the sweeping glance of the optimistic philosopher, the aesthetic power of the picturesque is reclaimed; as Nietzsche's Ruler artist will eventually discover, the superior and healthful individual has the power to impose harmony on the most abject images of poverty and suffering, repressing the dirt and detritus of social existence for the happiness and cheerful well-being of fully realized, fully synthesized individual life. The picturesque persists, well into the twentieth century, because it remains the battleground of the sanitary aesthetic; the place where anaesthesia still challenges aesthesia, the place where the power of the pure gaze still confronts the panic and anxiety, the guilt, the pity and the nose of the social reformer. In contemplating the power of the picturesque, nothing less than the political definition of humanity is perpetually at stake.

IV. Intensive Culture:
Sarah Grand's Eugenic Reconciliation

Sarah Grand's planned "trio" of eugenic novels written in the beginning of the twentieth century clearly exploits the ideological overlapping of mid-century environmental reform and late-century human engineering, and the way that both movements identified themselves by, through and as aesthetic discourse. I say "trio" of novels even though "duo" is more apt: Grand originally imagined a trilogy that, as Teresa Mangum explains, would have culminated in the healthy eugenic marriage of Adnam Pratt, the 1912 hero of *Adnam's Orchard,* and Ella Banks, the 1916 heroine of *Winged Victory.* Speculation on why the trilogy wasn't completed ranges from the cultural horrors and disillusionments of World War I to Grand's personal disillusionment with eugenics itself.[31] Impossible to ignore in the two novels Grand did write, however, is an emergent feminist investment in eugenic philosophy as a morally irreproachable strategy for seizing sexual and reproductive autonomy for women at a time of perceived declining national health. Contemporary scholars like Mangum and Beth Sutton-Ramspeck have productively struggled to address the seemingly unholy or at least unsavory alliance between feminist and eugenic purposes, and Sutton-Ramspeck does turn to the historical continuity between sanitary reform and racial hygiene in order to read

Grand's foregrounding of "cleanliness" as an essentially domestic concern.[32] But after recasting the ongoing work of nineteenth-century sanitation reform as an evolving aesthetic philosophy, it becomes plain that the shift in scene from *Adnam's Orchard* to *Winged Victory*, the shift between the protagonists, the landscape, and the reformist objectives of "intensive culture" that each novel pursues, also dramatizes the subtle shift in Socialist priorities from mid-Victorian environmental reforms to late-century genetic improvement.

Like *Middlemarch*, like *The Mating of Lydia*, *Adnam's Orchard* is set during a British agricultural depression blamed, in part, on aristocratic preferences for picturesque decay. Small tenant farmer Ellery Banks raises a family of ten children in the dilapidated Red Rose Farm, where it is damp in winter and stifling in summer, and he constantly petitions his landlord, Squire Pointz, for improvements. But

> it was such a picturesque little place that no one of any taste could have the heart to alter it—so said the Duchess, and the neighboring gentry cordially agreed; and all the more cordially because Red Rose Farm was a pretty object for a drive for London guests, who loved to sketch it, and photograph it, and sentimentalize about it and the Simple Life, when the Simple Life became the last luxury of fashionable talk.[33]

While the cottages on Squire Pointz's picturesque property contain weak children with decayed teeth and undersize adults who demonstrate "that general want of stamina which is a sure indication of degeneracy in the race" (38), the generalizing impulse of aristocratic taste represses all evidence of suffering and decay, and works to preserve the material space of its imaginative pleasure and power. The natural taste of the gentry, moreover, is aided and abetted by what Grand characterizes as a kind of bureaucratic optimism which meets the symptoms of racial decline and biological degeneracy by cheerfully "lowering the standard of height for men in the army," and troubling itself no further with what is clearly, in *Adnam's Orchard,* a physiological crisis (38). While Grand explicitly connects the worship of picturesque decay with the physical decay of the British laboring classes, she also suggests that the upper classes are going through a similar biological decline: not only is the wealthy Pointz family vulgar and animalistic, they are described as luxuriously "living in a vitiated atmosphere" where there is "no health" (429). The weakly, degenerate Pointz children suggest a tentative reproductive future for the upper classes which is matched at the other end of the social spectrum by the Malthusian implications of Squire Pointz's outright refusal to build additional housing for his own agricultural workers. At the start of the story, all the still-healthy sons of the soil have left Pointz for the eugenically dangerous London because there is no land for them to farm and no houses for them to take wives and begin families of their own. This plot point is the one that inspires our hero Adnam to build his orchard: he wants to import new agricultural techniques to England to allow a revitalized farming class "house room to bring up a healthy family," and thus turn the tide of degeneracy and decline that has infected the British population (57).

Given that Adnam's program of intensive culture resembles, so strongly, the ideological labor of mid-Victorian sanitary fiction, it is not surprising to find him surfacing within our now-ubiquitous sanitary mise-en-scène. Wandering the Pointz property at sunset, Adnam helps the reader evaluate the view:

> To the eye of the artist the sun, low down in the west, gave the last touch of beauty to the quiet land; but, as to the eye of the physician who knows that some much admired beauty is not the beauty of health but the symptom of a deadly disease, so to the eye of the modern agriculturalist, those peaceful pastures on either hand, sparsely sprinkled with cattle, were symptomatic of a threatened decay of a great nation, a danger signal not to be ignored for a moment if the situation were to be saved. . . . The fields looked lovely by the waning light in their vivid green, but it was not their loveliness that appealed to Adnam's intelligence. What he noticed was the neglect that had fallen upon them and the barrenness which was the result of neglect. The loneliness also struck him. Not a human being was there anywhere in sight except himself. (155)

Passing from the aesthetic gaze to the medical gaze, and finally resting with the eye of our modern agriculturist, Adnam, what we experience in this shrewdly overfamiliar passage is actually a reinvented sanitary narrative, where the shifting cultural meaning of the picturesque landscape is made to accommodate a new story of hygiene and social improvement. Adnam Pratt's reaction to the picturesque environment is certainly marked by an appropriate anxiety about its endemic pollution, but for Adnam, the lack of human presence in the landscape is what degrades the picture. Reversing the aesthetic instinct that would need to empty picturesque environments of vulgar people in order to preserve the beauty of the landscape, Adnam seeks to introduce a healthy set of human subjects into the barren landscape, to repopulate the brown emptiness with a selection of robust and vigorous British bodies. In this way, Adnam's goal is both aesthetically driven and biblically inspired: by repurposing a segment of his Yeoman father's wasteland for his agricultural experiment, the French system of "intensive culture" becomes a British pro-gram for racial improvement.

"Intensive culture" is a robustly ambiguous term in the novel, figuring literally as a system of greenhouse cultivation that requires a great deal of glass and a large number of strong workers; despite these difficulties, Adnam effortlessly amasses the money and the thirty men required for his proj-ect. Reading in the newspaper that anxieties about military efficiency have prompted the British army to purchase new tents, Adnam promptly pur-chases the old tents for his laborers, clearly underscoring the idea that his own application of intensive culture participates in the domestic program of national defense. In a chapter called "A Labour Camp Idyll," we learn that Adnam's men live in these tents, eating fish they catch and cook themselves, and that the healthy sport and food improves them both mentally and phys-ically (247). They eventually found their own library, and begin to create together an intellectual and artistic community of healthy laboring men. The aristocrats in the neighborhood complain about Adnam's labor camp, how-ever, misinterpreting the agricultural project of intensive culture as a form of dirt rather than cleanliness: the Duchess of nearby Castlefield Saye, for example, complains to Adnam's mother Ursula Pratt that his working field "looks like the abomination of desolation and mud pies" (109). The Duchess tries to sympathize with Ursula, exclaiming that it was such a pity "to spoil your picturesque old Orchard and that dear old field," even adding that the "dear weeds" which choked the Orchard in times past were so pretty (109). Mrs. Pratt, however, replies that they weren't "wholesome," and calmly offers her support for her son's agricultural endeavors by observing, somewhat chillingly, "I want to see the weeds killed everywhere" (109).

Indeed, Adnam's instinct for a highly controlled, carefully regulated environment for the superior growth of both crops and men seems to be part of his maternal inheritance. As we learn, Ursula Pratt has long experi-mented with a more biological form of intensive culture herself: years ago, Ursula left her own highly bred German Catholic family to deliberately mix her bloodline with the healthy bedrock of British Protestantism, the Yeoman class. Adnam's regular features, well-proportioned frame, endemic health and enlightened self-interest all become genetically legible when his mother is revealed to be a hidden Countess and actually the second wife of Adnam's father, Yeoman Pratt. By contrast, Pratt's elder son, Seraph, is the result of the Yeoman's less careful mating of earlier days:

> His mother had been an anemic girl of town stock, the child of tradespeo-ple, with impoverished blood, bred in the days when municipal ignorance,

mismanagement, and neglect of interest in the health of the community
generally was enough to make microbes in the milk carts stand on their
tails and cheer. . . . She lived long enough to infect him, her only child with
her innate defects of character and manner. (21)

Just as in Ward's *The Mating of Lydia*, in *Adnam's Orchard* we encounter some
mixed messages about germ theory, contagion, and the effects of heredity
on offspring. Seraph's mother is the product of an insanitary period in British municipal history, and microbe-infected milk seems to have degraded a
character that was already prone to degradation; her ill-favored physiology,
moreover, lingers in the body of her dark, poorly proportioned, bad-tempered
son. Grand insists that the differences between these two wives of Yeoman
Pratt, and thus the differences between their respective offspring, prove that
"qualities good or bad are inherent in the blood, things neither to be acquired
nor eradicated" (22). Indeed, Grand writes under a set of assumptions about
race culture that depends upon the superior maternal blood of her eugenic
hero: Adnam's aristocratic blood has been improved by being grafted upon
a pure, healthy British stock, and suggests that his inheritance will be more
than a talent for farming or a knack for agriculture.

This inheritance becomes most apparent when one of Adnam's work-
men in his labor camp reveals himself, suddenly, to be a masterful orator and
musician, seizing a violin to accompany Mrs. Pratt during a piano performance, and astounding everyone, except Ursula, with his virtuosity. Through
a bewildering series of unmaskings that occur toward the end of the novel,
the soulful and literate laborer Mickleham is revealed to be: a) a well-known
philanthropist who specializes in agricultural reforms; b) a famous art collector and connoisseur; c) a wealthy German prince named Strelletzen; and
d) Ursurla Pratt's brother and, therefore, Adnam's uncle. This enigmatic man
with the hands of an artisan and the voice of a gentleman, a man who knows
French and German and music, made a mysterious fortune "in the colonies"
after being disinherited by his Catholic family and now devotes his time to his
hobbies: agriculture and philanthropy (553). The incognito Prince Strelletzen
further reveals that he came to his sister's neighborhood out of interest in
his nephew and the orchard he was creating, and a desire to further Adnam's
agricultural program if intensive culture suited his own reformist objectives.
But when the degenerate, inebriate landowner Colonel Kedlock disparagingly
dubs Strelletzen the "artist-man," the Prince's most important function in the
novel is ironically confirmed: as the Ruler artist and consummate overman,
Strelletzen clarifies that Adnam's Orchard actually represents and reflects his
nephew's aesthetic inheritance, a natural aristocratic power to compose and

harmonize his own environment, to establish order out of chaos and to assign value and meaning to the various ranks of people in his newly constructed social ecology. In essence, Adnam recomposes his picturesque landscape as a painter would introduce people to an empty canvas, using his labor camp as a material hothouse for a healthy race with its own sphere of existence.

Prince Strelletzen's Nietzschean title also suits him particularly well after the artist-man manages to solve the central sanitary crisis in *Adnam's Orchard*. While still disguised as Mickleham, Strelletzen visits Squire Pointz to discuss the potential use of intensive culture in and around Red Rose Farm. On the wall of the Squire's luxuriously appointed private library, Mickleham notices a Goya painting, and surprises Pointz by mentioning that he knows a collector who would give a great deal to possess it. At this point in the novel, Pointz has been so harassed by the Sanitary Authorities and so exposed by local newspapers that he is willing to rethink his preference for the picturesque; he ruefully agrees to Mickleham's brokered sale of the Goya and to the investment of the money from the sale in the purification and agricultural improvement of his property. It is ideologically important that the Squire's aesthetic paradise is sacrificed for environmental cleanliness; throughout the novel, the library is the morally weak, physically diminished Squire's retreat from the "harassing recollections" of his failures as a paternalist and as a father (429). In *Adnam's Orchard,* as in so many late-Victorian novels, art and aesthetic philosophy are the spoils of a corrupt economic system that must be returned to the earth as manure for new forms of beauty and fertility.

On the other hand, Pointz's hoarded, overvalued painting is not a muddy landscape by Cuyp or a hideously embrowned Rembrandt portrait, not a typical object of mid-Victorian realist revulsion that can be symbolically exchanged for what I earlier identified as the sanitary aesthetic. The sudden surfacing of a Goya in *Adnam's Orchard* is, I would suggest instead, a telling index of the evolving aesthetic anxieties I've been discussing throughout *The Sanitary Arts:* the last of the Old Masters, Goya was also discovered around the time *Adnam's Orchard* was published to be the first of the Moderns. D. S. MacColl, a British art critic who was an early supporter of the Impressionist movement, claimed that the "devil" entered nineteenth-century art with the appearance of Goya, and that he manifested through his painting the bloodlust, cruelty, and terror of his home country: "What is the pride of Velasquez besides this fierce decorum and mad disdain; the pitiful night of Rembrandt changes to a horror of darkness, ambiguous with all that is furtive and unclean, featureless things that mop and mow, the bald harpy, the incubus and the bat."[34] Grand is maddeningly vague about what Squire

Pointz's Goya looks like; it could, after all, be a conventional, highly finished portrait of Spanish aristocracy or a canvas from the altar of a Church. But the significance of Goya at the beginning of the twentieth century was usually extracted, as MacColl's words imply, from his later Black Paintings: images of insanity, death, depravity, torture and illness that were thematically and visually at home during the post-impressionist and expressionist movements in Modern art. It would make a certain amount of ideological sense if Pointz's Goya was from this "unclean" period of the painter's career, the banishment of a Black Painting from the landowner's library would imply that degenerate, bloody, disturbing art must be bartered, at the end of this particular sanitary fiction, for public health and physiological revival. But the only clue to the subject of Pointz's Goya painting is the fact that at the moment of the Squire's strangely orchestrated bargain with Mickleham/Strelletzan, he is confronted by his angry wife who tries to prevent the sale. Pointz looks at her,

> The skin roughened by gluttony, and brick-red now with rage; the ugly pepper and salt of her coarse, ill-dressed hair; the gaunt form bared of all grace of womanly softness by the attrition of mean thought and strife; every repulsive detail of her personality he took in at a glance, and his distaste for her showed as never before in the expression of his face. With a contemptuous smile, the Squire glanced from her to the Goya. (445)

As the Squire's gaze shifts from his hideous wife to the mysterious Goya, visual metonymy provides one possible and possibly significant answer to the question of genre. Rejecting degenerate art and his ill-bred wife simultaneously, the Squire purifies his own aesthetic standards and prepares the way for his return to social responsibility through sanitary work.

Unlike, say, Max Nordau, who believed all Modern art was degenerate and fundamentally dangerous to the preservation of racial types,[35] Nietzsche believed that the Ruler artist was so strong and so racially healthy that he could actually derive sustenance from ugly, horrible, sensational art; by definition, the Ruler artist must "have all the morbid traits of the century, but to balance them through a superabundant, recuperative strength":

> Health and sickliness: one should be careful! The standard remains the efflorescence of the body, the agility, courage, and cheerfulness of the spirit—but also, of course, how much of the sickly it can take and overcome—how much it can make healthy. That of which the delicate man would perish belongs to the stimulants of *great* health.[36]

Weak men, as Nietzsche indicates, become overexcited when they listen to Wagner; they are too physiologically compromised, too much at the mercy of our "anarchy of the atoms" to resist the further fragmentation and terror that Modern music, like Modern painting, inflicts on the human nervous system.[37] One reason that Grand denies us the opportunity to "see" the Goya painting that Strelletzen removes from Pointz's library might be that we, like the Squire himself, are part of the degenerate herd that cannot survive an encounter with such terrifyingly abject art. The Goya painting that is whisked away by Strelletzen will no doubt be placed in healthier hands, with a curator who can withstand physiological shocks and injuries much more successfully than the "small, sallow, hopeless, ill-nourished" Squire Pointz (429).

The other significant landowner in *Adnam's Orchard* is an aristocrat who continues to be important in Grand's sequel, *The Winged Victory,* primarily because he takes an unusual interest in Adnam's would-be eugenic bride, Ella Banks. Stronger, richer, and more intelligent than Squire Pointz, the Duke of Castlefield Saye must similarly purge himself of perverse aesthetic instincts before he can move on to the next novel, and he accomplishes this through a much more traditional story of sanitary conversion. Although the Duke dearly loves the artistic proportions of his Village, and "at the back of his mind was a feeling that [his tenants] should have found comfort enough in the picturesque" (211), he voluntarily institutes necessary reforms on his properties, and even builds a new fever hospital like the one imagined in the 1830s by poor Lydgate. Interestingly, the Duke's hospital is called "Her Repose," and it opens just in time to admit victims of not only typhoid, but also diphtheria and tuberculosis from Squire Pointz's fetid cottages. The fever hospital itself is a great triumph of intensive culture, not because it makes use of Adnam's system of greenhouses, but because it forces health and prosperity from a repressive and exploitive class system. "Everything there bespoke wealth well spent, and if the money did come from the slums, like manure which deserves to be called dirty, it became transformed in the application also like manure, and lost its bad character when it was considered the source of so much deservedly admired fertility" (499). The sanitary plot of *Adnam's Orchard* is finally shaped by this kind of ideological transformation of dirt: through both agricultural reform and eugenic reform, "intensive culture" forces the bloom of health and the promise of fertility from the degraded soil, transforming dirt into art for the benefit of the British race.

Any social reconciliation provided by the sanitary aesthetic in *Adnam's Orchard* is premature, of course; Grand's subtitle for this novel is "A Prologue," implying that environmental sanitation is simply the first and most traditional form of cleansing that her eugenic trilogy will accomplish. Indeed, the hygienic work of agricultural reform in this first novel is obstructed by the entrenched degeneracy of Adnam's physiological foil, his elder brother Seraph. In a fit of rage, jealousy, and inebriation, the underbred Seraph sets fire to his brother's progressive greenhouses, burning Adnam's edenic labor camp to the ground. Emery Pratt dies, Seraph inherits the farm, and the solitary Adnam bravely sets off for London. Undaunted by his agricultural failure and by the temporary triumph of the degenerate herd, Adnam's program of intensive culture suggestively dilates at the end of the novel: according to Grand's closing sentence, "Henceforth, Adnam's Orchard was the World" (623).

I've suggested that mid-Victorian sanitary fiction is less revolutionary than evolutionary, that Socialist narratives of sanitation reform rarely demand that the aristocratic landowners be eliminated, only that their aesthetic perversities be cleansed. But the most conservative turn-of-the-century sanitary stories treat democracy itself as a filthy perversion, and can only negotiate cleanliness as a kind of physiological reinvention and reinscription of aristocratic power. Eugenic cleansing must originate from within the aristocracy, even if it superficially seems like the heroic sanitarian emerges *de novo* from the unwashed herd. Accordingly, Adnam's eugenic counterpart, Ella Banks, who grows up in the dilapidated Red Rose Farm, and who is the apparent daughter of a tenant farmer, passes from *Adnam's Orchard* to *Winged Victory* without suspecting that she is actually the illegitimate daughter of the Duke of Castlefield Saye. Ella's instinctive grace, surpassing beauty, and innate aesthetic taste are genetically unmoored and therefore controversial for most of the two-part trilogy. Ella is "pure aesthetic emotion made visible" according to Col Drindon, the London writer who also gives Ella the nickname of "Winged Victory" because she is a perfect unity of form and function. Her vocation also transfers Adnam's metaphoric program of intensive culture from the agricultural to the industrial: Ella's plan is to revive "the intensive craft of lace" in Great Britain and thus revitalize a degraded and degrading industry that is also a lost aesthetic resource for England.[38] A broad goal, perhaps, but Ella has a strategy with two separate tactics. The first is to eliminate the middlemen who sweat the labor of poor workers, and to open a shop where she can sell lace directly to a wealthy aristocratic clientele. The second is to revive the practice of aristocratic lace making itself, which she can accomplish by admitting the daughters of the wealthy to a school attached to her shop. The Duke of Castlefield Saye, knowing Ella to be his daughter, engages to be her benefactor and installs her in the family's dowager house in London: a worthy structure for both of Ella's purposes. "The rich and the great are the natural Guardians of Art," the lawyer for the Brabant family, Mr. Bosc, explains to her when he informs Ella of the Duke's generous intentions, and Ella accepts his gift accordingly as a rightful extension of aristocratic power. The house is decorated in eighteenth-century style, but refit for Ella with contemporary sanitary objectives that make cleanliness attainable even during the long season of London smuts. "My rooms must look healthy and fresh," Ella insists to Bosc. "Everything in it must be cleanable. It must be clean before everything. And not to be made stuffy and enervating with a surplus of cushions and easy chairs" (15). Throughout the novel, Ella's domestic sanitation is linked not only to her pursuit of exercise, and to the way that she comes to secretly imagine a marriage to the Duke's eldest son Melton as a way to get "good new blood" into a degenerating aristocratic tree (542), but to the scientist, Gregor Strangworth's, identification of "the intensive craft of lace" itself as what he calls a "hygienic" ritual:

> The attitude of the whole body which sewing necessitated and the steady rise and fall of the arm, have a healthy effect on the—er—centre, in fact, of a woman's being, the condition of which determines her conduct. (89)

Strangworth is a mysterious and powerful character in *Winged Victory*, a member of an "elect who are shaping life to its finest issues, a Spiritual Aristocracy" according to the decadent Lord Terry, a man who even organizes his dinner parties homogenously rather than episodically because "Dining is a great art" that maintains physiological health and digestive integrity of the body (165). Lace making, according to Strangworth, will strengthen the individual female body at the same time it strengthens the social body, uniting rich and poor women as fellow artisans, and reviving a "link in the chain of descent" that connects the current and currently degraded aristocratic family of women with their purer and more worthy ancestors. The Princess Anna, who graciously opens Ella's lace shop, and brings a whole train of wealthy customers in her wake, reveals herself to be a lace maker, and the two women momentarily forget ostensible class differences and as equals "enjoy the freemasonry of their craft" (77). "Lace can be patriotic," Ella insists to the agreeable Princess, and for most of the rest of the novel Ella's healthy and particularly female art is created and sold in the service of an imagined aesthetic nationalism, an harmonious union of classes of strong women for the greater glory of England (81).

This would seem somewhat more subversive if we didn't suspect throughout *Winged Victory* that Ella's true biological status would eventually minimize the class difference between our heroine and Princess Anna, and make the democratic discourse of freemasonry seem less free after all. The only real clue to her identity, however, is a Gainsborough portrait of the Duke's grand-

mother, a portrait that hangs in the Duke's private library and that remains
covered until its revelation can harmonize the biological family in *Winged
Victory* the way the Goya painting harmonized the social family in *Adnam's
Orchard*. The Duke is personally *cleaning* the painting when his eldest legitimate son enters the library one afternoon late in the latter novel, and its
details and colors stand out "as purely as if the picture were fresh from the
studio" (629). Unfortunately the Duke's recognition and reclamation of Ella as
the pure and fresh daughter he always wanted, the child produced by a liaison
with a woman of healthier, cleaner blood than that of his own lawful wife,
is forestalled by the fact that she has secretly become his son Melton's wife,
and is therefore doubly and more dangerously a daughter. When Melton sees
Ella herself in eighteenth-century lace and satin stepping forward from the
gleaming canvas, his incestuous crime is immediately legible. Devastated, he
orchestrates his own accidental death to spare everyone else the aftereffects,
and while this ending strikes Teresa Mangum as apocalyptic and as a radical repudiation of eugenic philosophy, it strikes me as the exemplification of
intensive culture's inevitable purpose: enhanced natural selection.

Throughout *Winged Victory*, the Duke interests himself in the study of
heredity, realizing gradually that his own choice in marriage was an unfortunate violation of his biological responsibilities, his aristocratic privilege and
burden to reproduce a strong and vibrant race.

> He had observed that bad traits came out worse in the next generation.
> His wife was foolish; his daughter was a fool. He hesitated in his speech,
> Eustace stuttered; he had direct intentions, but procrastinated; Melton, the
> hope of his house was a drifter. . . . He needed another kind of child, one
> to be proud of; but another kind of child would require another kind of
> mother, and his initial mistake must stand. He had not chosen the right
> woman to produce the child he would have gloried to have. (232–33)

Both Ella and the Duke have separately registered Melton's passivity, his weakness, his insufficiently evolved racial features; both also feel that a regenera-
tive marriage with a woman of healthy stock will right what is wrong with
Melton in his offspring. But by eliminating himself from the reproductive
cycle altogether, Melton repairs the biological family in keeping with the best
eugenic policies: Ella is now a legitimate daughter of the Duke of Castlefield
Saye and can legally possess her racial and aristocratic destiny, granting the
Duke, belatedly, the child he "would have gloried to have." Given that the
Duke's stuttering son, Eustace, marries the barren daughter of an alcoholic,
and that his foolish daughter Anne marries Squire Pointz's degenerate and

possibly syphilitic son Algernon, illegitimate Ella, otherwise the "Winged Victory" of the title, is the perfect unity of form and function, the healthy biological resource for aristocratic continuity, and the art that has sprung from the dirt after all.

Of course, we are finally denied the eugenic reconciliation prepared for us by the isolation of Adnam and Ella from the herd into which they were born, and by the revelation that their innate aesthetic powers are the rightful inheritance of a natural aristocracy. For whatever reason, Sarah Grand's eugenic story ends abruptly in 1916, and leaves hanging a whole host of possible outcomes for the physiological overmen she so carefully prepares for reproductive dominance. A eugenic program that relies on fortuitously discovered aristocratic bloodlines rather than rigorous breeding systems seems like a singularly ineffective method of racial improvement, one that resurrects the sentimental Dickensian story of the foundling child in order to invent a new Nietzschean parable of the exceptionally well-born. But if we remember the intellectual history of the aesthetic; if we remember, with Eagleton and Bourdieu, that conservative strain of aesthetic philosophy that is central to the work of political hegemony, the class system and the economic hierarchy, the "natural" taste for clean environments and beautiful people can be seen as a claim to aristocracy after all.

On Methods, Materials, and Meaning

[For] art is nothing less that the world as we ourselves make it, the world re-moulded nearer to the heart's desire. In this construction of a world around us, in harmonious response to all our senses, we have at once a healthy exercise for our motor activities, and the restful satisfaction of our sensory needs. Art, as no mere passive hyperaesthesia to external impressions, or exclusive absorption in a single sense, but as a many-sided and active delight in the wholeness of things, is a great restorer of health and rest to the energies distracted by our turbulent modern movements. . . . The satisfaction of the art-instinct is now one of the most pressing of social needs.

—Havelock Ellis, *The New Life* (1892)

*E*llis's words nicely capture the physiological meaning of beauty that became a dominant strand of sanitary discourse at the end of the nineteenth century. In its physiological phase, the Sanitary Idea worked as an aesthetic power to make the human body healthy through the enlightened sensory mechanism of taste. Taste is not represented by the exploitation of a single sense, moreover, but by a holistic sensory experience and awareness, an "art-instinct" that is inherently social because it can be satisfied only by the harmonizing perception of beauty in environments and in people. Ellis's aesthetic concept looks back to Shaftsbury and Kant, but with a new awareness of the extent of dirt and degeneracy that art must repress in order to function as a harmonizing social philosophy. The eugenic movement in socialism at the end of the nineteenth century may have been an unintended development of mid-Victorian sanitary thinking, but when eugenic advocacy is reexamined as an aesthetic philosophy within a formidable intellectual tradition that also includes sanitary thinking it seems less like a moral misstep or a political aberration than a collaborative and evolving cultural development. Self-organization is a morally neutral mechanism; as Paul Krugman somewhat ruefully explains, it is "something we observe, not necessarily something we want" (6).

Throughout *The Sanitary Arts,* Bourdieu and Eagleton have helped me to understand the power of the aesthetic to disguise ambivalent and repressive social programs as natural instincts for beauty. They have also helped me to interpret the resurrection of John Ruskin as the unwitting, unintentional father of eugenic advocacy as a chilling example of how that aesthetic functions to redefine sociological and statistical depravity as artistic taste. But when we find Ruskin operating as a eugenic bellweather, we must also realize that aesthetic history is robustly unstable and contingent, and that any causal narrative of cultural change must reflect the active, adaptive, and collaborative work of a variety of overlapping events, discourses, and people. The Ruskinian sanitary aesthetic is, on the one hand, a revolutionary overthrow of reigning artistic and political conventions; the cleanliness campaigns, after all, made *aesthesis* more social, more democratic, by leveling the senses. But sanitation reform is still a political philosophy imagined as an aesthetic philosophy, and it eventually recapitulates and reinvigorates some of the very artistic conventions most outrageous to mid-Victorian sanitarians. Even the ability to recognize and enjoy the picturesque, I argued in my last chapters, returns as a sign of individual health and vitality for neo-Kantian philosophers like Frederick Albert Lange, who celebrated the "synthetic thinking" and the "optimism" of powerful individuals who were able to ignore poverty and filth for the sake of aesthetic experience.[1] Lange, who significantly influenced both Nietzsche and Havelock Ellis, returns the concepts of disinterest, detachment and generalization to high aesthetic regard, encouraging his post-Chadwickian readers to let the haziness and blurriness of distance once again elide all of the depressing things they now know about the reeking, revolting, and reckless poor.

In this way, my methodology has followed my story. Rather than developing or "tracing" a new genealogy of sanitation reform that emanates from John Ruskin instead of Edwin Chadwick, I have been arguing for the deliberately constructed and highly political work of genealogical thinking, trying to call into question the institutionalization of intellectual and scientific history around sharply delineated points of origin and persons of interest. Ruskin and Chadwick played central roles in the story of the cleanliness campaigns, to be sure, but so did Frederick Albert Lange and Havelock Ellis, Friedrich Nietzsche and Francis Galton. However, it is also the case that my story has followed my methodology. In trying to resist the genealogical power of certain mutually exclusive narratives about sanitation and aesthetics, I have also attempted to resist the authoritative pull of those canonical Victorian voices who are most commonly associated with the genre of writing I privilege in *The Sanitary Arts:* the novel. While Dickens, Eliot, Gaskell and Collins have all made important appearances in these pages, they have been thrown into a broader, more collaborative conversation with their own less celebrated, less memorialized peers. It may be the case that the story I have been trying to tell about the sanitary aesthetic is more vividly available to me in noncanonical fiction because my interpretive strategy is less rigidly constrained by well-litigated authorial conventions, formal aesthetic qualities and entrenched critical protocols. It may also be true that noncanonical texts are noncanonical because they grapple, often quite unsuccessfully, with complex and even contradictory narratives about seemingly unrelated social and aesthetic problems. Sidestepping cause, I can still readily embrace effect: those less formidable voices—Charlotte Mary Yonge, Charles Reade, Sarah Grand, Grant Allen—have provided a much more robust and more complicated picture of my undisciplined topic over a longer nineteenth century, allowing me to identify significant cultural change represented by a set of discursive collisions, overlaps, and reconciliations that have not been conventional sites of interest for Victorian Studies.

Just as the distinction between high- and middle-brow fiction has prematurely limited the kinds of questions we have been able to ask about how the Victorian novel represents cultural change, the disciplinary separation of scientific discourse from aesthetic discourse has forced our answers to accommodate one semantic domain or the other. The production and circulation of the sanitary aesthetic within Victorian fiction, art criticism, home decoration guides, architectural handbooks, and eugenic propaganda can only be appreciated if we understand the idiosyncratically collaborative outcomes that emanate from unintentionally shared discoveries and objectives. More work needs to be conducted at the reclusive borders of seemingly unrelated disciplines and discourses; if my necessarily limited proddings at the interface between sanitation and aesthetics have been productive, I hope they have demonstrated that interactions among apparently uncongenial subjects and actors can be rich environments for some remarkable but forgotten causes of cultural change. Intent here needs to be separated from effect: as Levine explains, "there is a gap between ideology as a comprehensive group-based attempt to impose order and the kinds of successes and failures that particular ordering tactics actually achieve" (637). I would extend Levine's argument to include the possibility that the "ordering tactics" that emanate from the chasm between intent and effect can become, in turn, the conditions for the

intentional work of other actors, other participants in the ongoing collaborative work of cultural change. My own conclusion is that aesthetic stances and
scientific discoveries have political meanings that cannot finally be entirely
repressive or revolutionary. They shift in their encounters and their confron-
tations with each other, and it is only the attempt to sort cultural events into
the strict divisions of disciplinary discourse that imposes ideological coherence and temporal clarity on the much richer, longer, and more complex
story of nineteenth-century culture.

NOTES

Introduction

1. Poovey, *Making a Social Body* 99.
2. Foucault, *Discipline and Punish.*
3. Childers, *Novel Possibilities* 89.
4. Childers, *Novel Possibilities* 73. Of course, Childers does argue that the *Sanitary Report* borrows "representational strategies" from the Victorian novel, so while aesthetic forms are not his primary interest the formal conventions of fiction are implicit in his discussion of Chadwick.
5. Levine, Teukolsky.
6. Crary, Shires, Carlisle, Flint, Goodlad, Kennedy.
7. Chadwick, "The Manual Labourer as an Investment of Capital" 504.
8. Corbin 5.
9. Stallybrass and White 134.
10. Chadwick, *Report on the Sanitary Condition of the Labouring Population of Great Britain* 16–21. Sanitary crusaders' investment in describing foul stenches in detail in order to mobilize reform efforts is also discussed in Classen et al. 78.
11. Classen et al. 82.
12. Trotter 38.
13. Dowling.
14. Pease, *Modernism, Mass Culture and the Aesthetics of Obscenity* 20.
15. Eagleton 42–43.
16. Kant 50.
17. See Cohen's fascinating "Locating Filth," the introduction to his edited collection of essays, *Filth: Dirt, Disgust and Modern Life;* see also Allen, *Cleansing the City.*
18. Carlisle 16.
19. Quoted in Wohl 101; also quoted in Schama 416.
20. The term "self-organizing" is a familiar one in both biology and economics, explored most thoroughly by bioethicist Henri Atlan in his 1998 article "Intentional Self-Organization."

21. Krugman 3.

22. See Ward, *The Medea Hypothesis,* for a particularly grim look at self-organization in the ecosystem. In economics, Krugman's *The Self-Organizing Economy* entertains the notion of the ambivalent and not necessarily moral effects of free markets: self-organization is "something we observe, not necessarily something we want" (6).

23. Douglas 104.

24. While Carlisle argues that novels of the 1860s reflect a more highly refined sensitivity to the subtle aromas of class difference than the putrid, noxious, and poisonous smells of the 1840s could stimulate (Carlisle 17), the sluggish pace of the sanitary revolution allows me to focus more broadly on novels that span several decades and are much less subtly offended by dirt and disease.

25. Goodlad discusses waning interest in the Sanitary Idea (87), as does Allen (*Cleansing the City* 174).

26. Pater, *The Renaissance* 152.

Chapter 1

1. See Chadwick, *Report on the Sanitary Condition of the Labouring Population of Great Britain.*

2. Chadwick, "The Manual Labourer as an Investment of Capital," 504.

3. See Poovey, *Making a Social Body*; Childers, *Novel Possibilities.*

4. Douglas 36.

5. Carroll 59.

6. It is important to note what Ruskin himself clarified in the first pages of *Modern Painters*: "Speaking generally of the Elder Masters, I refer only to Claude, Gaspar Poussin, Salvator Rosa, Cuyp, Berghem, Both, Ruysdael, Hobbima, Teniers (in his landscapes), P. Potter, Canaletto, and those various Van somethings and Back somethings, more especially and malignantly those who have libelled the sea" (Ruskin, *Modern Painters* I, 48).

7. Ruskin, *Modern Painters* III, 241. This realization appears to have comforted Ruskin, who, by the time the third volume of *Modern Painters* was published, was agonizing over John Milton's use of the color brown to describe the air and water in *Paradise Lost.* In the 1860 *Elements of Drawing,* Ruskin would warn novice artists against the use of not only browns, but "dirty yellowish greens," comparing such pigments to a form of refuse deplored by sanitarians: "a decaying heap of vegetables" (III, 235).

8. Lindsay 108. Lindsay also notes that Gilpin had disparaged the Isle of Wight for the chalkiness of its coast; and though at times he found a small area of white acceptable, he and [Uvedale] Price both rated it a glaring hue that should be avoided" (108).

9. In the third volume of *Modern Painters,* Ruskin impatiently addresses the "careless readers" who need to ask such a question: such readers inquire "'Turner cannot draw, Turner is generalizing, vague, and visionary; and the Pre-Raphaelites are hard and distinct. How can anyone like both?'" Ruskin responds: "But *I* never said that he was vague or visionary. What *I* said was that nobody had every drawn so well: that nobody was so certain, so *un*visionary; that nobody had ever given so many hard and downright facts" (Ruskin, "Of the Use of Pictures," *Modern Painters* III, 356-57).

10. Ruskin, "Light" 187.

11. Teukolsky 5.

12. Ruskin, "Preface" I, xxxviii, li. All further citations of the preface to *Modern Painters* will refer to this 1844 edition, rather than the 1842 edition that was reissued in 2000.

13. For these definitions, see Fairholt 217, or Spooner xxviii.

14. Ruskin, *The Elements of Drawing* 235.

15. Nightingale 91.

16. Ruskin, "The Cestus of Aglaia" 446.

17. William Hazlitt, qtd. in Ruskin, "The Cestus of Aglaia" 499.

18. Ruskin, "The Relation of Art to Use" 73.

19. Burke 55.

20. Jameson 8.

21. Cozens 167–68.

22. Leonardo da Vinci, qtd. in Cozens 168.

23. William Gilpin, qtd. in Andrews, *The Search for the Picturesque* 28.

24. "The Turner Gallery" 144.

25. Lindsay 191.

26. Hazlitt, "An Inquiry" 16.

27. Hazlitt, "Pictures at Wilton, Stouhead, & c." 448.

28. Hazlitt, "The Pictures at Hampton Court" 425.

29. Ruskin, *Modern Painters* IV, 429–30. Ruskin locates the purer elements of sublimity in Turner's landscapes, of course; for Ruskin, sublimity is sanitized only when the artist can enter into full "communion of heart" with his subjects. There is no beauty or delight to be found in Turner's contemplation of decay, only pride, purpose and "largeness of sympathy" (429).

30. Punch 3.

31. For more information about Eastlake's career at the National Gallery, see Robertson.

32. Moore 16.

33. Coningham.

34. *Reports from the Select Committee on Fine Arts and on the National Gallery* 6.

35. Leslie 216.

36. Waagen, "Thoughts on the New Building to be Erected for the National Gallery of England" 121.

37. "The Report on the National Gallery."

38. "The Pictures' Petition".

39. McClintock includes an interesting chapter on racism, imperialism and the commodification of hygiene (207–31).

40. In "The Cestus of Aglaia" (1866) Ruskin rather insensitively compares the fight for freedom from the art preferences of the past to the struggle for black emancipation currently underway in America. "Perhaps a little white emancipation on this side of the water might be still more desirable, and more easily and guiltlessly won. . . . Of all the sheepish notions on our English public 'mind,' I think the simplest is that slavery is neutralized when you are well paid for it!" (494).

41. Mogford 7.

42. *Protest and Counter-Statement against the Report of the Select Committee* 90.

43. Ruskin, "Evidence from the Report of the National Gallery Site Commission" 547–48.

44. *A Handbook to the Gallery of British Paintings in the Art-Treasures Exhibition of Manchester* 26.

45. Redgrave 4.

46. "The National Gallery."

47. Waagen, "The National Gallery."

48. "Picture Cleaning in the National Gallery."

49. Waagen, "The National Gallery."

50. "Bravo, Boxall!"

51. Henry Merritt 3.

52. Collins, *A Rogue's Life* 68.

53. Thackeray 198.

54. Ritchie.

55. Clarke 213.

56. Yates 19.

57. Lysaght.

58. Douglas writes, "In these cases the articulate, conscious points in the social structure are armed with articulate, conscious powers to protect the system; the inarticulate, unstructured areas emanate unconscious powers to provoke others to demand that ambiguity be reduced. When such unhappy or angry interstitial persons are accused of witchcraft it is like a warning to bring their rebellious feelings into line with their correct situation. . . . Witchcraft, then, is found in the non-structure" (Douglas 102).

59. Ruskin, *Lectures on Landscape* 20

60. Hunt 57.

61. Bate 7.

Chapter 2

1. Ruskin, *Unto This Last* 156.

2. Eliot, *Middlemarch* 369–70. All further references will be found within the body of the text.

3. See Poovey and Childers, but also the fascinating discussion of Dickens's *Our Mutual Friend* in Gilbert 86. Gilbert explores the moral meanings of epidemic diseases, as well as the sanitary work of the reform novel.

4. Chadwick's famous concept of the "fever nest" was usefully explored in Stallybrass and White and extended in more specific geographical meaning by many other critics, including Gilbert and also Allen, *Cleansing the City.*

5. For a discussion of the literature that considers the picturesque to be a largely pre-Victorian concept, see Copley and Garside. For an excellent discussion of the ideological function of the picturesque within Romantic and Regency debates about agriculture and enclosure, see Bermingham.

6. Janowitz.

7. Andrews, "The Metropolitan Picturesque."

8. Ruskin, *Modern Painters* IV, 5.

9. Hawthorne 232.

10. Eliot, "The Natural History of German Life" 262.

11. Bourdieu 3–4.

12. Barrell 98.

13. Dickens 160–61. Andrews also discusses this passage in "The Metropolitan Picturesque."

14. Eliot, "The Natural History of German Life" 264.

15. Gaskell 26–27.

16. Garson 307.

17. Richardson, "Salutland" 9.

18. Carpenter, "Education by Proverb in Sanitary Work" 408.

19. Carpenter, *Civilisation* 11.

20. Morris 62.

21. Carpenter, *Civilisation* 20.

22. Edmund Burke, quoted in Eagleton 52.

23. Arnold 409.

24. Ruskin, *The Elements of Drawing* 235.

25. Beaumont 133.

26. A similar argument is made in Tomes.

27. On the conservative impact of sanitation reform, see the excellent Childers, "Observation and Representation"; more recently, Allen, *Cleansing the City,* provides an interesting and useful analysis of the sanitary and social regulation of the Victorian working classes.

28. Richardson, *Hygeia* 13.

29. Caddy, *Artist and Amateur* 18–19.

30. Broughton, *Second Thoughts* 217.

31. Robins.

32. Richardson, "Woman as a Sanitary Reformer" 178.

33. Nightingale 132.

34. Tomes, Bashford.

35. Yonge, *Astray.*

36. Halse 31.

37. Gissing 94–95.

38. Arnold 419.

39. Levine 647.

Chapter 3

1. Chadwick, "The Manual Labourer as an Investment of Capital" 504.

2. Smiles 263.

3. Stallybrass and White 129–30. Pamela K. Gilbert and Michelle Allen have followed Stallybrass and White's lead, in their own geographically interested research on sanitation reform: see Gilbert's "Medical Mapping," and Allen's *Cleansing the City.*

4. See Armstrong; Gallagher; Poovey, *Uneven Developments.*

5. Flint 42.

6. Day.

7. Carpenter 228.

8. White, "Undrained London."

9. Leighton 367.

10. Bayliss 241

11. Richardson, *Hygeia.*

12. Pater, *The Renaissance.*

13. Schaffer and Psomiades 3.

14. Pater, *The Child in the House* 12.

15. Broughton 60.

16. Caddy, *Lares and Penates* 43.

17. Yonge, *The Pillars of the House* I, 301–2.

18. Yonge, *The Pillars of the House* I, 302. Edgar's dirty propensities in art are matched by an equally decadent moral philosophy, and negative reviews of his painting *Brynhild* at the

Royal Academy exhibition send him into a downward spiral of degradation; he eventually runs away to the American West, where he dies an appropriately horrible death at the hands of Indians.

19. Edis, "Internal Decoration" 313.
20. Edis, "On Sanitation in Decoration" 324.
21. Carpenter, "Domestic Health" 228.
22. Murphy 8.
23. Smith and Young 127.
24. Garrett and Garrett 89.
25. White, "Hygenic Value of Colour in the Dwelling" 142.
26. Edis, "Healthy Furniture and Decoration" 321.
27. Gilman 5.
28. Stacpoole 39.
29. Marcus 94.
30. Tyndall 18.
31. Richardson, *Diseases of Modern Life* 55.
32. Bardwell ii.
33. A. L. O. E. 25.
34. Murdock 131.
35. Collins, *The Haunted Hotel.*
36. Panton 12.
37. Hardy 64.
38. Benjamin Richardson, qtd. in Fletcher 177.
39. Conway 230.
40. Katz 31.
41. E. W. Godwin, qtd. in Kinchen 106.
42. Kinchen 106.
43. Martineau 463.
44. Prettejohn 6.
45. Chesterton 7.
46. Hitchens 27.

Chapter 4

1. Pater, *The Renaissance* 150–51.
2. Bourdieu, qtd. in Eagleton 196.
3. Broughton 60.
4. Pease, *Modernism* 88.
5. Foucault, *The Birth of the Clinic* 155.
6. Morton 6.
7. Richards 147.
8. Buck-Morss.
9. Snow discusses this assumption about the morality of painless surgery in *Blessed Days of Anaesthesia* 157. The argument was at times made by B. W. Richardson, himself a proponent of animal experimentation.
10. Tellet 7.
11. Bronfen 5.

12. Bigelow.

13. Snow, *Operations without Pain* 72.

14. Bernard.

15. Twain.

16. Bernard, *An Introduction to the Study of Experimental Medicine* 103

17. Holmes-Forbes 162.

18. Allen, *Hilda Wade* 8.

19. Leach 44.

20. Allen, *Physiological Aesthetics* vii.

21. Meegan Kennedy has also noted that a concept of "medicine as an art" challenged the more mechanical, objectivist discourse of clinical medicine during the Victorian period, but she describes medical aesthetics as a form of human insight that surfaces "in case histories coded variously as sensibility, sentiment, sympathy, and even speculation" (Kennedy 5).

22. Richardson, "Salutland" 10.

23. De Chaumont, "Sanitary Science as Preventive Medicine" 4.

24. Bagshawe 218.

25. Ellis, *The Nationalisation of Health* 20.

26. Richardson, *The Field of Disease* 19.

27. Pease, *The History of the Fabian Society* 32.

28. Carpenter, *Vivisection* 12.

29. Carpenter, *The Need of a Rational and Humane Science* 25.

30. Berdoe 8, 147.

31. Carpenter, *Civilisation* 26.

32. Wootton 184.

33. Carpenter, *Civilisation* 19.

34. Wootten 213, Bashford 64.

35. Shaw, "What Is to Be Done with the Doctors?" 42.

36. Shaw, *The Doctor's Dilemma* 12.

37. Shaw, "Sanitation vs. Inoculation" 126.

38. Osler 186.

39. Carpenter, *Civilisation* 2.

40. Ellis, *The Nationalisation of Health* 20, 17.

41. Shaw, qtd. in Boxhill 62.

42. Pearson, *George Bernard Shaw* 311.

43. Carpenter, *The Need of a Rational and Humane Science* 26.

44. Yonge, *The Long Vacation* 183.

45. Aescalapius Scalpel [Edward Berdoe] 111.

46. Charles Reade's *Foul Play* (1877), for example, features a sanitary clergyman, Robert Penfold, who falls in love on the high seas with Hazel, a beautiful, dying consumptive. Penfold is infuriated when Hazel's physician allows her to eat sweets, and he convinces her to come under his medical care instead. "Disease of the lungs is curable, but not by drugs and unwholesome food" (43) he insists, but his remedies seem dubious until the ship is scuttled by pirates, and Penfold and Hazel are stranded on a sunny island paradise. Fed on turtles and their eggs, Hazel's health improves so miraculously that she is eventually able to commandeer a passing sailboat, repair it, and sail around the island by herself while chased by sharks.

47. Collins, *Heart and Science*. Benjulia's bold assertion that he practices vivisection primarily because he likes it epitomizes the Victorian anxiety about surgical *aisthesis*: "Knowl-

edge for its own sake is the one true god I worship. . . . Knowledge sanctifies cruelty. . . . In that sacred cause, if I could steal a living man without being found out, I would tie him on my table, and grasp my grand discovery in days, instead of months" (157).

48. Ouida 42.

Chapter 5

1. For a helpful discussion of the influence of germ theory on sanitation reform see Mort 26–33.
2. Tyndall 20, 41.
3. Budd, quoted in Tyndall 42–43.
4. Pelling 29.
5. Allen, *At Market Value.*
6. Allen, *The Woman Who Did* 3.
7. Bashford 128.
8. Sutton-Ramspeck 3.
9. Reade, *A Woman-Hater* II, 161.
10. This is discussed in Mangum 198.
11. Masterman 5.
12. Mort 27.
13. White, *Efficiency and Empire* 99.
14. Shee 797.
15. Ellis, *Eugenics Made Plain* 1.
16. Ellis, *The Task of Social Hygiene* 1.
17. Carpenter, "The First Principles of Sanitary Work" 44.
18. Richardson, "Salutland" 34.
19. Richardson, "Storage of Life as a Sanitary Study."
20. De Chaumont, "Sanitary Science and Preventive Medicine" 259.
21. Richardson, *Love and Eugenics in the Late-Nineteenth Century* 8.
22. Reynolds.
23. Koch's use of seed imagery in his discussions of anthrax and its isolation in 1876 is discussed in Tomes (36).
24. Tomes 38.
25. Richardson, "The Seed-Time of Health"; Richardson, The Health of the Mind" 6.
26. Eagleton 43.
27. Simon 477.
28. Bond 144.
29. Ellis, *The Dance of Life* 265.
30. Richardson, "The Seed-Time of Health" 1.
31. Ward, *The Mating of Lydia* 326.
32. Pease, *Modernism, Mass Culture and the Aesthetics of Obscenity* 21.

Chapter 6

1. Galton 17.
2. Pearson, *The Grammar of Science* 30.

3. Richardson, *Hygeia* 13.
4. Lehmann, *Natural Hygiene* 15.
5. Lehmann 188.
6. Ellis, *Eugenics Made Plain* 61.
7. Spencer 41.
8. Saleeby 33.
9. Rentoul 104.
10. Solomon 208.
11. Read 6.
12. Nearing 88.
13. Advertisement for Helen Baker's *Race Improvement, or Eugenics.*
14. Ruskin, "The Relation of Art to Use" 134.
15. Shee 804.
16. Saleeby 32.
17. Nietzsche, *The Will to Power* 465.
18. Ellis, *Eugenics Made Plain* 39. As Ivan Crozier points out, Ellis's own philosophy of sex, race, and art often follows "a Nietzschean line, which can first be detected in an article he published in the decadent *Savoy* magazine in 1896" 189.
19. Pearson, *The Grammar of Science* 369.
20. Ellis, *The Dance of Life* 265.
21. Saleeby 31.
22. Stone 39.
23. Cobbe, *The Peak in Darien* 89.
24. Bagshawe 219.
25. Ludovici 4.
26. Fry, "An Essay in Aesthetics" 26.
27. Fry, "Art and Science" 81.
28. Fry, "Art and Life" 14.
29. Hinton 280.
30. Lange.
31. Mangum 19, 218.
32. Sutton-Ramspeck.
33. Grand, *Adnam's Orchard* 38.
34. MacColl 43.
35. Nordau.
36. Nietzsche, *The Will to Power* 523–24.
37. Nietzsche, "The Case of Wagner" 25.
38. Grand, *Winged Victory* 89.

Coda

1. Lange 338.

WORKS CITED

Primary Texts

Advertisement for Helen Baker's *Race Improvement, or Eugenics. The Bookman* 36, Sept. 1912–Feb. 1913. New York: Dodd, Mead and Co., 1913, 97.

Aescalapius Scalpel [Edward Berdoe]. *St. Bernard's: The Romance of a Medical Student.* London: Swan, Sonnenschein, Lowry, 1887.

Allen, Grant. *At Market Value.* London: Chatto and Windus, 1894.

——. *Hilda Wade.* London: Grant Richards, 1900.

——. *Physiological Aesthetics.* London: Henry S. King, 1877.

——. *The Woman Who Did.* London: John Vane, 1895.

A. L. O. E. *Haunted Rooms.* London: T. Nelson and Sons, 1876.

Arnold, Matthew. "Culture and Anarchy." *Poetry and Criticism of Matthew Arnold.* Ed. Dwight Culler. 1869; New York: Riverside, 1961.

Bagshawe, Frederick. "The Preventive Side of Medicine.". *Transactions of the Hastings & St. Leonard's-on-the-Sea Health Congress.* Hastings: F. J. Parsons, 1890.

Bardwell, William. *What a House Should Be, versus Death in the House.* London: Dean and Son, 1873.

Bate, Percy H. *The English Pre-Raphaelite Painters: Their Associates and Successors.* London, 1899.

Bayliss, Wyke. "Sanitary Reform in Relation to the Fine Arts." *Transactions of the Hastings & St. Leonard's-on-the-Sea Health Congress.* Hastings: F. J. Parsons, 1890.

Beaumont, Averil. *Magdalen Wynard, or The Provocations of a Pre-Raphaelite.* London: Chapman and Hall, 1872.

Berdoe, Edward. *The Origin and Growth of the Healing Art.* London: Swan Sonnenschein, 1893.

Bernard, Claude. An Introduction to the Study of Experimental Medicine. 1865. New Brunswick: Transaction Publishers, 1999.

——. "On Curare." *Revue des Deux Mondes* 53, 1 September 1864): 164–190. Quoted in *Modern Rack: Papers on Vivisection* by Frances Power Cobbe. London: Swan Sonnenschein, 1889. 185.

Bigelow, Henry Jacob. "Insensibility during Surgical Operations Produced by Inhalation." *Boston Medical and Science Journal* 35 (1846); rpt. *The Source Book of Medical History.* Ed. Logan Glendenning. New York: Dover, 1960. 364.

Bond, C. J. "Health and Healing in the Great State." *The Great State: Essays in Construction.* Ed. H. G. Wells, Francs Evelyn Warwick, and G. R. S. Taylor. London: Harper and Brothers, 1912.

"Bravo, Boxall! Well-Done, Wornum!" *Punch,* 24 November 1866, 8–9.

Broughton, Rhoda. *Second Thoughts.* 1880; London: Macmillan and Co., 1899.

Burke, Edmund. *Essay on the Sublime and the Beautiful.* 1756; New York, 1909.

Caddy, Florence. *Artist and Amateur, or The Surface of Life.* London: Chapman and Hall, 1878.

———. *Lares and Penates, or The Background of Life.* London: Chatto and Windus, 1881.

Carpenter, Alfred S. "Domestic Health." *Transactions of the Brighton Health Congress, 1881.* London: E. Marlborough and Co., 1881.

———. "Education by Proverb in Sanitary Work." *Transactions of the Sanitary Institute of Great Britain* 6, 1884-85. London: Office of the Sanitary Institute, 1885. 397–419.

———. "The First Principles of Sanitary Work." *Report of the Third Congress of the Sanitary Institute of Great Britain*, Vol. 1. Ed. Henry C. Burdett. London: Office of the Sanitary Institute, 1880. 41–64.

Carpenter, Edward. *Civilisation: Its Cause and Cure.* 1889; London: Swan Sonnenschein, 1903.

———. *The Need of a Rational and Humane Science.* London: Humanitarian League, 1896.

———. *Vivisection.* London: Humanitarian League, 1904.

Chadwick, Edwin. "The Manual Labourer as an Investment of Capital." *The Journal of the Statistical Society.* London: Harrison and Sons, 1862.

———. *Report on the Sanitary Condition of the Labouring Population of Great Britain.* London: W. Clowes and Sons, 1843.

Chesterton, G. K. *The Man Who Was Thursday.* 1908; New York: Dodd, Mead, & Co., 1975.

Clarke, Charles. *Lord Falconberg's Heir.* London, 1868.

Cobbe, Frances Power. *Modern Rack: Papers on Vivisection.* London: Swan Sonnenschein, 1889.

———. *The Peak in Darien.* Boston: George Ellis, 1882.

Collins, Wilkie. *Miss or Mrs?; The Haunted Hotel; The Guilty River.* New York: Oxford University Press, 1999.

———. *Heart and Science.* London: Chatto & Windus, 1883.

———. *A Rogue's Life.* New York, 1970.

Coningham, William. "Letter to the Editor." *The London Times,* 8 December 1846. 4.

Conway, Moncure D. *Travels in South Kensington.* New York: Harper and Brothers, 1882.

Cozens, Alexander. "A New Method of Assisting the Invention in Drawing Original Compositions in Landscape"; rpt. A. P. Oppé. *Alexander & John Robert Cozens.* 1786; Cambridge, MA: Harvard University Press, 1954.

Day, Lewis F. "How to Hang Pictures." *The Magazine of Art* 5 (1882): 58–60.

De Chaumont, F. "Sanitary Science and Preventive Medicine." *Transactions of the Sanitary Institute of Great Britain* 8 (1886–87). 67–75.

———. "Sanitary Science as Preventive Medicine." *Report of the Fourth Congress of the Sanitary Institute of Great Britain, 1880.* London: Office of the Institute, 1880.

Dickens, Charles. *Pictures from Italy and American Notes.* 1846; London: Chapman and Hall, 1880.

Edis, Robert. "Healthy Furniture and Decoration." *International Health Exhibition Literature, Volume I: Health in the Dwelling.* London: William Clowes and Sons, 1884.

———. "Internal Decoration." *Our Homes and How to Make Them Healthy.* Ed. Shirley Forster Murphy. London: Cassell and Co., 1883.

———. "On Sanitation in Decoration." *Transactions of the Brighton Health Congress, 1881.* London: E. Marlborough and Co., 1881.

Eliot, George. *Middlemarch.* 1872; New York: Oxford University Press, 2008.

———. "The Natural History of German Life." *George Eliot: Selected Critical Writings.* Ed. Rosemary Ashton. New York: Oxford University Press, 1992. 260–95.

Ellis, Havelock. *The Dance of Life.* Boston: Houghton Mifflin, 1923.

———. *Eugenics Made Plain.* Girard, KS: Haldeman-Julius Co., 1923.

———. *The Nationalisation of Health.* London: T. Fisher Unwin, 1892.

———. *The Task of Social Hygiene.* New York: Houghton Mifflin, 1913.

Fairholt, F. W. *A Dictionary of Terms in Art.* London, 1854.

Fry, Roger. "Art and Life: A Lecture Given to the Fabian Society." *Vision and Design.* 1917; London: Chatto and Windus, 1923.

———. "Art and Science." *Vision and Design.* 1919; London: Chatto and Windus, 1923.

———. "An Essay in Aesthetics." *Vision and Design.* 1909; London: Chatto and Windus, 1923.

Galton, Francis. *Inquiries into Human Faculty and Its Development.* London: Dent, 1911.

Garrett, Rhoda, and Agnes Garrett. *Suggestions for Home Decoration.* Philadelphia: Porter and Coates, 1877.

Gaskell, Elizabeth. *North and South.* 1855; New York: Penguin, 2000.

Gilman, Charlotte Perkins. "The Yellow Wallpaper." *The Charlotte Perkins Gilman Reader.* Ed. Ann J. Lane. New York: Pantheon Books, 1980.

Gissing, George. *The Emancipated.* 1890; Chicago: Way and Williams, 1895.

Grand, Sarah. *Adnam's Orchard: A Prologue.* London: Heinemann, 1912.

———. *Winged Victory.* New York: D. Appleton, 1916.

Halse, George. *Graham Aspen, Painter.* London: Hurst and Blackett, 1889.

A Handbook to the Gallery of British Paintings in the Art-Treasures Exhibition of Manchester. London, 1857.

Hardy, Thomas. *A Laodicean.* 1881; New York: Oxford University Press, 1991.

Hawthorne, Nathaniel. *The Marble Faun.* 1860; New York: Oxford University Press, 2002.

Hazlitt, William. "An Inquiry: Whether the Fine Arts Can Be Promoted by Academic and Public Institutions." *Essays on the Fine Arts.* 1814; London, 1873.

———. "The Pictures at Hampton Court." *Essays on the Fine Arts.* London, 1873

———. "Pictures at Wilton, Stouhead, & c." *Essays on the Fine Arts.* London, 1873.

Hinton, James. *Chapters on the Art of Thinking.* London: C. Kegan Paul, 1879.

Hitchens, R. S. *The Green Carnation.* New York: Mitchell, Kennedy, 1894.

Holmes-Forbes, Avary W. *The Science of Beauty: An Analytical Inquiry into the Laws of Aesthetics.* London: Trubner & Co., 1881.

Hunt, William Holman. *Pre-Raphaelitism.* London, 1913.

Jameson, Anna. *Companion to the Most Celebrated Private Galleries of Art in London.* London, 1844.

Kant, Immanuel. *Anthropology from a Pragmatic Point of View.* Ed. Robert B. Louden. 1798; Cambridge: Cambridge University Press, 2006.

Lange, Frederick Albert. *The History of Materialism.* Trans. E. C. Thomas. London: Trubner and Co., 1881.

Lehmann, Heinrich. *Natural Hygiene, or Healthy Blood, the Essential Condition of Good Health and How to Attain It.* London: Swan Sonnenschein, 1901.

Leighton, Sir Frederick. "An Artist's View of the Smoke Question." *The Builder*, 25 March, 1882.

Leslie, C. R. *A Handbook for Young Painters*. London, 1855.

Ludovici, Anthony M. *Nietzsche and Art*. London: Constable and Co., 1911.

Lysaght, Elizabeth J. *The Veiled Picture, or The Wizard's Legacy*. London, 1890.

MacColl, Donald Sutherland. *Nineteenth-Century Art*. Glasgow: James Maclehose, 1902.

Martineau, Harriet. *Health, Husbandry and Handicraft*. London: Bradbury and Evans, 1861.

Masterman, Charles F. G. "Realities at Home." *The Heart of Empire: Discussions of Problems of Modern City Life in England*. London: T. Fisher Unwin, 1907.

Merritt, Henry. *Dirt and Pictures Separated in the Works of the Old Masters*. London, 1854.

Mogford, Henry. *Instructions for Cleaning, Repairing, Lining and Restoring Oil Paintings*. London, 1851.

Moore, Morris. "The Abuses of the National Gallery." *The London Times*, 18 January 1846; rpt. *The Abuses of the National Gallery*. London, 1847. 16.

Morris, William. "The Socialist Ideal in Art." *Forecasts of the Coming Century*. Ed. H. S. Salt. 1891; Manchester: The Labour Press, 1897.

Morton, William James. "Memoranda Relating to the Discovery of Surgical Anesthesia and Dr. William T. G. Morton's Relation to this Event." *The Post-Graduate* (April 1905).

Murdock, J. E. *The Shadow Hunter: The Tragic Story of a Haunted Home*. London: T. Fisher Unwin, 1887.

Murphy. Shirley Forster, ed. *Our Homes and How to Make Them Healthy*. London: Cassell and Co., 1883.

"The National Gallery: The Brown Mania." *Art-Journal* 5 (1853): 66.

Nearing, Scott. *The Super Race: An American Problem*. New York: B. W. Huebsch, 1912.

Nietzsche, Friedrich. "The Case of Wagner." *The Works of Friedrich Nietzsche*. Ed. Alexander Tille. New York: Macmillan & Co., 1896.

———. *The Will to Power*. Ed. Walter Kaufmann. 1888; New York: Vintage, 1968.

Nightingale, Florence. *Notes on Nursing: What It Is and What It Is Not*. New York: Dover, 1969.

Nordau, Max. *Degeneration*. 1895; London: William Heinemann, 1898.

Ouida. *Toxin*. London: T. Fisher Unwin, 1895.

Osler, William. *Counsels and Ideals*. Boston: Houghton Mifflin, 1905.

Panton, Jane Ellen. *From Kitchen to Garret: Hints for Young Householders*. London: Ward & Downey, 1893.

Pater, Walter. *The Child in the House*. Oxford. 1894.

———. *The Renaissance*. 1873; New York: Oxford University Press, 1998.

Pearson, Karl. *The Grammar of Science*. London: Adam and Charles Black, 1900.

"Picture Cleaning in the National Gallery." *The London Times*, 29 November 1852; rpt. *Art-Journal* 5 (1853): 30–31.

"The Pictures' Petition." *Punch* 24 (1853): 3.

Protest and Counter-Statement against the Report of the Select Committee. London, 1853.

Punch, "Hospital for Decayed Pictures." *The London Times*, 19 September 1844, 3.

Read, Mary Lillian. *The Mothercraft Manual*. Boston: Little, Brown and Co., 1922.

Reade, Charles. *Foul Play*. New York: Harper and Brothers, 1877.

———. *A Woman-Hater*. 3 vols. London: William Blackwood and Sons, 1877.

Redgrave, Richard. *A Century of Paintings of the English School*. London, 1865.

Rentoul, Robert Reid. *Race Culture or Race Suicide? A Plea for the Unborn*. London: Walter Scott Pub., 1906.

"The Report on the National Gallery." *Art-Journal* 19 (1857): 331.

Reports from the Select Committees and Commissioners on Fine Arts and on the National Gallery: With Minutes of Evidence, Appendices and Index: 1847–63. Shannon: Irish University Press, 1971.

Reynolds, J. Russell. "Sanitary Science and Preventive Medicine." *Transactions of the Sanitary Institute of Great Britain* 9 (1887–88): 81.

Richardson, Benjamin Ward. *Diseases of Modern Life.* New York: Bermingham and Co., 1882.

——. *The Field of Disease: A Book of Preventive Medicine.* Philadelphia: Henry C. Lea, 1884.

——. "The Health of the Mind." *Transactions of the Hastings & St. Leonard's-on-the-Sea Congress, 1889.* Hastings: F. J. Parsons, 1890.

——. *Hygeia: A City of Health.* London: Macmillan, 1876.

——. "Salutland: An Ideal of a Healthy People." *Transactions of the Sanitary Institute of Great Britain* 1 (1880). 1–37.

——. "The Seed-Time of Health." *Transactions of the Brighton Health Congress, 1881.* London: Marlborough and Co., 1881.

——. "Storage of Life as a Sanitary Study." *Transactions of the Sanitary Institute of Great Britain* 9 (1887–88): 500.

——. "Woman as a Sanitary Reformer." *The Commonhealth: A Series of Essays on Health and Felicity for Every-day Readers.* London: Longmans, Green and Co., 1887.

Ritchie, Leitch. *Wearyfoot Common.* London, 1854.

Robbins, Edward Cookworthy. "The Artistic Side of Sanitary Science." *Transactions of the Sanitary Institute of Great Britain* 8 (1886–87): 325–38.

Ruskin, John. "The Cestus of Aglaia." *On the Old Road.* 1865; rpt. London, 1885.

——. *The Elements of Drawing: In Three Letters to Beginners.* London: Smith and Elder, 1860.

——. "Evidence from the Report of the National Gallery Site Commission." *The Works of Ruskin.* Ed. E. T. Cook and Alexander Wedderburn. London, 1904.

——. *Lectures on Landscape.* 1871; London, 1897.

——. "Light." *Lectures on Art.* 1870–1878; rpt. with an introduction by Bill Beckley, New York: Allworth Press/School of Visual Arts, 1996.

——. *Modern Painters: Their Superiority in the Art of Landscape Painting to All the Ancient Masters.* 4 vols. Ed. and abridged David Barrie. 1842; rpt. London: Pilkington Press, 2000.

——. "On Usury." *On the Old Road: A Collection of Miscellaneous Essays and Pamphlets Published 1834–1885.* London: 1885.

——. "Preface." *Modern Painters: Their Superiority in the Art of Landscape Painting to All the Ancient Masters.* 2nd ed. London, 1844. Vol. 1, xxxviii; li.

——. "The Relation of Art to Use." *Lectures on Art.* New York, 1900.

——. *Unto This Last.* 1862; London: George Allen, 1890.

Saleeby, Caleb Williams. *Parenthood and Race Culture.* London: Cassell and Co. 1909.

Shaw, George Bernard. *The Doctor's Dilemma: A Tragedy.* London: Constable and Co., 1911.

——. "Sanitation vs. Inoculation." *The New Statesman,* 10 July 1915; rpt. *Doctors Delusions, Crude Criminology and Sham Education.* By George Bernard Shaw. London: Constable and Co., 1931. 126.

——. "What Is to Be Done with the Doctors?" *English Review,* Dec. 1917–March 1918; rpt. *Doctors Delusions, Crude Criminology and Sham Education.* By George Bernard Shaw. London: Constable and Co., 1931.

Shee, George."The Deterioration of the National Physique." *The Nineteenth-Century and After.* Ed. James Knowles. London: 1903.

Simon, John. *English Sanitary Institutions*. London: Cassell and Co., 1890.

Smiles, Samuel. *Character*. London: John Murray, 1890.

Smith, Percival Gordon, and Keith Downes Young, "Architecture." *Our Homes and How to Make Them Healthy*. Ed. Shirley Forster Murphy. London: Cassell and Co., 1883.

Solomon, Meyer. "The Science and Practice of Eugenics or Race Culture." *International Clinics: A Quarterly of Clinical Lecture*. Ed. Henry W. Cattell. London: J. B. Lippincott, 1912.

Spencer, Herbert. *Education: Intellectual, Moral, Physical*. London: G. Manwaring, 1861.

Spooner, S. *A Biographical History of the Fine Arts*. London, 1873.

Stacpoole, Florence. *A Healthy Home and How to Keep It*. London: Wells Gardner, 1905.

Tellet, Roy. *A Draught of Lethe: The Romance of an Artist*. London: Smith, Elder and Co., 1891.

Thackeray, William Makepeace. *The Newcomes*. 1855; Cambridge: Cambridge University Press, 1955.

Transactions of the Brighton Health Congress, 1881. London: E. Marlborough and Co., 1881.

"The Turner Gallery." *Art-Journal* 7, (1861): 144.

Twain, Mark. *Pains of Lowly Life*. London: Anti-Vivisection Society, 1900.

Tyndall, John. *Essays on the Floating Matter of the Air, in Relation to Putrefaction and Infection*. London: Longmans, 1883.

Waagen, Gustave. "The National Gallery." *Art-Journal* 5 (1853): 175.

———. "Thoughts on the New Building to Be Erected for the National Gallery of England." *Art-Journal* 5 (1853): 121.

Ward, Mrs. Humphry. *The Mating of Lydia*. New York: Doubleday, 1913.

White, Arnold. *Efficiency and Empire*. London: Metheun, 1901.

White, William. "Hygienic Value of Colour in the Dwelling." *International Health Exhibition Conferences, Volume 7: The Sanitary Construction of Houses*. London: William Clowes and Sons, 1884.

———. "Undrained London: A Fog Factory." *The Builder*, 25 March 1882, 367.

Yates, Edmund. *Land at Last*. London, 1866.

Yonge, Charlotte Mary. *Astray: A Tale of a Country Town*. London: Hatchards, 1886.

———. *The Long Vacation*. New York: Macmillan, 1895.

———. *The Pillars of the House*. 2 vols. London: Macmillan, 1873.

Secondary Texts

Allen, Michelle. *Cleansing the City: Sanitary Geographies in Victorian London*. Athens: Ohio University Press, 2008.

Andrews, Malcolm. "The Metropolitan Picturesque." *The Politics of the Picturesque: Literature, Landscape and Aesthetics since 1770*. Ed. Stephen Copley and Peter Garside. Cambridge: Cambridge University Press, 1994. 282–98

———. *The Search for the Picturesque: Landscape Aesthetics and Tourism in Britain, 1760–1800*. Stanford, CA: Stanford University Press, 1989.

Armstrong, Nancy. *Desire and Domestic Fiction: A Political History of the Novel*. New York: Oxford University Press, 1987.

Atlan, Henri. "Intentional Self-Organization: Emergence and Reduction, Toward a Physical Theory of Intentionality." *Selected Writings on Self-Organization, Philosophy, Bioethics, and Judaism*. Ed. Stephanos Geroulanos and Todd Meyers. New York: Fordham University Press, 2011. 65–94

Barrell, John. "Visualising the Division of Labour: William Pyne's *Microcosm*." *The Birth of Pandora and the Division of Knowledge*. Philadelphia: University of Pennsylvania, 1992. 89–111.

Bashford, Allison. *Purity and Pollution: Gender, Embodiment, and Victorian Medicine*. New York: Palgrave, 1998.

Bermingham, Ann. *Landscape and Ideology: The English Rustic Tradition, 1740–1860* Berkeley: University of California Press, 1986.

Bourdieu, Pierre. *Distinction: A Social Critique of the Judgment of Taste*. Trans. Richard Nice. Cambridge, MA: Harvard University Press, 1984.

Boxhill, Roger. *Shaw and the Doctors*. New York: Basic Books, 1969.

Briefel, Aviva. *The Deceivers: Art Forgery and Identity in the Nineteenth Century*. Ithaca. NY: Cornell University Press, 2006.

Bronfen, Elisabeth. *Over Her Dead Body: Death, Femininity and the Aesthetic*. New York: Routledge, 1992.

Buck-Morss, Susan. "Aesthetics and Anaesthetics: Walter Benjamin's *Artwork* Essay Reconsidered." *October* 26 (1992): 3–41.

Carlisle, Janice. *Common Scents: Comparative Encounters in High-Victorian Fiction*. New York: Oxford University Press, 2004.

Carroll, David. "Pollution, Defilement, and the Art of Decomposition." *Ruskin and Environment: The Storm-Cloud of the Nineteenth Century*. Ed. Michael Wheeler. Manchester: Manchester University Press, 1995. 58–75.

Childers, Joseph W. *Novel Possibilities: Fiction and the Formation of Early Victorian Culture*. Philadelphia: University of Pennsylvania Press, 1995.

———. "Observation and Representation: Mr. Chadwick Writes the Poor." *Victorian Studies* 37 (1994). 23–50.

Classen, Constance, David Howe, and Anthony Synnott. *Aroma: The Cultural History of Smell*. New York: Routledge, 1994.

Cohen, William A. "Locating Filth." *Filth: Dirt, Disgust and Modern Life*. Ed. William A. Cohen and Ryan Johnson. Minneapolis: University of Minnesota Press, 2005. vii–xxxvii.

Copley, Stephen, and Peter Garside. "Introduction." *The Politics of the Picturesque: Literature, Landscape and Aesthetics since 1770*. Ed. Stephen Copley and Peter Garside. Cambridge: Cambridge University Press, 1994. 1–12.

Corbin, Alain. *The Foul and the Fragrant: Odor and the French Social Imagination*. Cambridge, MA: Harvard University Press, 1986.

Crary, Jonathan. *Techniques of the Observer: On Vision and Modernity in the Nineteenth Century*. Cambridge, MA: MIT Press, 1990.

Crozier, Ivan. "Havelock Ellis, Eugenicist." *Studies in History and Philosophy of Biological and Biomedical Sciences* 39:2 (2008): 187–94.

Douglas, Mary. *Purity and Danger: An Analysis of the Concepts of Pollution and Taboo* London, 1989.

Dowling, Linda C. *The Vulgarization of Art: The Victorians and Aesthetic Democracy*. Charlottesville: University Press of Virginia, 1996.

Eagleton, Terry. *The Ideology of the Aesthetic*. Oxford: Basil Blackwell, 1990.

Fletcher, Ian. "Bedford Park: Aesthete's Elysium?" *Romantic Mythologies*. Ed. Ian Fletcher. London: Routledge and Kegan Paul, 1967. 169–207.

Flint, Kate. *The Victorians and the Visual Imagination*. Cambridge: Cambridge University Press, 2000.

Foucault, Michel. *The Birth of the Clinic*. New York: Vintage, 1994.

———. *Discipline and Punish: The Birth of the Prison*. New York: Vintage, 1995.

Gallagher, Catherine. *The Industrial Reformation of English Fiction, 1832–1867*. Chicago: University of Chicago Press, 1985.

Garson, Marjorie. *Moral Taste: Aesthetics, Subjectivity, and Social Power in the Nineteenth-Century Novel*. Toronto: University of Toronto Press, 2007.

Gilbert, Pamela K. "Medical Mapping: The Thames, the Body, and *Our Mutual Friend*." *Filth: Dirt, Disgust and Modern Life*. Ed. William A. Cohen and Ryan Johnson. Minneapolis: University of Minnesota Press, 2005. 78–102.

Goodlad, Lauren M. E. *Victorian Literature and the Victorian State: Character and Governance in a Liberal Society*. Baltimore, MD: Johns Hopkins University Press, 2003.

Janowitz, Anne. "The Chartist Picturesque." *The Politics of the Picturesque: Literature, Landscape and Aesthetics since 1770*. Ed. Stephen Copley and Peter Garside. Cambridge: Cambridge University Press, 1994. 261–81.

Katz, Tamar. *Impressionist Subjects: Gender, Interiority, and Modernist Fiction in England*. Urbana: University of Illinois Press, 2000.

Kennedy, Meegan. *Revising the Clinic: Vision and Representation in Victorian Medical Narrative and the Novel*. Columbus: The Ohio State University Press, 2010.

Kinchen, Juliet. "E. W. Godwin and Modernism." *E. W. Godwin: Aesthetic Movement Architect and Designer*. Ed. Susan Weber Soros. New Haven, CT: Yale University Press, 1999. 93–114.

Krugman, Paul. *The Self-Organizing Economy*. Cambridge: Blackwell, 1996.

Leach, Neill. *The Anaesthetics of Architecture*. Cambridge, MA: MIT Press, 1999.

Levine, Caroline. "Strategic Formalism: Toward a New Method in Cultural Studies." *Victorian Studies* 49:1 (2006): 636–57.

Lindsay, Jack. *J. M. W. Turner: His Life and Work: A Critical Biography*. London: Cory Adams and Mackay, 1966.

Mangum, Teresa. *Married, Middlebrow and Militant: Sarah Grand and the New Woman Novel*. Ann Arbor: University of Michigan Press, 1999.

Marcus, Sharon. *Apartment Stories: City and Home in Nineteenth-Century Paris and London*. Berkeley: University of California Press, 1999.

McClintock, Anne. *Imperial Leather: Race, Gender, and Sexuality in the Colonial Contest*. New York: Routledge, 1995.

Mort, Frank. "Health and Hygiene: The Edwardian State and Medico-Moral Politics." *The Edwardian Era*. Ed. Jane Beckett and Deborah Cherry. London: Phaidon, 1987. 26–33.

Pearson, Hesketh. *George Bernard Shaw: His Life and Personality*. 1942; Boston: Atheneum, 1963.

Pease, Allison. *Modernism, Mass Culture and the Aesthetics of Obscenity*. Cambridge: Cambridge University Press, 2000.

Pease, Edward R. *The History of the Fabian Society*. 1918; Open Source: BiblioBazaar LLC, 2009.

Pelling. Margaret. "Contagion/Germ Theory/Specificity." *Companion Encyclopedia of the History of Medicine*. Eds. W. F. Bynum and R. Porter. 2 vols. London: Routledge, 1993. 309–34.

Poovey, Mary. *Making a Social Body: British Cultural Formation, 1830–1864*. Chicago: University Chicago Press, 1995.

———. *Uneven Developments: The Ideological Work of Gender in Mid-Victorian England*. Chicago: University of Chicago Press, 1988.

Prettejohn, Elizabeth. *Art for Art's Sake: Aestheticism in Victorian Painting*. New Haven, CT: Yale University Press, 2007.

Richards, Stewart. "Anaesthetics, Ethics and Aesthetics: Vivisection in the late Nineteenth-

Century Laboratory." *The Laboratory Revolution in Medicine.* Ed. Andrew Cunningham and Perry Williams. Cambridge: Cambridge University Press, 1992. 142–69.

Richardson, Angelique. *Love and Eugenics in the Late-Nineteenth Century: Rational Reproduction and the New Woman.* New York: Oxford University Press, 2003.

Robertson, David. *Sir Charles Eastlake and the Victorian Art World.* Princeton, NJ: Princeton University Press, 1978.

Schaffer, Talia, and Kathy Alexis Psomiades. *Women and British Aestheticism.* Charlottesville: University of Virginia Press, 2000.

Schama, Simon. *A History of Britain: The Fate of Empire, 1776–2000.* New York: Hyperion, 2002.

Shires, Linda M. *Perspectives: Modes of Viewing and Knowing in Nineteenth-Century England.* Columbus: The Ohio State University Press, 2009.

Snow, Stephanie J. *Blessed Days of Anaesthesia: How Anaesthetics Changed the World.* New York: Oxford, 2008.

———. *Operations without Pain: The Practice and Science of Anaesthesia in Victorian Britain.* Hampshire: Palgrave Macmillan, 2006.

Stallybrass Peter, and Allon White, *The Politics and Poetics of Transgression.* Ithaca, NY: Cornell University Press, 1986.

Stone, Dan. *Breeding Superman: Nietzsche, Race and Eugenics in Edwardian and Interwar Britain.* Liverpool: Liverpool University Press, 2002.

Sutton-Ramspeck, Beth. *Raising the Dust: The Literary Housekeeping of Mary Ward, Sarah Grand, and Charlotte Perkins Gilman.* Athens: Ohio University Press, 2004.

Teukolsky, Rachel. *The Literate Eye: Victorian Art Writing and Modernist Aesthetics.* New York: Oxford University Press, 2009.

Tomes, Nancy. *The Gospel of Germs: Men, Women and the Microbe in American Life* Cambridge, MA: Harvard University Press, 1998.

Trotter, David. "The New Historicism and the Psychopathology of Everyday Life." *Filth: Dirt, Disgust and Modern Life.* Ed. William A. Cohen and Ryan Johnson. Minneapolis: University of Minnesota Press, 2005. 30–50.

Ward, Peter. *The Medea Hypothesis: Is Life on Earth Ultimately Self-Destructive?* Princeton, NJ: Princeton University Press, 2009.

Wohl, Anthony. *Endangered Lives: Public Health in Victorian Britain.* London: J. M. Dent, 1983.

Wootton, David. *Bad Medicine: Doctors Doing Harm since Hippocrates.* New York: Oxford University Press, 2006.

INDEX